Human Intelligence

Perspectives and Prospects

Robert Kail
Purdue University

James W. Pellegrino
University of California,
Santa Barbara

W. H. Freeman and Company
New York

Library of Congress Cataloging in Publication Data

Kail, Robert V.
  Human intelligence.

  (A Series of books in psychology)
  Bibliography: p.
  Includes index.
  1. Intellect   2. Cognition   I. Pellegrino,
James W.   II. Title.   III. Series.
BF431.K354   1985   153   84-18751
ISBN 0-7167-1688-7
ISBN 0-7167-1689-5 (pbk.)

Printed in the United States of America

3 4 5 6 7 8 9 0   VB   7 6 5 4 3 2 1 0 8 9

Human
Intelligence

A Series of Books in Psychology

Editors: Richard C. Atkinson
Gardner Lindzey
Richard F. Thompson

To our parents,
Alice and Robert Kail
Emily and Vincent Pellegrino

Contents

Preface

Probably no aspect of contemporary psychology is as familiar to—and misunderstood by—the general public as intelligence and intelligence testing. For both lay people and psychologists, the mental testing movement is often thought to represent *the* psychological approach to human intelligence. In fact, there are at least two other major theoretical perspectives on intelligence within modern psychology: cognitive psychology and the developmental tradition exemplified by Piaget's theory. Our aim in this book is to present and evaluate each of these perspectives on intelligence, as well as to describe some new theories that have emerged in the 1980s. In describing this work, our goal has been to present the essentials of each approach, shorn of many details, so that readers with a limited background in psychology can understand the contributions of each approach.

We want to acknowledge the help of many individuals during the writing of this book. W. Hayward Rogers, our editor at W. H. Freeman, maintained enthusiasm throughout the long period between the presentation of the first outline for this book and its completion. Jeff Bisanz, Robbie Case, Buzz Hunt, Dick Snow, Bob Sternberg, and Jim Voss provided detailed and incisive comments on drafts of this book, comments that were extremely helpful in the final stages of writing. Ed Cornell brought our attention to the material on Wayne Gretzky that appears in Chapters 3 and 4. To each of these individuals, many thanks.

Portions of this book were written while one of us, RK, was a visiting faculty member at the University of California, Santa Barbara, and at the University of Alberta. Many individuals at both institutions made these visits productive and fun. Special thanks are due to Susan Goldman and Jeff Bisanz, who made possible the visits to Santa Barbara and Edmonton, respectively.

Robert Kail

January 1985 James W. Pellegrino

1

Introduction: Issues and Approaches

Intelligence and intelligence tests are often in the news, usually at the heart of some controversy. Consider the following stories carried by the *Los Angeles Times:*

> IQ testing that leads to the placement of an unusually large number of black children in so-called mentally retarded classes has been ruled unconstitutional by a federal judge. Chief U.S. District Court Judge Robert F. Peckham, ruling in a statewide class action suit filed in 1971 on behalf of five black children, said the use of standardized IQ tests to place children in educable mentally retarded (EMR) classes violated recently enacted federal laws and the state and federal constitutions. . . . In his decision, Peckham said the history of IQ testing and special education in California "revealed an unlawful discriminatory intent. . . . The intent was not necessarily to hurt black children, but it was an intent to assign a grossly disproportionate number of black children to the special, inferior and dead-end EMR classes." [October 18, 1979].

> A controversial Escondido sperm bank for superbrains has produced its first baby—a healthy, nine-pound girl born to a women identified only as a small-town resident in "a sparsely populated state.". . . Founded by inventor Robert K.

Graham of Escondido in 1979, the facility contains sperm donated by at least three Nobel Prize winners, plus other prominent researchers. . . . The sperm bank was founded to breed children of higher intelligence. The goal has been denounced by many critics, who say that a child's intelligence is not determined so much by his genes as by his upbringing and environment. [May 25, 1982].

Becky Swanston frequently taps out notes on a pure-pitch xylophone for her daughter Kelly, age $9\frac{1}{2}$ months, and plays classical music for her "all the time." . . . Melenie Petropolous shows oversized flashcards to her son Tommy, age 3, with bits of information ranging from the names of different birds to the parts of a plant. . . . Karen Garber flashes cards with words, shapes and colors at her son Nicholas, who will be 3 in June and who can count to 10 and identify shapes and colors. . . . The three mothers are among the graduates of a $490, weeklong course offered by a Philadelphia organization called the Better Baby Institute entitled "How to Multiply Your Baby's Intelligence," designed to teach parents how to make their infants, toddlers and preschoolers smarter. [May 1, 1983].

Each of these stories provoked much impassioned debate, as one might expect. Some arguments concern the ethical and moral implications of, for example, selective breeding of bright children or selective placement of children in different classes (e.g., Lambert, 1981). Other arguments deal with the statistical basis of various conclusions, for instance, whether tests are really biased if the data are analyzed "properly" (e.g., Jensen, 1980). What one hears less often, however, is discussion of the construct of intelligence itself. What is intelligence? How should a psychological theory of intelligence be conceptualized? Questions like these, which should be central to any discussion relating to intelligence and intelligence testing, are rarely raised, much less answered. Psychologists and lay persons alike seem too quick to accept the cliche that "intelligence is what intelligence tests measure."

In fact, the definition of intelligence emanating from the tradition of mental testing is not the only psychological perspective; there are others. We have written this book because we believe that to resolve the scientific and ethical dilemmas depicted in these and other similar news stories, we must broaden our views of intelligence. The social, ethical, and theoretical issues at stake are too great to base the discussion on a single view of intelligence, whatever its apparent virtues; a broader perspective is called for.

Much of the controversy surrounding intelligence stems from the fact that, on the one hand, it is a possession prized by most people and yet, on the other hand, the term has no objective, agreed-upon referent. Individuals agree upon the proper referent for characteristics such as height, weight, or age. For intelligence, however, we cannot point to a single observable characteristic of a person as indicating his or her intelligence.

In fact, the term *intelligence* can be used in two ways. First, we can refer to intelligent *acts:* discovering a new element in nature, writing a symphony, or designing a new computer—each of these is a major feat that we would agree is an intelligent act. Second, we use intelligence to refer to *mental processes* that give rise to intelligent acts such as those just described. Terms like *smart, bright, talented, sharp,* and *quick* are all adjectives we casually use to describe people who are (we believe) well endowed with the mental entities underlying intelligent behaviors.

Most psychological theories of intelligence address the processes underlying intelligence rather than the behaviors themselves. This emphasis stems from an assumption regarding the number of distinct mental processes that are necessary to account for the full range of intelligent acts. At one extreme, one could propose that each intelligent act is associated with a unique mental process. Somehow Beethoven was born with the specific talent to write nine symphonies, just as Marie Curie was born with the specific ability to discover radium. The other extreme is to propose that a single mental ability underlies all intelligent achievements. In this view, it was simply an accident of time and place that Beethoven wrote the *Eroica* instead of discovering radium.

Neither of these extreme views is attractive. In fact, most psychologists take an intermediate view: The number of distinct mental processes is greater than one but less than the number of intelligent acts. There is hardly consensus, though, on what this intermediate number is. Estimates range from two to several hundred. These disparities notwithstanding, there is agreement that some finite set of mental processes is sufficient to give rise to the full range of intelligent human acts.

An immediate obstacle is that these processes of intelligence cannot be observed directly. We cannot peel back the scalp and watch the processes in action, nor is there reason to expect that we shall be able to do so in the near future. Hence, the only way to study mental processes is indirectly, by examining the intelligent acts that they produce. In effect, much of this book concerns the different ways that theorists have bridged the gap between acts and processes. But if all theories use intelligent acts as a starting point, we need to be more precise in defining those acts.

As we noted earlier, one recurring approach has been to define intelligence as those behaviors that are measured by intelligence tests (e.g., Boring, 1923). This has never been very satisfying, though, because of the underlying circularity in the logic: Defining intelligence in this fashion is feasible only if one can distinguish tests of intelligence from tests that may look like they measure intelligence but really do not. But we cannot make this distinction, for the only way to snare these ersatz measures of intelligence is to show that they really do not measure intelligence, which we have not yet defined.

Another approach is to recognize that throughout much of the history of Western civilization, intelligence has been associated with knowledge and reasoning. And today, when educated persons are asked to mention behaviors that typify intelligence, the usual list would include such things as the ability to reason logically, the ability to solve novel problems and the ability to learn new information. In saying these behaviors are intelligent, we assume that people are simply reflecting the values of society at large, or more candidly, the values of influential persons within that society. But should we equate the educated individual's definition of intelligence with that of society at large?

Sternberg and his colleagues (Sternberg, Conway, Ketron, & Bernstein, 1981), addressed this question in a series of studies. They asked people to judge whether each of 250 behaviors was characteristic of a "prototypic" intelligent person. Experts—psychologists doing research on intelligence—made these judgments, as did lay people (who, importantly, were not simply a group of college students, who might be influenced by their knowledge of psychology). Both groups judged the behaviors similarly; the experts' views of intelligent behaviors were certainly *not* at odds with the conceptions held by the population at large. Even more interesting is the similarity between groups in terms of general categories of intelligent acts. Both experts and lay people divided intelligence into two primary categories. One, *verbal ability*, encompassed behaviors such as "displays a good vocabulary," "reads with high comprehension," "is knowledgeable about a particular field of knowledge," and "displays curiosity."

The second general category concerned *problem-solving skills* as indicated by "reasons logically and well," "able to apply knowledge to problems at hand," and "makes good decisions."

These, then, form the core of the large number of behaviors that we call intelligent, a core that is reasonably similar for lay people and experts in the field of intelligence. The issue that will occupy much of the rest of the book is to identify those mental processes that enable people to engage in these behaviors that their peers call intelligent.

Before proceeding, we need to sound an important warning. All of our examples of intelligent acts have been decidedly Western; intelligent acts in other cultures may be quite different. One frequently cited example involves navigation among Pulawat islanders. These men sail canoes hundreds of miles through the Pacific Ocean to reach islands that may be less than a mile wide (Gladwin, 1970). Such a feat is just as remarkable as those listed earlier. The key question concerns the mental processes that are involved. Do the processes underlying intelligence also vary from culture to culture? Or is it reasonable to assume that members of *Homo sapiens* worldwide have much the same mental apparatus, which responds to produce culturally appropriate acts of intelligence? There are no definitive answers to these questions. Hence, most of our claims regarding intelligence will pertain to individuals living in literate, industrialized societies, where we can identify the core set of intelligent behaviors with some confidence.

In this book we describe three different psychological perspectives on intelligence. The *psychometric tradition* represents the branch of psychology that has been concerned primarily with the measurement of intelligence; essentially all extant tests of intelligence have been devised by psychologists associated with the psychometric tradition. A second view on intelligence, the *information processing perspective*, is an outgrowth of work in experimental psychology. It provides elaborate descriptions and theories of the specific mental activities that comprise intelligence. A third view of intelligence, that provided by *cognitive developmental psychology*, is associated with the theory of intellectual development proposed by the Swiss psychologist Jean Piaget. This tradition is a rich source of information on the growth and development of intelligence.

There is agreement among the perspectives, at a very general level, concerning the skills and activities that are associated with being or becoming intelligent: *Reasoning* and *problem-solving* skills are the principal components of intelligence in each of these perspectives. Moreover, in each perspective adaptability is considered an important aspect of intelligence. This is implicit in the research conducted within each tradition, where individuals must deal with a succession of novel stimuli and tasks; performance depends on the ability to adapt rapidly to the new situations. Such adaptation to changing environmental demands is also an explicit component of Piaget's theory, although the period of adaptation and change is more extended, usually being measured in months and years rather than in minutes. Although reasoning and adaptability are common general themes to each of the three approaches, they are elaborated differently.

Organization of the Book

Each of the three traditional perspectives has led to theory, research, and methodology that are useful for addressing certain aspects of a theory of intelligence. However, as we shall see, no single perspective provides a truly comprehensive, integrative view of intelligence. Consequently, our goal in this book is to determine how each of the three major perspectives uniquely furthers our understanding of human intelligence. In Chapters 2 through 4 of this book, we shall consider, respectively, the psychometric, information processing, and cognitive developmental perspectives on intelligence. In Chapter 5, we first compare the three traditional perspectives, then we present some new developments in the study of intelligence, instances that bridge the gaps between the different traditions and that suggest the nature of future comprehensive theories of intelligence. Finally, in Chapter 6, we turn to the implications of these different perspectives for some of the controversies described at the beginning of this chapter.

2

The Psychometric Approach

Throughout the twentieth century, mental tests and the assessment of intellectual ability have served two major functions. Historically, the most visible function of mental tests, generally called intelligence tests, has been in education. Objective tests of intellectual ability were developed initially to aid in educational assessment and placement. That is, they were designed to help educators match instruction to a student's abilities. Thus, on the basis of a low IQ score, together with other test information as well as parent and teacher observations, a child would be placed in a class of retarded children, where the child could receive instruction geared to his or her intellectual level. In like manner, scores from an aptitude test battery might be cited to encourage an adolescent to pursue literature rather than mathematics or mechanics. The issues involved in deciding an appropriate instructional match are as much philosophical as scientific, and it is these philosophical issues that have fueled the controversy over mental tests and their use.

Mental tests have also served another function that is less visible than the use of tests in educational practice but is no less important. Performance on mental tests has provided the raw data for psychometric theories of intelligence. Use of mental tests for this purpose began in the 1880s in Europe, and we begin our account there.

Early History

The German scientists who established psychology as a separate discipline in the 1870s (notably Wilhelm Wundt) were not concerned with intelligence and its assessment. For these psychologists, the proper subject matter of psychology was the study of sensation and perception. They ignored the "higher mental processes" like thinking and problem-solving that most psychologists and lay persons today equate with intelligence. In addition, the early German psychologists were interested in formulating *general laws of behavior.* Hence, they viewed differences between people as errors reflecting the imprecision of a young science, not phenomena of interest. Before the end of the nineteenth century, however, came many proposals for a psychology of intelligence and individual differences.

Sir Francis Galton

Sir Francis Galton—British biologist, psychologist, and statistician—is generally regarded as the "father of mental tests" (Boring, 1950). Like the German psychologists, Galton believed that simple sensory, perceptual, and motor processes formed the fundamental elements of human intelligence. However, Galton the biologist was concerned with problems of human evolution and thus the study of differences between species and differences between members of the same species was quite familiar to him. (In fact, he was a half-cousin of Charles Darwin.)

Galton the statistician was also profoundly impressed by the pioneering work of the Belgian astronomer and statistician Quételet, who had discovered that physical characteristics such as height and weight had a bell-shaped, or normal distribution in human populations. Seeing that individual differences in physical characteristics conformed to a well-known mathematical equation, Galton set out to determine if psychological differences between persons were equally systematic. In 1884 he established a laboratory in which he administered simple tests of vision, hearing, and reaction time. Over the course of six years, nearly 10,000 persons were tested. Given the scope of the project, it was disappointing that no important findings emerged regarding psychological differences between persons. It may well be the case that Galton was a victim of the sheer amount of data he collected. (Analyzing Galton's data 100 years later with a computer, Johnson, McClearn, Schwitters, Nagoshi, Ahern, and Cole, 1984, found systematic individual differences in response time.) Nevertheless, many of the important questions about intelligence—its measurement, heritability, nurturance, and the like—had been raised. In addition, a scientist of Galton's stature had raised the study of human psychological variation to a position of eminence and had devised a series of psychological tests for that purpose.

James McKeen Cattell

The first North American proponent of a psychology of individual differences and mental testing was James McKeen Cattell. As was the case with Galton, Cattell's primary contribution lay in establishing the priorities of a developing science rather than in the impact of his research. From his earliest contact with psychology in Wundt's laboratory in the 1880s, Cattell apparently was struck by the differences among persons in their performance on psychological tasks. His dissertation, in 1886, was a study of individual differences in reaction time. Two years later he lectured at Cambridge University, where meetings with Galton fostered and refined his ideas regarding the nature of individual differences. He returned to the United States in 1888 and conducted most of his notable research on individual differences during the next decade.

Like Galton, Cattell believed that sensory, perceptual, and motor processes were the fundamental elements of thought. Consequently, he sought to measure individual differences in these phenomena by testing college students' abilities to select the heavier of two weights and by measuring the speed with which they responded to a tone, to name just two of the tests included in his battery. Cattell first described this work in an article published in 1890, in which he coined the term *mental test.* Over the next several years, Cattell's tests were used to evaluate large numbers of college students, and it was expected that the scores would indicate which individuals would succeed in college. In fact, relationships between Cattell's tests and college achievement were consistently small, thus providing little support for the use of these tests as predictive instruments (Wissler, 1901). This outcome surprised and disappointed Cattell (Woodworth, 1944), but it did little to dissuade him from the belief that the study of individual differences should be at the heart of psychological research.

Cattell provided more direct impetus as well for psychological research on individual differences. From 1891 to 1917, Cattell was the head of the psychology department at Columbia University. During this period Columbia granted more doctoral degrees in psychology than any other university in the United States. Cattell granted students considerable freedom to pursue problems of their own choosing, yet he was constantly encouraging them to grapple with applied problems in education, industry, and medicine (Woodworth, 1944). As a result, many of the pioneers of the testing movement were trained at Columbia during Cattell's tenure.

Alfred Binet

Galton is known as the father of the testing tradition, and Cattell is credited with originating the phrase *mental test,* but Alfred Binet, a French psychologist, is recognized as the creator of the first intelligence test. In 1904 the minister of public instruction in Paris appointed a commission to study education for retarded children who were unable to profit from the instruction typically given in schools. The commission recommended that retarded children should attend special schools where they could receive more appropriate instruction. This decision meant that an objective means of identifying retarded children was essential. Binet, who was already well-known for his work on intelligence in retarded and nonretarded persons, and his student, Theophile Simon, were responsible for developing an intelligence test to meet this need. The result was a test, usually referred to as the "1905 Scale," consisting of thirty different tests ranging from touching one's nose or ear on request to drawing designs from memory to defining abstract terms. To provide norms for the scale, fifty nonretarded children ranging from 3 to 11 years of age were tested. It was found, for example, that 7-year-olds but not 5-year-olds could explain the difference between paper and cardboard (Peterson, 1925). Children suspected of mental retardation could be given the tests, and their performance could be compared with that of children of the same chronological age in the normative sample.

The 1905 Scale was greeted with great enthusiasm in both Europe and the United States. Previously, judgments of mental retardation had often relied heavily on an examiner's intuition and little else. Binet and Simon, however, seemed to have viewed the 1905 Scale as a preliminary instrument, for in 1908 a new scale appeared. New items were included, a new method was introduced for calculating a child's intellectual level, and a larger standardization group was used. The 1908 Scale, like its predecessor, was immediately recognized as an invaluable tool that fulfilled an important practical need and fulfilled it well (or so the psychologists of that era thought).

The next significant step in the development of the Binet–Simon intelligence tests took place in 1916, when Lewis Terman of Stanford University published an extensive revision of Binet's tests that was the result of six years of research and development. Prior versions of the Binet Scales used in the United States had essentially been literal translations of the Binet scales into English, with a few culturally inappropriate items changed. Terman's modifications were so extensive that the outcome was a completely new scale, one usually referred to as the "1916 Stanford–Binet."

Several features contributed to the widespread popularity of the Stanford–Binet (Goodenough, 1949). First, Terman expressed a child's level of performance in terms of an intelligence quotient (IQ). This measure, devised in 1912 by William Stern, consisted of a child's mental age (MA) divided by the child's chronological age (CA) multiplied by 100:

$$IQ = \frac{MA}{CA} \times 100$$

This new measure provided a straightforward means of describing a child's level of intellectual development relative to the norm for children of the same age. Scores less than 100 indicated below-average ability and scores greater than 100 above-average ability.

Second, Terman provided clear, detailed instructions for each problem appearing on the scale. Binet had provided only general instructions; examiners were never certain whether questions could be repeated, whether certain infrequent responses should be considered correct, and so on. The final change worth noting in the 1916 Stanford–Binet concerns the standardization of the test. In standardizing the 1908 Scale, Binet and Simon had tested 203 boys attending school in Paris. Terman, in contrast, included about 1400 individuals in his standardization sample, all of whom were tested within two months of their birthday and who attended what were judged to be "typical" schools. Notwithstanding the obvious problem in defining a typical school, Terman's procedures were by far the most sophisticated efforts at standardizing a psychological test to that time.

The Binet–Simon scales are significant historically because they represent a distinct departure from the approach to intelligence and individual differences espoused by Galton and Cattell. Both Galton and Cattell—like most psychologists of their time—felt that sensory, perceptual, and motor processes were the basic elements of intelligence; accordingly, tests were designed to measure these processes. In contrast, throughout the 1890s Binet had argued that human intelligence could not be reduced to simple perceptual–motor "building blocks." He proposed instead that more complex processes like memory, mental imagery, comprehension, judgment, and autocriticism constitute the core of human intelligence (Binet & Henri, 1896; Binet & Simon, 1908). The Binet–Simon scales reflect this bias, including many items that test memory, imagery, comprehension, and judgment but none that primarily test sensory, perceptual, or motor skill.

A second difference is related to the first. For Galton and Cattell, research on individual differences went hand in hand with constructing psychological theories of human thinking. Binet was as much interested in a theory of intelligence as he was in developing a practical diagnostic instrument, but practical advances quickly outstripped theoretical advances—much to Binet's dismay. Thus, early on a division occurred between psychologists interested in intelligence tests primarily as a basis for psychological theories and those interested in tests as diagnostic and predictive instruments.

A third difference emerging in the tests of Binet and Simon was an emphasis on a developmental approach to the measurement of intelligence. Galton and Cattell, like most of their contemporaries, studied only adults, for children were not seen as reliable or trustworthy participants in psychological research. Of course, the very reason for which Binet and Simon were constructing their tests necessitated that they test children. More important, however, Binet and Simon (1908) argued that the nature of intelligence changes as children grow older, and with the 1908 Scale they introduced the concept of mental age as a means of expressing a child's level of intellectual development.[1] On earlier tests a person's score had simply been the number of problems solved successfully. Binet and Simon included in the 1908 Scale four problems that the typical 4-year-old should solve, four problems that a typical 5-year-old should solve, and so on through age 13. A child's mental age was established by first determining the basal level, defined as the most advanced level at which a child missed no more than one problem. For each additional five problems that were passed, one year was added to the basal level. This notion of mental age did much to popularize the Binet–Simon scales, both because it was so easy to grasp and because it seemed to provide a simple, objective means of quantifying a child's intellectual level.

Finally, in fairness to Binet, we should emphasize that he was not only concerned with quantification and scaling but equally concerned with the diagnostic value of his test when used by a skilled examiner.

Charles Spearman

In examining the work of Binet, we have seen the emergence of the practical side of testing, that of using tests to determine and diagnose a person's level of intellectual development. The other side of the testing movement is the use of tests to generate theories of intelligence and individual differences. For this part of the testing movement, we must return to Europe at the turn of the century.

The great debate among psychologists interested in intelligence was whether it was best thought of as a series of independent specific mental faculties or whether intelligence was more general and global, not amenable to division into separate com-

---

[1]Strictly speaking, Chaille (1887) was the first to express the outcome of a psychological test in a metric similar to Binet and Simon's concept of mental age. However, because Chaille's work was published in a journal with only limited circulation, Binet and Simon are traditionally credited with introducing the concept to the psychology community at large.

ponents. If intelligence was general and global, it was argued that "well-endowed" persons should attain high scores on all measures, while less well endowed persons should perform poorly on all measures.

To assess such consistency in performance across tasks, a *correlation coefficient* is computed. A correlation coefficient is simply a statistic used to quantify the relationship between two variables. The statistic, usually denoted r, can take on values from −1 to 0 to +1. Values of r that are close to +1 or −1 indicate a strong relationship between two variables; when r is close to 0, the two variables are completely unrelated. Some examples may clarify how relationships are expressed quantitatively with a correlation. The correlation between height and weight is approximately .6: As a general rule, taller people are heavier than shorter people, but the correlation is not perfect (i.e., +1), reflecting the existence of short, heavy persons as well as tall, thin ones. An example of a negative correlation is the relationship between age and running speed in adults. Typically, adults run slower as they get older. This correlation is negative because increases in one variable (age) are associated with decreases in the second variable (running speed). The correlation is not perfect (i.e., −1), reflecting the existence of young adults who run at speeds slower than some middle-aged and elderly persons.

Now, as we said earlier, if intelligence is general and global, the result would have been consistently large, positive correlations among scores on mental tests. In fact, correlations among measures were low and nowhere near as large as was expected according to the generalist view, giving support by default to the separatist group.

All of this changed in 1904 when Charles E. Spearman, a British psychologist, published two landmark papers. In the first (1904b), Spearman showed that the size of a correlation is limited by the reliability of the two measures being correlated. Reliability refers to the consistency or reproducibility of a set of results. A measure or test is considered reliable if it produces consistent scores for the same individual and consistent differences among individuals when administered at two different times. Spearman showed that the maximum *possible* correlation between two measures decreases as the reliabilities of the measures decrease.

In the second paper (1904a), Spearman presented correlations among test scores for children. He concluded that when the correlations were evaluated in light of the reliabilities of the tests, there was evidence for a two-factor theory of intelligence. A general factor, or g, was involved in performance on all measures. In addition, test-specific intellectual factors, each referred to as *s* (for specific), were thought to be involved at some level in all measures of intelligence. This bold new view, the first psychological theory of intelligence to be developed with some degree of mathematical precision, touched off a vigorous debate in the testing movement, a debate that continues today.

   In the work of Spearman, as well as that of Galton, Cattell, and Binet, we see two developments that have come to characterize this tradition. First, although many of the pioneers of the testing movement came from within experimental psychology, there were also many experimental psychologists who were hostile to the idea of a psychology of individual differences. Separation between differential and experimental psychology increased throughout most of the twentieth century, with the result that psychological theories of intelligence and individual differences were increasingly formulated without regard to theoretical and empirical advances in experimental psychology. Second, in the work of Spearman we saw that an advance in theory was linked to refinement in mathematical and statistical techniques. This was hardly a unique event; throughout the ensuing eighty years, theories of intelligence have been shaped by advances in statistics. Many of the statistical advances were actually a direct consequence of the need to invent new ways to deal with large and complex sets of test-score data to address theoretical issues.

The First Factor Theories

Spearman's seminal work on the interpretation of correlational patterns became the cornerstone of *factor analytic* theories. Such theories represent an attempt to explain a large set of data in terms of the simplest possible psychological and mathematical model. To understand differences between major theories and their evaluation, we shall use a hypothetical example drawn from the area of athletics to illustrate some of the logic of data collection and analyses in the context of two different types of theories.

An Illustrative Example: Athletic Ability

The first type of theory to consider is very simple. We assume that a *single general athletic ability* is required to excel in any athletic event. As an example, consider the ten events of the modern decathlon: 100-, 400-, and 1500-meter runs, 110-meter high hurdles, javelin, discus, shot put, pole vault, high jump, and broad jump. One further assumption is required, namely, that individuals vary with respect to general athletic ability. That is, some individuals are more skilled athletically than others.

If we begin with these assumptions, then a particular set of results should be obtained when we take a group of individuals and have them compete in each of the ten events. For each of fifty individuals we obtain a score on each event, giving us a total of 500 different scores. Our theory predicts that individuals who possess higher degrees of athletic ability will have better scores on all events. To determine if this is true, we calculate correlations between the scores of individuals on all pairs of events. When the correlations between scores on all events are computed, a new and smaller set of data is obtained, which is shown in Table 2-1. This table, known as a *correlation matrix*, shows how individuals' scores on each event are related to their scores on all other events.[2]

The data in Table 2-1 can be examined in light of our simple theory of athletic ability. Note that all of the correlations are large, exceeding .9 in every case. What this means, literally, is that individuals who score well in any particular event are highly likely to excel in other events as well. There are many theories that could account for this consistency in performance across tasks. Perhaps the officials are crooked, so the winners of each event are the wealthy, because they can offer the largest bribes. If we can eliminate this and other far-fetched explanations, probably the most

---

[2]Actually, the correlations presented in Tables 2-1, 2-3, and 2-4 would be based on a person's *position* in the event, not the time to complete the event (as in the track events) or the distance or height achieved (as in the field events). We would not use the latter values because *smaller* times are associated with excellence in track events while *larger* distances represent excellence in field events. This means that some of the correlations would be positive and others negative. Computing correlations based on position in an event eliminates this problem, because excellence is denoted by a small number (indicating a high finish) in all events.

Table 2-1   *Correlations for decathlon events consistent with a theory of general athletic ability*

	400-m run	1500-m run	Hurdles	Javelin	Discus	Shot put	Pole vault	High jump	Broad jump
100-m run	.95	.93	.96	.92	.91	.92	.94	.92	.94
400-m run		.92	.91	.91	.92	.93	.91	.95	.91
1500-m run			.91	.92	.94	.91	.95	.96	.92
Hurdles				.93	.91	.92	.96	.95	.94
Javelin					.95	.94	.91	.92	.91
Discus						.95	.92	.91	.93
Shot put							.93	.92	.94
Pole vault								.95	.94
High jump									.95

plausible explanation is our notion of a general athletic ability: namely, that people have a certain level of athletic skill that determines their performance in each athletic event.

Two parts of this argument are worth emphasizing, for they turn out to be critical when we return to psychological theories of intelligence. First, saying that people have a certain level of athletic skill does not address *in any way* how they acquired that skill. People may have the skill because they inherited it or because they practiced endlessly. The origins of the skill are not germane to our argument; all that counts is that the level of general athletic ability remains stable throughout the period in which individuals participate in the decathlon.

Second, notice that our argument does not depend on our ability to measure general athletic ability per se. Instead, we infer this quantity. This is particularly evident in Table 2-2, which depicts hypothetical general athletic ability for a subset of the fifty individuals as well as their performance on three specific events. We assume only that general athletic ability is greater for the first individual than for the second, and it in turn is greater than for

Table 2-2   Relations between g values and performance in three events

Event	Person 1	Person 2	Person 3	Person 50
100-m run (seconds)	10.2	10.8	12.2	18.5
Javelin (meters)	80	78	77	60
High jump (meters)	2.4	2.3	2.1	1.5
	g_1 ≥	g_2 ≥	g_3 ≥	g_{50}

the third person, and so on. Actual values of g_j are unknown and unnecessary; what is essential is that if $g_1 > g_2$, then the first individual should outperform the second on *any* athletic event.

Now let us consider a different theory of athletic ability, one in which we assume *separate* and *independent* athletic abilities. For present purposes, we suppose that these correspond to *speed* and *strength* factors. Our theory now leads us to the principle that the correlation between scores on any two athletic events will depend on whether events involve the same specific athletic skills. If speed is critical in both events, then the correlation should approximate 1, as it should if both events emphasize strength. If our theory is correct that strength and speed are independent, then the correlation between a speed event and a strength event should be 0.

An ideal pattern of correlations corresponding to a speed–strength theory of athletic ability is shown in Table 2-3. Correlations between track events (100-, 400-, and 1500-meter runs and the high hurdles) are all 1.0. Correlations between the field events (javelin, discus, shot put, pole vault, broad jump, and high jump) are also 1.0. However, the correlation between any specific field event and any specific track event is 0. This pattern of correlations does not *prove* our speed–strength theory. It might be the case that the track officials were crooked but the field officials were honest. Hence, wealth determined success in track events but general athletic prowess determined success in field events. Assuming we can document the honesty of the officials, the speed–strength theory provides a parsimonious account of the correlations in Table 2-3.

The speed–strength theory as it stands is undoubtedly wrong, for it assumes that an event is either a speed event *or* a strength event. It would be more realistic to assume that both

Table 2-3   *Correlations for decathlon
events predicted by a speed–strength theory
of athletic ability*

	400-m run	1500-m run	Hurdles	Javelin	Discus	Shot put	Pole vault	High jump	Broad jump
100-m run	1	1	1	0	0	0	0	0	0
400-m run		1	1	0	0	0	0	0	0
1500-m run			1	0	0	0	0	0	0
Hurdles				0	0	0	0	0	0
Javelin					1	1	1	1	1
Discus						1	1	1	1
Shot put							1	1	1
Pole vault								1	1
High jump									1

speed and strength can be involved in varying amounts in a person's performance on an event. The runs, for example, would emphasize speed over strength; the shot put and discus would emphasize strength over speed. The remaining events would involve both. The hurdles, for example, might be primarily a speed event with a moderate strength component; the emphasis might be just the opposite in the javelin. Strength and speed might be equally important in the pole vault.

In this more sophisticated version of a speed–strength theory, the correlation between two events will be a function of the relative contribution of the two abilities to performance in the two events. Hence, a more realistic pattern of correlations is depicted in Table 2-4. Now all correlations are positive, as was the case with the general theory of athletic ability. The correlations are not uniform, though, with higher values obtained when events tap the same abilities (e.g., large strength components) than when they do not.

Table 2-4   Correlations for decathlon events consistent with a theory in which speed and strength jointly determine performance

	400-m run	1500-m run	Hurdles	Javelin	Discus	Shot put	Pole vault	High jump	Broad jump
100-m run	.95	.92	.94	.10	.05	.01	.50	.40	.45
400-m run		.93	.95	.08	.03	.02	.55	.43	.40
1500-m run			.92	.12	.07	.05	.52	.45	.46
Hurdles				.07	.02	.06	.51	.42	.44
Javelin					.93	.95	.45	.50	.47
Discus						.96	.48	.52	.46
Shot put							.49	.49	.50
Pole vault								.89	.92
High jump									.95

The Logic of Factor Analysis

The foregoing arguments concerning the nature of athletic ability hold equally well when applied to the nature of human intelligence. If human intelligence is general and global, correlations should be uniformly high; if human intelligence consists of separate, specific abilities, then we expect performance on certain tests to be highly correlated but unrelated to scores on tests that measure other abilities. If, for example, verbal ability is a separate component of human intelligence, then performance on tests of verbal ability should be highly correlated but unrelated to measures of quantitative skill.

A shortcoming to the logic developed thus far is that it works well only when the number of distinct abilities is small. When more than a few abilities are possible, simply scanning a correlation matrix for patterns of relations is impossible. Instead, *factor analysis* has been the procedure used by most psychometric theorists. The logic of analyzing correlation matrices to reveal underlying abilities was specified first by Spearman, who also expressed it mathematically in preliminary form. L. L. Thurstone, however, was one of the first to propose a formal mathematical procedure for conducting factor analysis on a pattern of correlations.

To illustrate the logic of factor analysis, consider the graph shown in Figure 2-1. This diagram is one way of representing the information contained in the correlation matrix in Table 2-4. Each axis represents a separate ability, or *factor;* the position of the point in the two-dimensional space defined by the axes represents the contribution of each factor to performance in an event. Thus, for events that fall on an axis, successful performance depends upon that factor alone. Points that fall somewhere off of the axes represent events in which both speed and strength are involved.

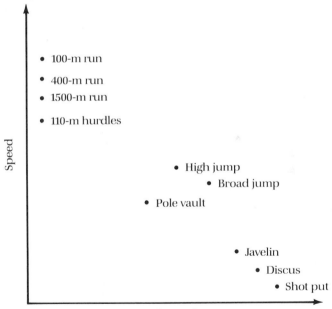

Figure 2-1   A two-factor theory of athletic ability in which the two factors are strength and speed.

The specific mathematical machinery used in factor analysis to translate a correlation matrix into a two-dimensional space such as that shown in Figure 2-1 is enormously complex, and we shall not address it here. Suffice it to say that what factor analysis does is (1) take a correlation matrix, (2) determine the number of factors present in the data, which can range from 1 to $n - 1$ where n is the number of different measures (i.e, tasks) represented in the correlation matrix, and (3) indicate the contribution of each factor to performance on each task, which is typically referred to as the *loading* of the task on a factor. What factor analysis does not do is indicate the nature—that is, the theoretical meaning—of any particular factor. That must be *inferred* by looking at tasks that load on a factor and trying to determine what they have in common. Thus, if we find that 100-, 400-, and 1500-meter runs all load on a factor, it is our knowledge of what people do on these tasks—not the mathematical wizardry of factor analysis—that leads us to label the y axis in Figure 2-1 as speed.

This issue leads to one of the interpretive problems frequently encountered in psychometric theories of intelligence. Consider Figure 2-2, in which the positions of the events relative to one another are the same but the axes have been rotated 45°. Again we have two factors, but they can no longer be interpreted as the speed and strength factors of before. Instead, one axis seems to represent a general athletic factor; the second factor corresponds to a continuum representing speed at one end and strength at the other. The result is that we have two mathematically equivalent solutions for the same set of data. In the initial solution (Figure 2-1), there are two independent athletic abilities that contribute differentially to performance on a series of athletic events. The second solution postulates a general factor and a combined speed–strength factor. (The latter could actually be decomposed further into two separate factors if we imagine a three-dimensional space: The general factor g represents the y axis, while the specific factors speed and strength, represent the x and z axes.)

Which type of theory is most appropriate? Unfortunately, there is no clear answer, because both provide mathematically equivalent solutions to the data. Different theoretical orientations have led to differences in the method used for factor analysis of a correlation matrix derived from performance on tasks.

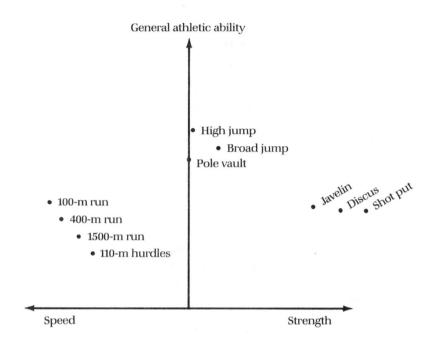

Figure 2-2 *A two-factor theory of athletic ability in which the horizontal axis corresponds to a speed–strength factor and the vertical axis corresponds to a general ability factor.*

General Versus Specific Mental Abilities

Much the same sort of debate has characterized the psychometric work on theories of intelligence. Spearman's two-factor theory of intelligence, with its emphasis upon the general factor *g*, initially appeared to account for correlations between scores on mental tests. This was true, however, so long as the mental tests involved dissimilar types of problems, not unlike the events of the pentathlon rather than the decathlon. However, the larger the set of tests or measures that is administered to a group of individuals, the greater the possibility of similarity among sets of measures, for example, track versus field events in the decathlon or verbal versus numerical versus spatial problems on mental tests. In cases such as these, a single general factor does not adequately account for the observed correlations between performance on the entire set of measures. Subsequently, Spearman (1927) modified his theory to include the idea of group factors in addition to the general factor g. Allowance for group factors such as verbal or spatial ability was demanded by correlational patterns not unlike our previous illustration of separate speed and strength factors in addition to a general athletic-ability factor. Nevertheless, Spearman maintained the concept of a general ability factor that pervades all intellectual tests.

Thurstone (1938) proposed an alternative theory of intelligence based upon his analyses of performance on a large battery of mental tests administered to undergraduates at the University of Chicago. He rejected the idea of a general factor and proposed instead a theory that focused on independent, primary mental abilities. His argument was based upon data similar to our hypothetical decathlon situation. Rather than postulating a general factor with either a speed–strength continuum or separate speed and strength factors, he favored the mathematically equivalent solution that postulated two independent speed and strength factors. The general factor was unnecessary to account for correlational data. In his research on mental abilities, he found evidence for a set of primary mental abilities that were labeled Space, Verbal Comprehension, Word Fluency, Number Facility, Induction, Perceptual Speed, Deduction, Rote Memory, and Arithmetic Reasoning. The fifty-seven individual tests that were administered could be mapped on to these separate factors, and his data indicated that these factors, or abilities, were independent.

To give some idea of what the factors illustrate, we need to examine some of the tests that are associated with individual factors. The Space factor is assessed by tasks that require the individual to judge whether two items rotated in space are the same or different. The items to be compared can be letters, abstract shapes, or flags. The space factor is thought to represent the ability to visualize how parts of objects fit together, what their relationships are, and what they look like when rotated in space. This is in contrast to the Perceptual Speed tests, where items must also be compared to determine if they are identical. However, the items are not rotated. An example would be to determine if the following strings are identical:

ahfgjel   ahfpjel

This factor is thought to represent the ability to recognize like-nesses and differences between objects and symbols quickly and accurately.

The Verbal Comprehension factor is assessed by tests measuring knowledge of synonyms and antonyms. An example of such an item might be to find the synonym for *ancient* among the following choices: *dry, long, happy, old, sloppy*. This factor is thought to measure the ability to understand ideas expressed in words. The Number Facility factor is assessed by problems like $16 \times 99 = \underline{\quad}$. This factor presumably reflects the ability to handle simple quantitative problems rapidly and accurately as well as to understand and recognize quantitative differences. The Induction factor is reflected in tests that require the individual to determine some rule or relationship in a pattern of figures, num-bers, or letters. For the series of letters *abcacdadea. . .*, the task would be to continue the series. This factor reflects the ability to solve logical problems where inference of a rule or relationship is demanded. This is in contrast to the Deduction factor, which requires the individual to reach a logical conclusion from a set of facts or premises. An example is a syllogism such as: "John is taller than Bill; Bill is taller than Jim. Who is the shortest?"

The debate between Spearman and Thurstone concerning general intellectual ability versus specific primary mental abilities was partially resolved by the development of *hierarchical* the-ories to account for correlational data. Such theories appeared necessary to accommodate data that fit neither the two-factor general and specific theory of Spearman nor the primary-abilities theory of Thurstone. To understand the problem, consider the difference between testing a group of Olympic contestants on the decathlon events versus testing a group of randomly chosen young adults. We would consider Olympic athletes as all pos-sessing superior general athletic ability compared with adults from the population at large. What differentiates the Olympic athletes is their prowess in specific track or field events. Thus, we might expect to obtain little evidence for a general factor differ-entiating them but considerable evidence for a set of specific abilities that appeared independent.

This analogy holds true if we consider the original group of students tested by Thurstone—University of Chicago under-graduates, a highly select intellectual group. All possess superior general intellectual ability; what differentiates them are specific abilities, such as verbal, numerical, and spatial reasoning. Thus, the data Thurstone (1938) collected from these individuals could readily be accounted for by a set of independent primary mental abilities; a general factor was unnecessary mathematically and psychologically.

The situation becomes very different, however, if we test a less select group of individuals on a set of athletic events or mental tests. Our data will tend to show a pattern in which performance on each event is correlated with performance on all other events; that is, there are no zero correlations in the correlation matrix. When this occurs, the data are more consistent with the idea that the individuals in our diverse group not only possess specific abilities but that these specific abilities are themselves correlated, giving rise to the notion of an overall ability.

Such a dilemma arose when Thurstone administered his primary-mental-abilities test battery to a group of schoolchildren (Thurstone & Thurstone, 1941). His data forced him to abandon a solution involving orthogonal or independent factors. He chose instead a set of *oblique,* or *correlated,* axes (factors) that best approximated his mathematical criterion for factor analysis. Figure 2-3 is an example of such a solution for a hypothetical set of test data representing spatial and numerical reasoning tests. In choosing a solution with correlated specific factors, one is left

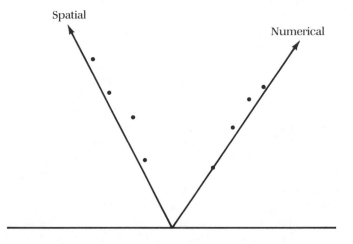

Figure 2-3   A two-factor solution in which the factors are oblique (i.e., correlated).

with the problem of explaining the pattern of correlations of the factors extracted from the pattern of correlations of the original tests. In Thurstone's case, he chose to resolve the problem in terms of a general factor, with the various specific or primary mental abilities loading differentially on this general factor. Ultimately, Thurstone agreed that such a second-order factor, obtained by factoring the correlations between the primary factors, was very similar to Spearman's g.

The outcome is partial agreement between the theories of Spearman and Thurstone. Both were forced to accept a hierarchical theory of intellectual abilities, a type of theory advocated by Burt (1949). The difference between Spearman and Burt on the one hand and Thurstone on the other is a difference in emphasis. Spearman and Burt represent the so-called British school, which emphasizes the importance of the general factor; factors lower in the hierarchy are considered less interesting or important. Thurstone and later Guilford represent the American school, which emphasizes the importance of primary ability factors and deemphasizes second-order factors extracted from the pattern of correlations of the first-order or primary factors.

Modern Factor Theories

Hierarchical Models of Intellect

From the 1940s to the present, factor theories have been developed that represent a reconciliation of the Spearman and Thurstone positions. Two major hierarchical theories have been proposed. The first of these, specified by Vernon (1965), represents an extension of Burt's theory and the British emphasis on the general factor. The second was described by Cattell (1963, 1971) and represents an emphasis on primary abilities characteristic of the American school.

Vernon's Theory. The theory proposed by Vernon (1965) is based upon a factor analysis approach that starts at the top of the hierarchy. The general factor is first determined for a correlation matrix. Relationships among tests based upon this general factor are factored out. The resulting residual correlations—that is, correlations between tests after the general factor is eliminated—are then factored further. This type of top–down approach can proceed through a number of successive levels, each level having less general significance than the preceding one. The result is a hierarchy similar to that shown in Figure 2-4. At the top of the hierarchy is *g*. Below *g* are two major group factors representing verbal–educational ability (*v:ed*) and spatial–practical–mechanical ability (*k:m*). The *v:ed* factor can be further decomposed into more specific abilities, such as verbal and numerical ability. Similarly, the *k:m* factor is further decomposed into specific abilities such as perceptual speed and spatial ability. In addition, there are certain cross-links, such as mathematical ability, which are influenced by both spatial and numerical ability.

Such decomposition can be continued in an effort to derive ever more specific factors in a hierarchy. Consider, for example, spatial aptitude, which falls under the spatial–practical–mechanical construct (*k:m*) in Vernon's (1965) theory (see Figure 2-4) and which has been elaborated by many theorists (Lohman, 1979; McGee, 1979; Smith, 1964). Spatial aptitude, in turn, can be decomposed into three further factors (Lohman, 1979). One is labeled *spatial orientation* and appears to involve the ability to imagine how a stimulus or stimulus array would appear from another perspective. Typically, in such tasks individuals must reorient themselves relative to some landmass.

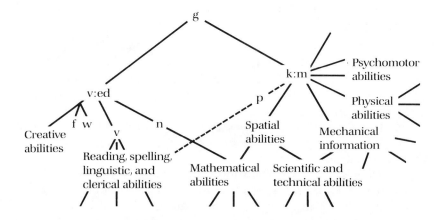

Figure 2-4   *Vernon's hierarchical model of intelligence. (Reprinted with permission from H. J. Eysenck,* The structure and measurement of intelligence *[New York: Springer-Verlag, 1979].)*

The other two factors are labeled *spatial relations* and *spatial visualization* (Lohman, 1979). The spatial relations factor seems to denote the ability to engage rapidly and accurately in mental rotation processes in order to decide if two stimuli are identical. Examples of common spatial relations tasks are shown in Figure 2-5. The first example is drawn from the Space Test of the Primary Mental Abilities (PMA) battery, (Thurstone & Thurstone, 1949). On this test individuals identify the alternatives that would be identical to the standard on the left if both appeared in the same orientation. The second type of problem shown in Figure 2-5,

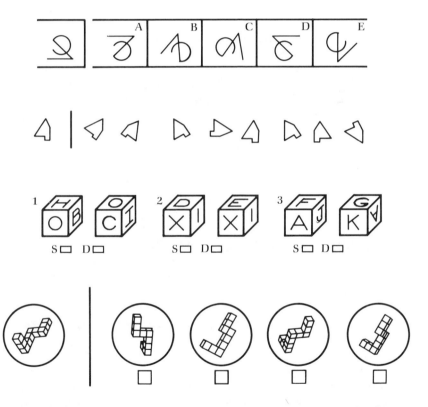

Figure 2-5   Examples of items from tests that tap the spatial-relations factor. See discussion in text. (Reprinted with permission from J. W. Pellegrino & R. Kail, Process analyses of spatial aptitude. In R. J. Sternberg (Ed.), Advances in the psychology of human intelligence, vol. 1 [Hillsdale, N. J.: Lawrence Erlbaum Associates, Inc., 1982].)

similar in format to the PMA Space Test, is the Cards Test from the French Reference Kit for Cognitive Factors (French, Ekstrom, & Price, 1963). The third example is the Cube Comparisons Test from the French Reference Kit. The individual's task is to determine if the two cubes could be different views of the same cube or not, which requires rotation of one or more surfaces to bring the cubes to the same orientation. The final example is taken from a test devised by Vandenberg (1971) based upon stimuli used originally by Shepard and Metzler (1971). The individual is to find the two stimuli that are rotated versions of the standard on the left.

The *spatial visualization* factor is defined by tests in which the stimuli are more complex than those on tests of spatial relations and in which the speed with which individuals respond is emphasized less than the number of problems solved correctly. Such tasks frequently involve the movement of internal elements of the stimulus or the folding and unfolding of flat patterns. Representative tasks are illustrated in Figure 2-6. The first problem shown in Figure 2-6 is taken from the Minnesota Paper Form Board Test. The individual's task is to select the completed figure that can be constructed from the set of pieces arranged randomly in the upper left corner. The second problem is from the Punched Holes Test of the French Reference Kit. The problem depicts a series of hypothetical folds of a square of paper followed by the punching of a single hole. The individual's task is to select the answer showing the number and location of the holes when the paper is unfolded. The third problem, illustrating paper folding or, as it is sometimes called, *surface development*, is from the Differential Aptitude Tests. Depicted is a flat, unfolded object and several completed objects. The individual's task is to select the object that will result from folding the flat object on the left.

The difference between spatial relations and visualization tasks seems to reflect two complementary aspects of performance (Lohman, 1979; Pellegrino & Kail, 1982), depicted in Figure 2-7. One is the *speed–power* dimension: Problems on the spatial relations tests are solved more rapidly than problems on spatial visualization tasks, and the tests themselves are administered in a format that emphasizes speed in the former case but both speed and accuracy in the latter. The second dimension involves the *complexity* of the stimuli presented, where complexity refers to the number of elements or parts of a stimulus that must be

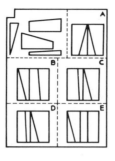

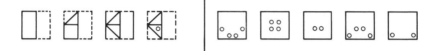

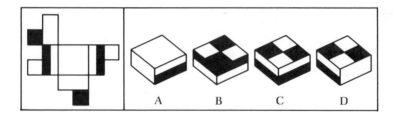

Figure 2-6   *Examples of items from tests that tap the spatial visualization factor. See discussion in text. (Reprinted with permission from J. W. Pellegrino & R. Kail, Process analyses of spatial aptitude. In R. J. Sternberg (Ed.),* Advances in the psychology of human intelligence, *vol. 1 [Hillsdale, N.J.: Lawrence Erlbaum Associates, Inc., 1982].)*

processed in solving the problem. Problems on spatial relations tests, although varying in complexity, nonetheless typically involve less complex stimuli than do problems appearing on tests of spatial visualization.

We have used spatial ability to illustrate both the content of typical mental tests and the type of hierarchical decomposition that can be done in examining test score relationships. A similar decomposition could be done for the verbal–educational factor, breaking down factors into specific subgroups of verbal and numerical tests with finer subdivisions within each of these two

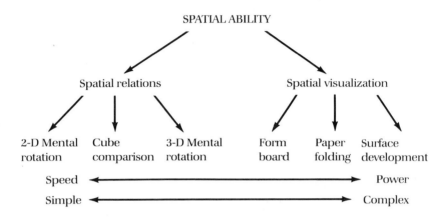

Figure 2-7 *Decomposition of spatial ability into the factors of spatial relations and spatial visualization. The factors are distinguished in terms of two dimensions: speed–power and the complexity of the stimuli. (Reprinted with permission from J. W. Pellegrino & R. Kail, Process analyses of spatial aptitude. In R. J. Sternberg (Ed.),* Advances in the psychology of human intelligence, *vol. 1 [Hillsdale, N.J.: Lawrence Erlbaum Associates, Inc., 1982].)*

content areas. But it must be remembered that there tend to be significant relationships among many tests. Thus, even though spatial orientation, relations, and visualization subfactors can be separated, scores on these tests tend to be highly correlated.

Cattell's Multiple-Factor Theory. The theory proposed by Raymond Cattell (1963, 1971) represents a major attempt to synthesize Thurstone's and Spearman's views of intellect. Cattell accepts the idea of primary abilities as well as the derivation of higher-order abilities from the relationships among the primary abilities or factors. However, Cattell also accepts the idea of general factors that are significant. The theory is based upon a bottom–up approach to factor analysis. Given a set of results such as Thurstone's correlated primary abilities, the next step is to conduct a second-order factor analysis utilizing oblique rotations. The result is a set of correlated second-order factors that can be further analyzed to determine more general third- and perhaps fourth-order factors. The result is that a hierarchy is built up from the bottom, in contrast to the type of top–down procedure advocated by British theorists such as Vernon.

Horn and Cattell (1966) reported the results of a second-order factor analysis of several primary abilities. They derived five second-order factors labeled g_f for fluid ability, g_c for crystallized ability, g_v for power of visualization, g_r for retrieval capacity, and g_s for cognitive speed. Cattell's theory places primary emphasis upon the g_f and g_c factors, where the former is often interpreted as representing the basic biological capacity of the individual and g_c represents the effects of acculturation upon intellectual ability.

The distinction between fluid and crystallized intelligence can be illustrated by considering results reported by Horn (1968) representing the loading of different primary abilities on each factor. Table 2-5 describes the general characteristics of tests representing specific factors and gives the g_f and g_c factor coefficients. The specific factors are listed in order from primary loadings on the g_f factor to primary loadings on the g_c factor. The g_f factor is best defined by primary abilities that closely follow Spearman's interpretation of g, the ability to educe and apply relations. The g_c factor is best defined by verbal comprehension ability, which is heavily dependent upon cultural context and prior experience.

Of interest is the fact that some primary abilities load on both higher-order factors. This is partly due to the fact that g_c and g_f are themselves correlated. The substantial correlation between them can be interpreted as support for the Spearman and Vernon position of a single higher-order g. Still higher-order factor analyses can be conducted. The result of such an analysis (Cattell, 1971) is a third-order factor g_f(h) and an educational-effectiveness factor. Both g_f and g_c load on the higher-order g_f(h) factor but only g_c loads on the educational-effectiveness factor. In addition, g_f has a higher loading than g_c on the g_f(h) factor.

Cattell's hierarchical theory is in many ways similar to Vernon's theory. One difference is the labels associated with factors at different levels in the hierarchy as well as their interpretation. Another difference is that Cattell has theorized about the causal relationships that exist among the different ability factors and their emergence over development. His ideas are reflected in the *investment and triadic theory*. The triadic theory differentiates three separate influences on cognitive performance. The most general are the *capacities*, which are presumed to be related to the structural and functional capacities of the brain. The most general capacity is g_f. Other capacities are g_s (speed),

Table 2-5   *Examples of loadings on g_f and g_c factors*

Factor label (test example)	g_f	g_c
Figural Relations (Induction of a relation among common figures, as in a figural analogy or matrix problem.)	.57	.01
Memory Span (Immediate recall of a series of numbers or letters.)	.50	.00
Induction (Induction of a rule from relations shown in a series of letters, numbers or figures.)	.41	.06
General Reasoning (Solving problems of area, rate, interest, etc., as in test of arithmetic reasoning.)	.31	.34
Semantic Relations (Induction of a relation among words as in verbal analogies.)	.37	.43
Formal (Deductive) Reasoning (Arriving at a conclusion from a set of facts or premises, as in a syllogism.)	.31	.41
Number Facility (Quick and accurate use of arithmetic operations, such as addition and subtraction.)	.21	.29
Experiential Evaluation (Solving problems involving protocol and diplomacy, as in a test of social relations.)	.08	.43
Verbal Comprehension (Advanced understanding of language, as measured by a vocabulary test.)	.08	.68

and g_r (retrieval capacity). The second class of influences are referred to as *provincials;* these are presumed to reflect localized brain areas. Generally, the provincials refer to sensory and motor skills that can influence performance. The clearest of these is p_v, visualization ability. The third class of influences are referred to as *agencies.* An agency is more associated with the cultural experiences of the individual. Agencies develop as a function of the investment of g_f and other capacities into a particular intellectual skill. The most general agency is g_c, crystallized ability.

The investment and triadic theory represents a speculative attempt to explain some of the patterns observed in factor analytic research. It is only loosely tied to the results of psychometric studies. However, the theory has a number of implications for influences on abilities. One such implication is that g_f is more a function of genetic and biological factors; in constrast, g_c is a function of both g_f and environmental influences. A second implication is that g_f and g_c should show differential changes as a function of aging. Specifically, as biological capacity diminishes with age, g_f should decline but no parallel decline is predicted for g_c. We shall shortly look at some of the data supporting this implication.

Guilford's Structure-of-Intellect Theory

One additional multiple-factor theory of intelligence has achieved prominence. Guilford (1967, 1982; Guilford & Hoepfner, 1971) proposed a theory that rejected the idea of a hierarchy of mental abilities. Furthermore, he argued against the concept of a single general intelligence factor, as proposed by Spearman, Burt, and Vernon. He also disagreed with Cattell and Horn's idea of a small group of general abilities. Instead, Guilford posited 120 distinct intellectual abilities representing the structure of intellect. He organized these factors along three dimensions that interact to determine different specific factors (see Figure 2-8). One dimension consists of five types of mental operations. The second dimension involves the content or areas of information in which the operations are performed. The third dimension represents the product or outcome that results from applying a given operation to a particular content.

Before going further, it will be useful to delineate briefly each of the categories along each dimension of the structure-of-

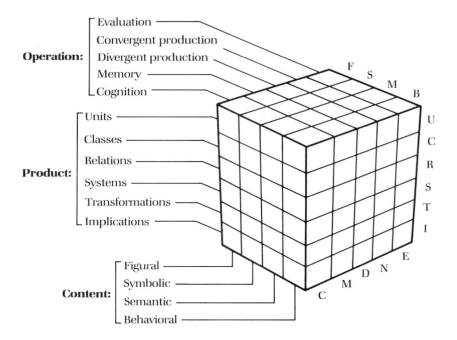

Figure 2-8   *The structure-of-intellect model proposed by Guilford.*
(Reprinted with permission from H. J. Eysenck, The structure and
measurement of intelligence *[New York: Springer-Verlag, 1979].)*

intellect model. The Content categories go beyond a simple verbal
(i.e., semantic) versus nonverbal (i.e., figural) contrast and include
a Symbolic category. This category refers to letters and numbers
as the specific item content. A critical feature of this category is
that the symbols or signs are organized into meaningful systems
such as the alphabet. The Behavioral category refers to problems
involving the actions of other people.

The Operation categories refer to mental activities performed upon a specific type of content. Cognition means discovery or recognition. Memory refers to retention of something cog-
nized. Divergent Production means thinking in different
directions, or seeking varied answers or solutions. In contrast,
Convergent Production refers to assembling or organizing information to generate a single best solution or answer. Evaluation
refers to decisions about the correctness or goodness of an answer.

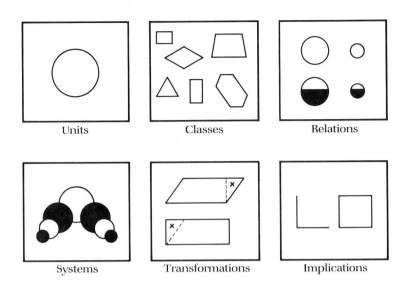

Figure 2-9   Illustrations of the six kinds of products in Guilford's structure-of-intellect model, using figural examples. (Reprinted with permission from J. P. Guilford, The nature of human intelligence [New York: McGraw-Hill, 1967].)

The Product categories refer to the desired result of applying a given operation to a given content. Figure 2-9 illustrates the different types of products with figural content. Units are single entities or chunks; Classes are sets of objects with one or more common properties; Relations are connections between two things; Systems are complexes, patterns, or organizations of inter-dependent or interacting parts; Transformations are changes of state for information products; finally, Implications are things expected, implied, or predicted from given information.

To concretize Guilford's efforts even further, we can provide some examples of the types of tests associated with individual cells in the structure-of-intellect model. A test of the Cognition of Symbolic Classes (CSC) is Number Classification. An example problem is

44   55   33

The individual must select a number that fits into this class. The individual must recognize the class rule for the symbolic content; that is, the operation is Recognition, the product is a Class, and the content is Symbolic. Cognition of Semantic Classes (CMC) is tested by a Verbal Classification test in which the individual must select a word that is consistent with a group of words such as *horse, mosquito,* and *snake.* Evaluation of Semantic Relations (EMR) is tested by analogy problems such as "Traffic is to signal as river is to _____" with choices such as *bank, dam, canal,* and *sandbags.* The operation is Evaluation, the product is a Relation, and the content is Verbal-Semantic. A final illustration is Cognition of Behavioral Implications (CBI). The individual is presented a statement such as "I'm just wondering how I'll act; I mean how things will turn out." The task is to pick the best psychological implication of this statement. The choices might be: (1) She's looking forward to it; (2) she's worried about it; and (3) she's interested in how things will turn out.

In the orginal structure-of-intellect theory, each ability is defined by its unique position on each of the three dimensions. No assumption is made about relationships among abilities sharing common positions on one or two dimensions. In fact, all abilities are presumed to be independent, and the dimensions of the model do not represent higher-order factors. Thus, the Cognition-of-Figural-Units ability is not presumed to share more in common with the Cognition-of-Symbolic-Units ability than with the Cognition-of-Symbolic-Classes ability. According to such a model, it should be possible to construct tests that separately measure each of the 120 unique abilities and that will load on only one of the many different factors extracted from a matrix of test score intercorrelations. A large part of Guilford's research program has been directed towards developing such tests and then attempting to validate the results in the context of the theory.

The structure-of-intellect model also provides a context within which to interpret other theories, such as Vernon's hierarchical theory. The distinction between the verbal–educational and spatial–practical–mechanical major group factors is partially parallel to the separation of semantic versus figural content. The further split of the verbal–educational factor into verbal and numerical abilities is seen as parallel to the distinction between semantic and symbolic content. Additional specific factors would correspond to product and operation categories in the Guilford model.

Why did Guilford argue for such a model as opposed to hierarchical models, such as the Vernon or Cattell model? Guilford (1964) pointed out that in his research, 17% of all correlations between mental tests fell in the −.10 to .10 range. In 1971, he indicated that 8677 of 48,140 correlation coefficients fell in this interval and that 24% of the correlations found in numerous studies were not significantly different from a value of 0. Guilford argued that such results do not support the assumption of a single general factor in intellectual ability. However, an alternative perspective was expressed quite clearly by Brody and Brody (1976 p. 43):

> Even if we accept Guilford's findings at face value, we find that the most comprehensive research on the most diverse intellectual abilities and measures specially constructed and selected to be independent of each other still leaves us with the finding that 76% of the time we can reject the null hypothesis that $r = 0$. . . . Strictly speaking, this finding is not compatible with Guilford's theory.

The data and analyses used by Guilford to support his theory have been criticized on several grounds. One issue concerns his use of targeted or Procrustean rotations to verify factors in the structure-of-intellect model.[3] In factor analysis with a Procrustean rotation, an investigator specifies prior to the analysis the kind of solution that one desires, then forces the final solution to match the prediction as closely as possible.

Horn and Knapp (1973) provided an interesting demonstration of the problems incurred by using such a method to verify a theory. They used data from three of Guilford's studies and compared the quality of the fit of the data to predictions from the structure-of-intellect model and from arbitrary models, that is, models based upon random selection. Using targeted rotations, they found that the data fit the random hypotheses as well as they fit the hypothesis based upon the structure-of-intellect model. Such a demonstration does not necessarily lead to rejection of the structure-of-intellect model but rather questions the methods used to provide support for it.

---

[3]In Greek legend, Procrustes was an innkeeper who adjusted the length of his guests by chopping off their feet if they were too long for his beds or stretching them on his rack if they were too short.

Related criticisms of the structure-of-intellect model involve the replicability of factor structures, the reliability of measures, and evidence of correlations between tests representing different factors. The details of these arguments involve statistical issues that are too technical for us to present here. Suffice it to say that many people advocate the basic position that a hierarchical theory is a more parsimonious representation of mental-test data and that the fractionalization of intellect into 120 distinct abilities appears unwarranted.

Recently Guilford has adopted a view partially reconciling his structure-of-intellect model with other theorists' views as well as with criticisms of his theory. Two changes are noteworthy. First, the Content dimension has been expanded from four to five categories, with the Figural category now replaced by separate Auditory and Visual content categories (Guilford, 1977). Thus, there are now 150 factors in the model.

The second major change is acceptance of the view that higher-order factors need to be considered. This is due to evidence of correlations between the individual specific factors of the model. Rather than treating them as independent entities with no overlap or relationship, they are now viewed as part of an interrelated system (Guilford, 1982). The basic, or first-order, factors are each of the 150 cells of the model. However, these combine in pairwise fashion to produce eighty-five second-order factors. Each second-order factor represents a pair of categories, such as Operations and Products, that are collapsed over the remaining dimension of the model. Five Operations and six Products yield thirty second-order factors, five Operations and five types of Content yield twenty-five more second-order factors, and six Products and five types of Content yield the remaining thirty second-order factors.

In addition, Guilford proposes sixteen third-order factors representing each of the sixteen major categories of his structure-of-intellect model. The sixteen categories are the five types of Content, the six types of Products, and the five types of Operations. Thus, Memory would be considered a third-order factor with second-order factors below it, such as Memory for Classes or Memory for Semantic Content. At the first-order level are each of the specific factors of the model representing a Content–Product–Operation triplet, such as Memory for Semantic Classes.

With these revisions to his theory, Guilford has moved closer to a hierarchical model that recognizes correlations among specific factors. Nevertheless, he still maintains that there is no evidence to support a fully hierarchical model with a general ability at the apex of the hierarchy. His reluctance to do so is based on his data indicating a number of zero correlations among various intellectual tests. Thus, we see in Guilford's recent modifications of his theory movement towards a hierarchical perspective, but one that remains distinct from those of theorists such as Vernon and Cattell. In addition, Guilford has made an important contribution by focusing attention on the issue of mental *processes* and *products* as important topics in understanding test performance and human abilities.

Development and Differentiation of Intellectual Abilities

When samples of adults are tested in factor analytic research, often there is evidence for many different abilities that appear uncorrelated. Good examples of this are Thurstone's original work with University of Chicago undergraduates and Guilford's studies of officer candidates in the Air Force, Navy, Coast Guard, and Marines (4534 of approximately 8000 individuals tested in several studies; see Guilford & Hoepfner, 1971). In contrast, when samples of elementary and secondary school children are tested, the data often support a general-abilities model with a single general factor and broad group factors accounting for the majority of the variance in the data.

Theorists have attempted to explain differences in factor structures obtained at different age levels in terms of a theory that intelligence becomes increasingly differentiated as a function of age, experience, and schooling. Support for such a theory is sought in changing patterns of test-score correlations. Garrett (1946) was one of the first to propose a theory of the increasing differentiation of abilities. Several sets of data appeared to be consistent with such an argument, including Thurstone's (1938) study of undergraduates and the Thurstone and Thurstone (1941) study of eighth grade children. Subsequently, Burt (1954) reviewed data in support of the Garrett thesis. Table 2-6 is an example of data offered by Burt in support of such a hypothesis. The

Table 2-6   *Percentage of variance accounted for by a general and three specific factors at three age levels*

| | Age | | |
Factor	8	10	12
General	52	36	28
Verbal	7	9	11
Arithmetical	3	3	13
Manual	3	6	7

Source: C. Burt. The differentiation of intellectual ability. *British Journal of Educational Psychology*, 1954, 24, 76–90. Reproduced courtesy of Scottish Academic Press (Journals) Limited.

data in the table indicate the contribution of a general factor and specific factors in accounting for test-score data obtained from 8-, 10-, and 12-year-old children. There is a decline in the importance of the general factor and a corresponding increase in the importance of specific factors.

Not all studies show this pattern of increasing differentiation of ability with age (e.g., Dye & Very, 1968; Vernon, 1961). Furthermore, there is an additional noteworthy problem of interpretation in this sort of research: Do tests administered at different age levels measure the same abilities with the same degree of reliability? For example, tests of numerical or verbal ability contain different sets of items at each age level. Although the tests administered to different age groups contain comparable content, the intellectual demands of, say, a vocabulary test may not be the same for all age groups. Thus, the differentiation due to age may actually reflect greater dissimilarity among items on tests for older individuals, not greater dissimilarity among older individuals. Because of these interpretive problems, the differentiation hypothesis remains plausible but unsubstantiated.

The differentiation hypothesis concerns changes in intelligence during childhood; earlier we noted that one implication of Cattell's hierarchical theory concerned changes in intelligence in adulthood. Recall that changes in g_f and g_c during adulthood should not be uniform: g_f is thought to decline more due to aging than does the culturally based g_c, which is thought to be relatively resistant to change.

A number of investigators have looked at age changes in various ability factors with particular emphasis on measures associated with the g_c and g_f factors. Some of the studies have involved *cross-sectional* designs in which individuals of different ages are tested at the same point in time. Thus, one might compare the performance of groups of 20-, 40-, and 60-year-olds. Cross-sectional designs have provided data that both g_f and g_c decline with age (e.g., Schaie & Strother, 1968). There are other cross-sectional data that support the decline in g_f with age but also indicate no decline in g_c (Horn & Cattell, 1967). In general, cross-sectional studies of age changes in g_f and g_c support the hypothesis of differential rates of decline with the suggestion that g_c remains stable and may in fact increase with age (Horn & Donaldson, 1976, 1979).

Longitudinal designs present quite a different picture of age changes in g_c and g_f. In a longitudinal design, the same individuals are tested at different ages; a sample of individuals might be tested at age 20 years, again at age 40, and a final time at age 60. Available longitudinal data indicate that g_c and g_f do not decline with age to the extent suggested by cross-sectional research and may not decline at all (Schaie & Strother, 1968).

One basis for the discrepant findings obtained with the cross-sectional and longitudinal research stems from the assumptions underlying the two designs. In a cross-sectional design, one assumes that the different samples are comparable in terms of their educational history, cultural experiences, and other pertinent variables. That is, one assumes that the 60-year-olds, when 40, were like the current sample of 40-year-olds, who in turn, are assumed at age 20 to have been like the current sample of 20-year-olds, and so on. To the extent that this assumption is false, cross-sectional designs can provide misleading data. For example, quality and quantity of education in North America have improved over most of the twentieth century. As a result, individuals in younger samples in a cross-sectional design will usually be better educated than persons in older samples. The result is that what may appear to be deficits due to aging may reflect differences in education.

This is not a problem for longitudinal research, for here the same individuals are tested throughout. Two other problems do crop up. First, in longitudinal research one focuses on the life span of one cohort of individuals, say those born in 1930. Is it reasonable to generalize findings from this group to cohorts born in 1950, 1970, or 1990, whose educational and cultural experiences are likely to be quite different? The only way to know for sure is to test the latter groups for their entire life spans. A second problem is that in a research project that spans sixty years, many individuals are lost from the sample. Some lose interest and refuse to participate, some move away, and, of course, some die. What is particularly troublesome here is that typically the individuals remaining in the sample are not a random sample of those who started. Those who continue to participate are often better educated, more affluent, and healthier than those who are lost from the sample.

In short, neither the cross-sectional nor the longitudinal design provides a foolproof approach to understanding changes that occur during adulthood. It is because of these shortcomings (and the enormous investment in time, literally generations, involved to resolve them) that the data are ambiguous with respect to the original Cattell hypothesis of age-related changes in various subfactors of intelligence. An alternative design has been proposed that combines the advantages of both the cross-sectional and longitudinal approaches and is known as the cohort-sequential design (Baltes & Schaie, 1973). In this type of design, individuals of different ages are simultaneously and repeatedly tested over several time periods. At each testing period, cross-sectional data are obtained. For each age group, the different testing periods also provide longitudinal data. In addition, the design allows for contrasts between different cohorts but at comparable ages to estimate whether the experience of being born at a particular point in history has differential effects.

As one might imagine, data conforming to such a design are limited. The data that are available suggest that both cross-sectional and longitudinal samples show similar patterns of decline in test scores and that declines do not occur until after the age of 50 (Schaie, Labouvie, & Buech, 1973; Schaie & Labouvie-Vief, 1974). (Those interested in reviews of data on age changes in intelligence test scores and in performance on cognitive, perceptual, and psychomotor tasks should consult Schaie, 1983; Willerman, 1979; or Willis, 1984.)

Theories and Tests

At the beginning of this chapter, we noted that mental tests have served two major functions. One of these is to provide the data base for theories of intelligence. The other is to assess and place students in educational systems. As we noted earlier, the original test developed by Binet and Simon was the first such test in the Western world devised for use in schools. On the Stanford–Binet, tests are arranged in order by age, and the examiner finds the age level at which the examinee passes all tests. Testing then continues until the examinee reaches the test level at which no tests are passed. The number of items passed is then used to determine an intelligence quotient, or IQ score. The IQ score is no longer determined by dividing mental age by chronological age and multiplying by 100. Instead, the score is based upon extensive normative data for examinees of a comparable age. The score reflects an examinee's relative position within a given age group, an IQ of 100 representing average ability. Despite this and other changes to the Stanford–Binet that have been made over the years, it remains remarkably similar to the test originally developed by Binet and Simon. In short, psychometric theories have had little impact upon the content and form of the Stanford–Binet.

Today, however, the Stanford–Binet is far from the only measure of intelligence; the number of mental tests available is enormous (see, for example, Buros, 1974, 1978), and the structure of many reflects the influence of psychometric theory. Consider, for example, the Wechsler Adult Intelligence Scale (WAIS) and the extension of the WAIS for children, known as the WISC, for Wechsler Intelligence Scale for Children (Wechsler, 1974). The WAIS and WISC contain items that more closely follow psychometric theory. The subtests of the WAIS and WISC are divided into two major groups, representing verbal and nonverbal (performance) scales. The WAIS and WISC report an overall IQ as well as separate verbal and performance IQs.

Much the same can be said for many of the widely used group intelligence and aptitude tests. The majority of these tests are targeted for childen of school age. Among the group intelligence tests used frequently in North America are the Lorge–Thorndike, Otis–Lennon, California Tests of Mental Maturity, Kuhlmann–Anderson, and Cognitive Abilities Test. The composition of these tests reflects psychometric theory in the sense that the items have a history of high loadings on either a general factor or a major group factor. Thus, group intelligence tests typically yield a single overall score, presumably reflecting g, as well as separate scores for verbal, quantitative, and nonverbal scales. The emphasis in group intelligence tests is on the assessment of abilities that have been shown to predict academic achievement. Hence, these tests tend to be associated with the *v:ed* group factor in Vernon's theory and the g_c and g_f factors in Cattell's theory.

A concrete illustration of the content and analysis of a frequently used intelligence test illustrates the emphasis on assessing general factors. The Cognitive Abilities Test contains ten different subtests grouped into Verbal, Figural, and Quantitative sections. Table 2-7 shows a factor analysis of the entire test battery for seventh grade students. The factor analytic technique is similar to that advocated by British theorists with the general factor extracted first followed by more specific verbal, nonverbal, and quantitative factors.

An alternative analysis following the Thurstone and Cattell approach would yield a solution more consistent with the g_f–g_c analysis of the tasks described above. The Verbal section consists of the following subtests: Classification, Analogies, Vocabulary (synonyms), and Sentence Completion. The latter two subtests would be considered measures of g_c; the former two represent measures of g_f as well as g_c because they are induction tasks. The Quantitative section consists of a Number Series subtest, a Quantitative Relations subtest, and an Equation Building subtest. The first of these is a measure of g_f; the latter two primarily reflect g_c.

Table 2-7   *Factor analysis of seventh grade pupils' performance on the Cognitive Abilities Test*

| | Factors | | | |
Subtest	General	Verbal	Figural	Quantitative
Vocabulary	.67	.51	−.02	.12
Sentence completion	.73	.51	.03	.07
Verbal classification	.70	.42	.10	−.07
Verbal analogy	.80	.29	.03	−.05
Quantitative relations	.74	.01	−.04	.25
Number series	.82	.02	.00	.06
Equation building	.79	−.02	.00	.21
Figure classification	.67	−.01	.39	−.05
Figure analogies	.77	.00	.40	−.07
Figure synthesis	.62	−.07	.39	.13

The Figural section consists of Analogy, Classification, and Puzzle Assembly subtests (form board). The former two clearly represent g_f tests, and the latter is a measure of both g_v and g_f.

In addition to general intelligence tests, sometimes known as omnibus tests, there are also specific-abilities batteries. Such batteries represent a difference in emphasis more in line with the primary-mental-abilities view of Thurstone. Examples of such batteries are the SRA Primary Mental Abilities (PMA) Tests developed by Thurstone and Thurstone, the Differential Aptitute Tests (DAT) developed by Bennett, Seashore, and Wesman, and the Comprehensive Abilities Battery developed by Hakstian and Cattell. The PMA battery contains tests representing five specific factors: Perceptual Ability, Numerical Ability, Verbal Ability, Spatial Ability, and Induction. The DAT contains tests representing eight factors: Verbal Reasoning, Numerical Ability, Abstract Reasoning, Space Relations, Mechanical Reasoning, Clerical Speed and Accuracy, and Language Usage. A similar range of abilities is assessed by the Comprehensive Abilities Battery.

The subtests found on these specific-abilities batteries partially overlap with subtests found on general intelligence tests. For example, measures of verbal ability are typically synonym or antonym tests; measures of induction include letter and number series completion as well as verbal and nonverbal analogy problems.

These aptitude batteries, like general intelligence tests, were developed with a specific criterion in mind: the prediction of academic achievement. Thus, one of the major criteria for any test of intelligence has come to be its predictive validity, that is, its ability to predict differences among individuals in some measure of social significance (usually but not always educational achievement). Individually administered intelligence tests, such as the Stanford–Binet and the Wechsler, and group tests, such as the Cognitive Abilities Test and the Differential Aptitude Tests, have been shown to have such predictive validity for academic performance.

As an example, we can consider predictive validity data, expressed as correlation coefficients, for the Cognitive Abilities Test. The technical manual for this test reports many different sets of results representing the correlation between test scores and measures of academic achievement such as reading grades, arithmetic grades, overall grade point average, and achievement test scores. For example, scores obtained on the CAT for children show an average correlation of .5 with reading or arithmetic grades obtained two to three years later. Similarly, CAT scores show an average correlation of .55 with college grades. Correlations in this range or higher are also obtained for scores on achievement tests.

Patterns such as these are characteristic of many intelligence tests. In part, this is attributable to the fact that scores on intelligence tests tend to correlate highly with each other. In fact, one way to validate a new intelligence test is to show that scores on the new test correlate with scores on the Stanford–Binet! The CAT has the following correlations with Stanford–Binet IQ scores for 9- to 11-year-old children: .72 for Verbal, .65 for Quantitative, and .60 for Nonverbal.

The story is not too different if we look at correlations with a specific-aptitude battery, such as the Differential Aptitude Test. For ninth grade students, the CAT Verbal score correlates .74 with the Verbal Reasoning subtest of the DAT, and the CAT Numerical score correlates .70 with the Numerical Ability subtest of the DAT. The Nonverbal subtest of the CAT correlates between .61 and .65 with the Numerical Ability, Abstract Reasoning, and Space subtests of the DAT.

All of these results are representative of two recurrent facts: (1) Scores on intelligence tests correlate highly with each other, and (2) scores on intelligence tests have moderate to high correlations with measures of academic performance. As the criterion to be predicted becomes more removed from the educational process—for example, job success or personal achievement—correlations decrease. This can be attributed to several factors beyond the scope of our present discussion. Suffice it to note, however, that one reason intelligence tests have persisted is that they did such a good job in meeting their original assignment— the prediction of academic performance!

Concluding Remarks

The critical element in the psychometric approach to developing theories about intelligence is the focus on individual differences. Mental tests are administered to large numbers of individuals, and the relationships among test scores become the basis for theories. We have seen that there are disagreements about the interpretation of different sets of results. Furthermore, results from different sets of test data often are not in complete accord. We can cite two reasons here for this disagreement, inconsistency, and controversy. First, there are many ways to analyze the same set of data. We have given some indication of this by illustrating independent versus correlated factors and the idea of top–down versus bottom–up factor analysis producing different hierarchies. Thus, different apparent solutions can be obtained for the same data, which lead to different psychological interpretations. Second, the data obtained in separate studies differ. The critical data for any type of factor analysis are correlations between test scores. The pattern of correlations depends upon the actual tests administered and the characteristics of the group taking the tests. Thus, studies vary with respect to the group tested (schoolchildren, armed service recruits, and criminals), the total number of tests administered, and the specific tests included in the test battery. The unfortunate outcome is a lack of comparability of separate studies, which is further complicated by alternative methods of analysis.

Despite such problems, some general facts and conclusions cannot be overlooked. One pervasive fact is that when a range of intellectual problems (tests) varying in content and format are administered to a sample of individuals, a matrix of positive test-score correlations is obtained. The pattern of the data supports a hierachical model with a general ability underlying all cognitive performance as well as several specific abilities. Although theorists may differ in their interpretations of a specific set of data, there is remarkable consistency in the general types of data that are typically obtained. For example, verbal and nonverbal abilities can be readily distinguished in children and adults.

Factor theorists have attempted to simplify the interpretation of correlations by way of general and specific abilities organized in a hierarchical or multidimensional scheme. One way to view factor theories is in terms of a structural model of human intellect. Unfortunately, factor theories do not provide a satisfactory way of defining exactly what a factor or ability might be. A factor is a hypothetical entity that an individual possesses to varying degrees. But what is it that an individual actually possesses when he or she has high levels of general intelligence or scores well on a specific ability, such as spatial visualization? Spearman could not provide a satisfactory answer to this question; when pressed, he attempted to define g as mental energy or force. In short, a factor is a mathematical abstraction that is interpreted after the fact by the psychometric theorist. The interpretation is based upon an *intuitive analysis* of the content of the tests that load on the same factor and the apparent intellectual demands for solving the individual problems, not unlike the analysis of spatial ability factors and tests illustrated earlier.

Many individuals working in psychometrics have been aware of some of the limitations of this approach to theorizing. For example, Thurstone pointed out that factor analysis was a technique for generating rather than testing hypotheses. For him, ideas emanating from factor analytic patterns constituted hypotheses to be tested in more controlled experimental research. One of the most significant criticisms of psychometric approaches to intelligence was offered by the psychometrician Quinn McNemar (1964, p. 881):

> Abilities or capacities, or aptitudes, or intellectual skills, or whatever you choose to call them, are measured in terms of response products to standardized stimulus situations. The stimulus is presented to an organism which by some process comes up with a response; thus any attempt to theorize and/or study intellect in terms of a simple stimulus–response (S–R) paradigm seems doomed to failure unless drastically modified and complicated by the insertion of O for organism and P for process. . . . Studies of individual differences never come to grips with the process or operation by which a given organism achieves an intellectual response. Indeed, it is difficult to see how the available individual difference data can be used even as a starting point for generating a theory as to the process nature of general intelligence or of any other specified ability.

As we noted in Chapter 1, understanding these processes that underlie mental acts has been the aim of cognitive psychologists, and it is this perspective that we consider next, in Chapter 3.

3

The Information
Processing Approach

For the moment, let us return to the topic of athletic or motor skill. Our goal is to understand how individuals perform tasks such as running, throwing the shot put, and high jumping. A reasonable way to approach the problem is to start by studying various aspects of body structure, organization, and functioning. This would include muscle structure, coordination of body parts, dynamics of motion, and physical principles applied to human body action. In short, we would approach the body as a system and try to understand how the elements of this system function together to achieve a given result. We would seek a theory of motor performance that can be applied to a wide range of motor activities. The applications would indicate how various elements of the system interact in running, jumping, throwing, and the like.

By adopting this type of approach, we would derive a general theory of human motor skill. This theory could then be used to develop smaller subtheories or models for the performance of different motor acts. The theory would not explain individual differences in athletic ability per se. However, it could be used as a framework for analyzing and understanding the nature of individual differences in performance or ability.

The approach outlined here is very different from trying to develop a theory of athletic skill by administering different motor tasks to many people and then observing how performances are correlated over tasks and individuals. In the previous chapter, we used exactly this second approach to illustrate the difference between a general athletic-ability factor versus specific ability factors. The key difference between the two approaches is that in one case we start with a wide range of tasks and individuals. We then attempt to deduce a general theory to explain our current data. The theory is empirically driven and not clearly constrained by a consideration of the organism producing the results. In contrast, the objective of the approach introduced in this chapter is to develop a theory of how the body is structured and how elements of that structure work together to achieve some outcome. Given the theory, we can apply it to a wide range of performances and a wide range of individual differences in the performance of a particular task.

This same contrast in approaches can be carried over to the analysis of intellectual performance. In the preceding chapter, we illustrated the psychometric approach to studying intellectual behavior. In this chapter, we shall consider an alternative approach in which the aims are to specify a general theory of how the human mind is structured and to determine the mental events and processes associated with achieving any intellectual response. Our goals in this chapter are threefold: first, to provide an overview of the basic components of such a theoretical perspective; second, to illustrate how such a theory can be used to develop models for performance in a wide range of cognitive tasks; and third, to show how we can use the theory and models to understand individual differences in cognitive performance.

The branch of experimental psychology that focuses on the structures and processes of the human mind is *cognitive psychology*. Cognitive psychologists study such related phenomena as perception, memory, comprehension, problem-solving, knowing, thinking, understanding, and, notably, intelligence. In studying these phenomena, most contemporary cognitive psychologists adhere to an *information processing* view of human cognition.

The term information processing is derived from computer science and provides a strong clue as to the nature of this approach. To understand the behavior of a cognitive system— whether computer or human—one must examine the processes that intervene between input and output. In a computer system, these processes are specified in a program that instructs the computer what to do. Consider the program represented in Figure 3-1, which can determine the sum of two numbers. The

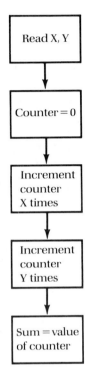

Figure 3-1   A simple flow diagram to add two numbers.

program involves a number of specific steps. First, the program reads two numbers, say 4 and 3. Second, a counter is set to 0. Third, the counter is incremented *x* times, which would be 4 in our example. Next the counter is incremented *y* times, 3 in our example. The resulting value of the counter, 7, provides the sum.

Each of the steps in this program may be referred to as a *routine*. The organization of these routines in a program is referred to as the *executive routine* or *control structure*. Each routine, in turn, may be composed of simpler subroutines that, when organized appropriately, carry out the function of the routine. Thus, the program is structured into hierarchical levels of operation, with each superordinate routine composed of an organized set of subordinate routines.

Now consider the cognitive processes of a person who is determining the sum of two numbers. In effect, the information processing perspective leads one to ask questions about human problem solvers that are analogous to those we would ask about the computer. We would attempt to discover the processes (routines) that are required to solve the problem and to identify the strategy or plan (executive routine) that integrates specific processes into a functional package that produces the desired results. We would also ask about the type of information that is needed to solve the task, how this knowledge is represented (formatted and interrelated) in memory, and how new information from the environment is incorporated into this system.

Figure 3-2 depicts a general diagram of the human information processing system, one that includes many of these notions. When information is detected in the environment, output from the receptors is analyzed—via a *pattern recognition process*—in an effort to identify it. If the pattern is indeed meaningful to the individual, then some of the individual's knowledge relevant to the pattern may be called upon. What happens next is hard to predict, because it depends on the nature of the identified pattern. The pattern may lead to the search for additional relevant

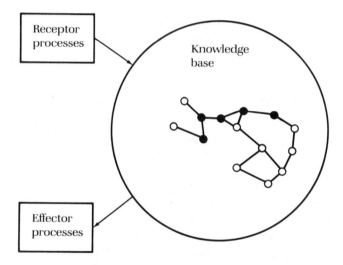

Figure 3-2   *A general representation of the human information processing system. The knowledge base consists of nodes (circles) linked by associations. The unfilled circles depict active nodes; the filled circles, inactive nodes. (Reprinted with permission from R. Kail & J. Bisanz, Information processing and cognitive development. In H. W. Reese (Ed.),* Advances in child development and behavior, *vol. 17 [New York: Academic Press, 1982].)*

knowledge (e.g., if the problem given above involved calculus instead of addition). Or the pattern may lead to an immediate response, as when in driving a car one swerves to avoid an oncoming vehicle. Still another possibility is that the pattern leads to a restructuring of some part of knowledge (i.e., learning occurs).

In the next three sections of this chapter, we shall elaborate this overview of the basic components of the human information processing system and examine some of the experiments that led to this view of cognition. We shall begin by discussing the characteristics of the *knowledge base*; then we shall consider *pattern recognition*; finally we shall examine *activated memory*.

The Knowledge Base

The human mind is certainly one important repository of knowledge, but it is hardly the only one. Egyptian pottery, Homeric poetry, libraries, and modern computers all share with the human mind the characteristic of providing relatively enduring records of information. Let us consider, briefly, one of these other stores of knowledge, a library. How might we characterize the knowledge in a library? Several possibilities come to mind. One would be simply to list all of the volumes in the library. A second approach would be to describe the scheme used to organize the volumes in the library. Yet another tack would be to describe the procedures used by individuals to gain access to the volumes. The list would certainly not end here, but these examples give some feel of the various ways one might try to understand the knowledge contained in a library.

Very similar strategies could be pursued in trying to understand human knowledge. One could identify (1) what a person knows, (2) how that knowledge is organized, and (3) the processes used to access the knowledge when it is needed. Information processing psychologists have rarely taken the first of these three avenues. The reason for not doing so is easy to understand. The average human adult knows a staggering amount of information. Simon (1981), for example, estimates that expert chess players know more than 50,000 chess-related bits of information, and this is in only one narrowly defined factual domain. Hence, cataloging the contents of a person's knowledge would be such a Herculean endeavor that it has rarely been attempted. Furthermore, the outcome of such an effort would be the description of but a single individual. Much adults' knowledge is common to individuals within a culture, but a good deal of human knowledge is idiosyncratic, varying enormously from person to person.

Consequently, information processing psychologists have focused instead on identifying the organization of human knowledge and the processes used to access that knowledge. They have done so on the assumption that although the contents of knowledge may differ from one person to the next, the organizing structure and mechanisms for accessing that structure are, at some level, common to all members of the species. In the present section of this chapter, we shall discuss the issue of organization; mechanisms for accessing knowledge are considered in subsequent sections.

Contents have not been ignored entirely, however. One fundamental distinction concerning the contents of knowledge is the difference between *declarative knowledge* and *procedural knowledge*, a distinction that corresponds to the difference between *knowing what* and *knowing how*. That is, declarative knowledge refers to the sorts of knowledge that we call facts, which we usually can describe verbally, such as "dogs have four legs," "Tallahassee is the capital of Florida," and "Matt's birthday is October 17, 1980." Procedural knowledge refers to knowing how to perform some activity. Examples would include knowing how to type, how to tie a necktie, or how to ride a bike. Procedural knowledge, unlike declarative knowledge, typically is not readily described verbally.

Declarative Knowledge

How might factual knowledge be organized in the human mind? One possibility is that knowledge is stored in the temporal order in which it is experienced, as if the mind were a tape recorder in which each experience is registered on the next segment of blank tape. This notion has a serious drawback: Just as it can be time-consuming to find a particular piece of music on a long tape, such a system is probably much too inefficient to be any kind of realistic representation of how humans organize the knowledge they have experienced.

Most information processing psychologists believe, instead,

that human knowledge is represented as a network in which conceptually similar entries are associated with one another. An example of such a network, depicting a person's knowledge about animals, is shown in Figure 3-3. The network is fundamentally associative, in that there are entries or *nodes* (the ellipses) linked together. Several characteristics of this network distinguish it from any simple associative structure. Consider the associations themselves. There are different types of associations: *isa* links are used to denote category membership; *can* and *has* are used to denote properties of the node; *lookslike* is used to denote the

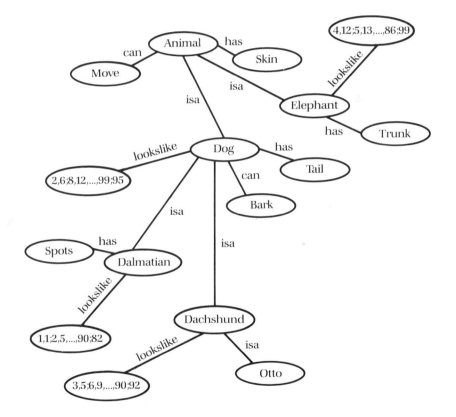

Figure 3-3   *A portion of a person's knowledge of animals. The ellipses correspond to nodes in the network that are linked by qualitatively different types of associations:* isa, has, can, lookslike. *See discussion in text. Adapted from Kail and Bisanz (1982).*

mental image associated with a node.[1] Note also that links vary in length, which is a way of indicating that they differ in strength: Shorter lines denote greater strength.

Prototypes. The nodes in an associative network refer to generic versions of concepts like dog, bird, and the like. Much of this knowledge, of course, is acquired from a person's experiences with specific exemplars of the concept. From experiences with different dogs, for example, we derive properties that differentiate the general class of dogs from the general class of cats. But dogs also differ considerably as a class, along a number of dimensions including size, color, length of hair, and ear shape, to name just a few. Hence, it is just as important that we also derive a concept that corresponds to our sense of the average or prototypic dog. Adults agree that a collie, for example, is somehow a more typical dog than a Chihauhau, presumably because a collie's size and other characteristics are more typical of dogs generally than are a Chihauhau's.

The process of establishing these generic nodes seems to involve establishing the properties associated with a concept and determining their centrality to the concept. Thus, of the properties *barks, has a tail,* and *eats,* the first would be a central or defining property of dogs and therefore associated strongly with the node for dog. *Has a tail* would be associated with dogs, but less strongly, because it is not a defining property. *Eats* is a property of all animals and hence would probably not be associated directly with dogs at all but be accessible only via inference.

The next step involves establishing a prototypic value for each of the associated features. For example, we need to determine whether a prototypic bark is more like the high-pitched yap of a Chihuahua or closer to the intimidating growl of a Doberman. Adults typically select the most frequently experienced value of that feature for their prototypes (Hayes-Roth & Hayes-Roth, 1977; Strauss, 1979).

One important implication of these generic nodes is that a person's representation of a concept, object, or person may not

---

[1]The node denoting a mental image contains pairs of numbers. These refer to x, y coordinates of points that would be used to generate an image. In other words, using the term *mental image* does not imply that a person has pictures stored in the mind. Instead, a mental image corresponds to a set of coordinates that would generate an image when activated, much as particular elements on a television screen are activated to generate a picture.

correspond to any actual instance of the concept, object, or person. Suppose, for example, you went to a political convention and asked party members the kind of car they own and their favorite vacation spots. Their hypothetical responses are shown in Table 3-1. The most frequent answers to the questions are Cadillac and Europe, hence, these would be part of your conception of members of this party (i.e., the node in your associative network). Yet this is misleading, for no individual member of the party who owns a Cadillac travels to Europe. This example illustrates that social stereotypes—views of individuals or groups of individuals that do not conform to reality—can easily arise from normal cognitive functioning.

Scripts. Prototypes represent a means by which an individual can abstract the common elements of experiences that occur over time. On occasion, the temporal order of experiences is critical in that it helps to define the knowledge. Consider, for example, knowledge of the activities involved in eating in a restaurant or going to see a movie. Both of these examples refer to a complex collection of *temporally organized* events. *Script* is the term used to refer to such knowledge (Schank & Abelson, 1977).

Scripts and prototypes share several characteristics. Scripts, like prototypes, are generic representations drawn from specific experiences. Just as experiences with Dalmatians, Chihuahuas, and Labradors give rise to a generic concept of dog, seeing different movies in different theaters results in a general scheme of the distinct episodes that are typically involved in seeing a movie. For example, adults' scripts for going to a restaurant seem to involve the following distinct episodes (Bower, Black, & Turner, 1979): (1) be seated; (2) look at the menu; (3) order the meal; (4) eat the food; (5) pay the bill; and (6) leave.

Table 3-1 *Hypothetical favorite vacation spots of political party members according to make of car owned*

	Favorite vacation spot				
Make of car owned	Europe	Rockies	Florida	Other	Total
Cadillac	0	250	250	250	750
Chevrolet	250	100	100	100	550
Ford	250	100	100	100	550
Other	250	100	100	100	550
Total	750	550	550	550	2400

Like prototypes, scripts can sometimes distort people's recall of experiences. For example, in describing a delicious meal at an elegant restaurant, most adults would not mention the fact that they looked at the menu because most listeners would assume that they had. Later listeners often have difficulty distinguishing what actually occurred from what they *infer* occurred (e.g., Bower et al., 1979). Similarly, if an experience does not conform to a script, people will be less likely to recall it accurately later. For example, if the episodes occurred in an order different from that specified in the script (e.g., a restaurant where one pays first, then eats), those experiences will often be recalled in the order dictated by the script, not in the order in which they were experienced.

Scripts and prototypes, then, are double-edged swords of sorts. They allow us to understand novel experiences (e.g., going to a new restaurant) that would be completely uninterpretable if the knowledge base consisted only of specific previous experiences. Yet they do so at the cost of introducing some distortions into our perception of experiences and our later recall of those experiences.

Procedural Knowledge

Recently, one of the authors was teaching his son, then 4 years old, how to tie his shoe. The instructions went something like this:

> Take the shoelace on your right and loop it over the other shoelace and back under, towards you. Then grab the ends of the lace and pull them until they are snug. Next, make a loop with the shoelace on your left and hold it. With your right hand take the other lace over the top of the loop. Then pull the lace under the loop, towards you, making it into a loop at the same time. Pull the ends of the loops until the knot is snug, but be sure you don't pull so hard that the ends of the laces come free.

Two characteristics of these instructions deserve comment. First, notice how awkward it is to express in words these actions that children and adults perform effortlessly. Somehow this verbal account, though accurate, does not readily capture the fluid, rapid movements of an adult performing the activity. Second, to generate these instructions (and write them here), the author actually had to tie his own shoes slowly, explaining each step of the process as he went. The knowledge simply was not readily available as a statement of facts (i.e., as declarative knowledge); indeed, the knowledge cannot be easily dissociated from performing the activity itself.

The phenomena described here certainly are not specific to tying one's shoes. To the contrary, they apply to all procedural knowledge ranging from simple skills mastered by all individuals to skills that are mastered by only a few (e.g., the skills of the .300 hitter in baseball). The dynamic properties of skill are often difficult to capture in associative networks like those we used to describe declarative knowledge (but see Norman & Rumelhart, 1975). Instead, information processing psychologists have tended to rely on *production systems* to represent procedural knowledge. The basic unit of such a system is the *production*, which consists of a condition or set of conditions and an associated action (or set of actions) to be taken whenever the conditions are met. For example,

If it is raining and you have no umbrella
THEN go indoors

is a very simple production. Whenever both conditions are met, the action is taken.

An Example. Because production systems describe actions, the best way to understand them is to see them in action. To illustrate a production system, we will consider the *water jug problem* studied by Luchins (1942; Luchins & Luchins, 1959): Individuals are given a set of jugs, told the quantity that each holds when full, and are told that they have access to unlimited amounts of water. The individual's task is to get an amount of water specified by the experimenter into one of the jugs. What complicates the problem is that the jugs have no quantity markings on them, so the only way to measure is by filling jugs entirely and pouring water back and forth between them. For example, given one jug with a capacity of 14 quarts, another of 36 quarts, and a third with 8 quarts, an objective might be to obtain exactly 6 quarts of water. To solve this problem, we need only fill the 14-quart jug, then transfer the water to the 8-quart jug; exactly 6 quarts are then left in the 14-quart jug.

Obviously this is a simple problem, and hence it is useful to illustrate the activities of a production system. The system,

modified from Anderson (1980, pp. 285–286), contains three productions:

P1. IF a jug is empty and its capacity exceeds the goal
THEN fill the jug.
P2. If one jug contains more than the goal and the capacity of the
other jug(s) is less than the contents of the first jug
THEN empty the smaller of the other jugs and fill it from the
first jug.
P3. If one jug contains the desired quantity
THEN stop.

These productions, like the examples listed above, contain a condition side and an action side. Whenever the conditions are met,
the associated actions are taken. This system includes two operating rules. First, productions are considered in sequence until
the problem is solved. Second, whenever a production refers to a
jug, we assume that the jugs are considered in sequence, from left
to right (i.e., A then B and C), and the first jug satisfying the
condition of a production will trigger that production.

Now consider the actions of this production system on the
problem just presented (see Table 3-2). The three productions are
considered in sequence. The conditions of P1 require that a jug
be empty. The first of the three jugs examined, A, satisfies this
condition, so it is filled. The status of the three jugs, depicted in
the first row of Table 3-2, is that jug A is full while B and C remain
empty. The next production to be considered is P2. Both of its
conditions are met, for (1) jug A contains 14 quarts, which is more
than the goal, and (2) the capacity of jug C, 8 quarts, is less than
the quantity in jug A. Consequently, we fill jug C from jug A, the
results of which are depicted in the second row of the table.
Proceeding through the set of productions, P3 is considered next.

Table 3-2   *Solution of a simple water jug problem by original production system*

	Content		
Production	*Jug A (14 quarts)*	*Jug B (36 quarts)*	*Jug C (8 quarts)*
P1	14	0	0
P2	6	0	8
P3	STOP		

The three jugs are considered in sequence, and finding that the contents of jug A is the desired amount, the system stops.

Now let us examine the production system as it deals with a more difficult problem: Given jugs of 21, 127, and 3 quarts, produce exactly 100 quarts. As before, P1 is considered first. Jug A does not meet the conditions of P1, because its capacity is less than the goal, but jug B does and it is filled. P2 is then examined and its conditions are met, for jug B contains more than the goal and the capacity of jugs A and C are less than the contents of B. Because jug C is the smaller of A and C, it is filled from jug B. The result is displayed in row 2 of Table 3-3. P3 is then considered; its conditions are not met, so the system returns to the first production in the sequence, P1. Its conditions are not satisfied, so we return to P2 and again its conditions are met. The outcome is that jug C is emptied, then filled again from jug B. This sequence repeats several times. The conditions of P2 are met, but not those of P1 and P3. Finally, after P2 has fired nine times in succession, the conditions of P3 are met and the problem is solved.

In this problem we start to see some of the shortcomings of this particular production system. Notice, in particular, what occurred when jug B had 121 quarts of water. The system went ahead and transferred three quarts to jug C. If instead the water had been transferred to jug A, the problem would have been

Table 3-3   Solution of difficult water jug problem by original production system

Production	Content		
	Jug A (21 quarts)	Jug B (127 quarts)	Jug C (3 quarts)
P1	0	127	0
P2	0	124	3
P2	0	121	3
P2	0	118	3
P2	0	115	3
P2	0	112	3
P2	0	109	3
P2	0	106	3
P2	0	103	3
P2	0	100	3
P3	STOP		

solved. The system, however, always transfers water to the smaller of the two jugs (i.e., P2); it has no way of "knowing" that a short cut was present, as a human probably would.

To make the production system behave in this more intelligent manner, P2 could be replaced with a more sophisticated production, P2A:

> P2A. IF one jug, I, contains more than the goal and the capacity of the other jugs is less than the contents of jug I
>
> THEN 1. calculate the difference between the contents of I and the capacity of jug J,
>
> 2. calculate the difference between the contents of I and the capacity of jug K,
>
> 3. find the difference closer to but not less than the goal, and
>
> 4. empty the water from the jug determined in part 3 and fill that jug from jug I.

P2A is considerably more complex than its predecessor, P2, yet the complexity is necessary to give the system the intelligence lacking in our original system.

Follow the sequence of actions as the modified production system tackles the same problem (i.e., measure 100 quarts from jugs of 21, 127, and 3 quarts). Production P1, unmodified from the original system, is considered first and its conditions are met. The result is that jug B is filled. P2A is next in sequence and its conditions, too, are satisfied. Taking the four steps on the action side results in the following:

> 1. The contents of B minus the capacity of A is 127 − 21 = 106.
> 2. The contents of B minus the capacity of C is 127 − 3 = 124.
> 3. Both 106 and 124 are not less than the goal, but 106 (obtained by subtracting the capacity of A) is closer.
> 4. Fill jug A from jug B.

The outcome of P2A is in the second row of Table 3-4: Jug A is full, jug B now has 106 quarts, and jug C is empty. The next production in sequence, P3, is not triggered, nor is P1. Returning to P2A, we find its conditions are satisfied once again, for jug B still contains more than the goal and the capacities of the remaining jugs are still less than the goal. The resulting actions are:

1. The contents of B minus the capacity of A is $106 - 21 = 85$.
2. The contents of B minus the capacity of C is $106 - 3 = 103$.
3. 85 is less than the goal but 103 (obtained by subtracting the capacity of C) is not.
4. Fill jug C from jug B.

Now jug A remains full, jug B has 103 quarts, and jug C is also full. In the next sequence of processing, P3 and P1 are again considered and rejected, P2A is set in motion, with the result that jug B now contains exactly 100 quarts. Hence, when P3 is considered, processing halts.

The greater complexity of P2A compared with P2 enabled the problem to be solved more rapidly—five productions fired compared with the original eleven. What is perhaps more important is that the behavior of the revised system has less of the mechanical or rote characteristics of its predecessor and seems to have more of the intelligent characteristics we like to attribute to human problem solving.

General Skills. Our version of Anderson's (1980) production system represents an *algorithm* for solving water jug problems in that the system is a complete set of actions that will consistently lead to the right answer if implemented accurately (and if the problem is indeed solvable). Similarly, the verbal description of tying one's shoe would be an algorithm, for it faithfully leads to tied shoes. *Heuristics*, in contrast, are general guidelines or rules of thumb that may make a solution likelier but do not guarantee one. For example, if the problem is to find where you left your car keys, one heuristic would be to check in all of the usual spots where you leave your keys.

Table 3-4   *Solution of difficult water jug problem by modified production system*

| Production | Content | | |
	Jug A (21 quarts)	Jug B (127 quarts)	Jug C (3 quarts)
P1	0	127	0
P2A	21	106	0
P2A	21	103	3
P2A	21	100	3
P3	STOP		

We can also illustrate the difference between heuristics and algorithms with a *problem space*. This is simply a diagram that allows us to represent the various states involved in solving a problem and the different operations that can be used to move between states. Part of such a problem space is shown in Figure 3-4. Literally any type of problem can be cast into this sort of framework as long as the initial state, goal, and operations are well defined. For example, the initial state might be "I'm hungry" and the corresponding goal state could be "I am stuffed"; legal operations could include (1) go to a restaurant and buy something to eat and (2) go to the kitchen to make something to eat. Thus, in terms of a problem space like the one shown in Figure 3-4, an algorithm refers to a *known* sequence of operations that links a start state with a goal state; a heuristic is a rule that one uses to select an operation in the absence of an algorithm.

One general heuristic that many adults use is called *means–ends analysis.* In this approach, a person first identifies the difference between the current state of affairs and the desired state of affairs and searches for actions that will eliminate the difference. If, to continue our earlier example, the initial state is one of hunger and the goal is to be sated, the difference is one of getting food in one's stomach. One action that would eliminate the difference would be to go to a restaurant, but to do so one needs money. If none is available, then there is a discrepancy between the current and desired states in terms of cash on hand. We can eliminate this difference by going to the bank, which means that the conditions for going to a restaurant are now satisfied, which in turn means that we can now eliminate the discrepancy between the initial and the goal states.

Means–end analysis is not always the most efficient heuristic. Consider the problem of flying from Santa Barbara, California, to West Lafayette, Indiana. The initial state is the current location; the goal state is the desired destination; the legal operators are all scheduled flights in the United States. Search of the available operations reveals no direct flight (that would make the problem too easy), so we establish as a subgoal flying to any large city east of the Rocky Mountains. A flight to Denver qualifies. We reassert the original destination—West Lafayette—and again search for a direct flight. Finding none, we create another subgoal: Seeing that West Lafayette is near Indianapolis, we establish the latter city as a suitable intermediate destination. Once there, though, we discover that the only flights to West Lafayette are from Chicago, so

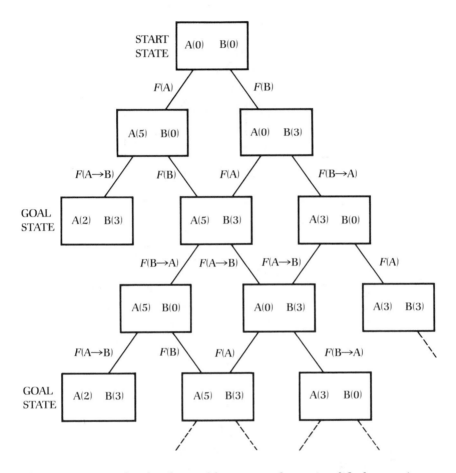

Figure 3-4   Five levels of a problem space for a simplified water jug problem. The objective is to measure 2 quarts of water given jugs that hold 5 quarts (jug A) and 3 quarts (jug B). Legal operations include filling jug A or jug B, represented as F(A) and F(B), respectively, as well as pouring from jug A to jug B and vice versa, denoted by F(A→B) and F(B→A), respectively.

we must either drive (not a legal operation) or fly north to Chicago and then south again to West Lafayette.

The difficulty here can be easily seen if we examine the problem space for this problem, shown in Figure 3-5. The number of legal operations leading from the initial state is large, but only one path leads from intermediate states to the goal state. Hence,

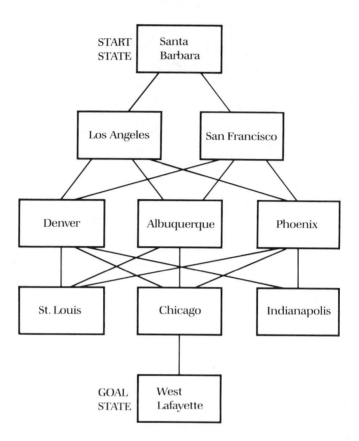

Figure 3-5 *A problem space depicting the problem of flying from Santa Barbara, California, to West Lafayette, Indiana.*

most intermediate states will lead to a dead end, sooner or later. In such cases, *working backwards* is a more useful heuristic than means–ends analysis. Here one begins with the goal and seeks an operation from some intermediate state that would lead directly to the goal. In this case, we would set the goal as West Lafayette and determine that the only relevant operation is a flight from Chicago. Once this operation was identified, we would set Chicago as our subgoal, and continue to work backwards through our projected trip.

Summary

The knowledge base refers to factual or declarative knowledge as well as to procedural knowledge. Information processing psychologists typically characterize the former as an associative network consisting of nodes connected by various types of links. Prototypes and scripts represent two ways in which a generic representation is formed from distinct experiences.

We distinguished two general categories of procedural knowledge. An algorithm is a set of actions that achieves a specified outcome when executed properly. A heuristic, in contrast, is a rule of thumb for solving a problem in the absence of an algorithm. Two useful heuristics that adults often use are means–ends analysis and working backwards.

Before discussing how knowledge guides information processing, we should consider some implications for issues of intelligence and individual differences. One of the hallmarks of human intelligence is the possession of a large body of organized knowledge that is readily accessible. As one example, we consider adults to be more intelligent than children simply by virtue of their greater knowledge and experience. Furthermore, we differentiate among individuals of the same age with respect to the amount and types of knowledge they possess. As we saw in Chapter 2, measures of verbal and quantitative ability contain vocabulary and arithmetic problems, respectively. Individuals who score well on such tests must have a declarative knowledge base sufficiently well elaborated to identify word meanings and subtle aspects of concepts, as well as highly efficient procedures for complex computations. Superior performance on mental tests may be attributable to what information is stored, the way in which it is organized, and perhaps the speed or relative ease of accessing this information.

Differences in the availability of information also have interesting implications regarding the likelihood of acquiring more knowledge. Recall our discussion of the importance of prototypes and scripts. What these constructs illustrate is that understanding new facts and concepts and incorporating them into the knowledge base is easier when they can be related to information that already exists. Perhaps this is why measures of verbal ability are good predictors of school success and achievement. Those who know more at a given point in time have a greater chance of acquiring still more information because new information can be incorporated into an existing, well-developed knowledge base.

Pattern Recognition

For external events to be translated into mental experience, physical stimuli must first be translated into neural activity. In the case of vision, for example, light passes through the pupil to the lens, where it is focused on light-sensitive receptors on the retina. This initiates a chemical reaction, which in turn generates a neural impulse. In hearing, vibrations from some object (e.g., a tuning fork or vocal cords) create pressure waves in the air; these changes in air pressure create movement in the tympanic membrane (i.e., the eardrum). The tympanic membrane is linked via bones in the middle ear to the *cochlea*, a cavity filled with fluid and lined with hair cells that are connected to auditory nerve cells. Movement of the tympanic membrane translates into distinct waves within the fluid of the cochlea, thereby stimulating the hair cells and the auditory neurons.

The consequences of stimulating either the eye or the ear (or other modalities, for that matter) is neural activity. However, the neural activity generated by the receptors does not, by itself, give rise to our subjective experience of the external world. Instead, the pattern of neural activity is analyzed in the brain. In other words, sensory systems function much like a card reader in a large computer system. Just as each human sensory system is responsive to only a particular type of external stimulation, the card reader is designed to be sensitive only to information of a well-defined type (i.e., the once ubiquitous IBM card). Furthermore, in both sensory systems and card readers, the product of this information–receptor interaction is a pattern of electrical activity that must be sent on—to the brain or to the computer's central processing unit—for it to be rendered meaningful.

In both vision and audition, processing by the sensory system seems to result in a representation called an *icon* that contains much of the information from the stimulus, but in a volatile medium that has a lifetime measured in seconds. During this brief interval, meaning must be given to the icon, a process referred to by information processing psychologists as *pattern recognition*.

Template Matching

One way that pattern recognition might occur would be through a process known as *template matching*. In this system, patterns of neural activity corresponding to known stimuli are stored in the knowledge base. Recognizing a pattern involves comparing the current pattern of neural activity with these stored representations or templates; recognition occurs when a match is found.

Template matching is the means by which bank checks can be read automatically. Numbers at the bottom of a check (see Figure 3-6) denote the bank and the account; these numbers are read off the check by an electronic analog to the eye and compared with templates stored in the computer. Template matching is well suited for this form of pattern recognition, because the number of potential patterns is small, consisting only of digits and a few other special characters. Also, the digits are printed in exactly the same position on every check and always appear in the same distinctive format.

These same circumstances that make template matching feasible for use with bank checks make it an unlikely candidate for human pattern recognition. Note first that humans are capable of recognizing an enormous number of patterns; for each pattern to be compared against all of these stored templates would be an unwieldy, time-consuming process. Furthermore, humans are

Figure 3-6   A bank check. The numerals in the lower left-hand corner are read by comparing them against templates.

capable of recognizing a pattern even though it appears in different orientations, and, in the case of letters and numbers, in different styles.

This fact alone does not rule out a template-matching system. One could propose that the knowledge base includes a separate template for each orientation and style, but the resulting system is hardly efficient. In addition, it could not recognize a familiar letter in a completely novel orientation or novel style, which humans certainly can do.

These logical arguments against template matching can also be supplemented by experimental evidence. Consider a task in which a person is asked to find some specific letter in a large array of letters. Suppose, for example, that a person were asked to find the letter Z in each of the two columns in Table 3-5.

Table 3-5   Lists for a visual search task

List A	List B
U R C	X V K
B G S	A N W
S U R	W X V
D B S	M A W
R C D	V K M
S G B	W N A
C G R	K N V
B D S	A M W
U G D	X N M
R U D	V X M
B G S	A N W
B D B	A M A
C B D	K A M
G B S	N A W
D U R	M X V
S B Z	W A Z

According to a simple template-matching scheme, the pattern of neural activation resulting from each letter in the array would be compared with the template in the knowledge base for Z. Finding the Z by this method should be equally rapid for the two columns in Table 3-5, because the Z appears in exactly the same location, and both contain the same number of highly familiar letters. Yet typically the Z is found much more rapidly in list A than in list B (Neisser & Bellar, 1965), a finding that cannot be explained readily with any simple template-matching scheme.

Feature Detectors

If template matching is not the basis for human pattern recognition, what is the mechanism? One clue comes from the experiment just described, in which people searched for a particular letter in an array. In list B, where finding the Z is usually more difficult, all of the letters were made of straight lines (e.g., A, K, and X) with no curves such as in B, R, S, or U. The easier of the two lists, in contrast, is just the opposite, consisting only of curved letters and including no letters with only straight lines. In other words, the similarity of the *features* of the letters seems to be critical in determining the ease with which a pattern is recognized.

One of the first pattern recognition schemes based on the detection of features was proposed by Selfridge (1959) and is called *Pandemonium*. As can be seen in Figure 3-7, Pandemonium's method of recognizing patterns involves a sequence of actions by different "demons." When a stimulus is presented, an internal representation or image is created that corresponds to a translation of the stimulus into a pattern of neural activity to be analyzed. The first level of analysis is done by the *feature demons*. Their job is to analyze the pattern of activity to determine if a single specific feature—such as a horizontal line, a vertical line, or an acute angle—is present. At the next level are *cognitive demons*, each corresponding to some known pattern. The job of these cognitive demons is to monitor the feature demons of interest to them, that is, those feature demons that collectively comprise a pattern. Thus, the cognitive demon for the letter A monitors feature demons for acute angles, horizontal lines, and oblique lines.

The cognitive demon attempts to attract the attention of the *decision demon* in direct proportion to the number of relevant

Feature demons   Cognitive demons

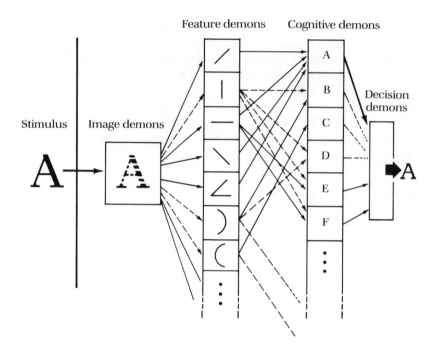

Figure 3-7   *Selfridge's Pandemonium model of pattern recognition.
(Reprinted with permission from R.* Klatzky, Human memory, 2nd ed.
[San Francisco: W. H. Freeman and Company, 1980].)

feature demons that are active. Thus, when a B is present, the
cognitive demon for O makes no attempt to attract the decision
demon, for none of its features have been activated. The cognitive
demon for F is moderately active, for Bs and Fs include many
common features. The cognitive demon for B, of course, is responding vigorously, for all relevant features are present. The
pattern will be recognized when the decision demon decides
which cognitive demon to attend.

The results of the experiment on scanning an array for a
specific letter can be handled neatly in a pattern recognition
system of this sort. The letters in list B share many features with
Z. In Pandemonium, the cognitive demons corresponding to Z as
well as A, K, and N would be clamoring for the attention of the
decision demon throughout the list. The result is that the decision demon needs more time to decide if, in fact, a given letter is
Z or merely a letter similar to a Z. In list A, by contrast, the
cognitive demon for Z is inactive throughout most of the list, for

its feature demons have not detected any features associated with a Z.

It would be misleading to leave the impression that feature-based pattern recognition is this simple. If one believes in such a system, an obvious first order of business would be to specify the features, for these are really the fundamental units of processing. Here there has been progress in identifying the distinctive features of alphanumeric stimuli (e.g., Gibson, 1969), but there is greater controversy (and less progress) regarding the features used as the basis for recognition of more complex patterns, such as human faces and landscapes.

Equally important, we should point out that features are, in effect, templates. That is, they are representations stored in the knowledge base against which incoming stimuli are compared. The difference is one of order of magnitude: Features refer to simple templates that are used collectively to recognize a stimulus. As we defined them originally, templates referred to a stored representation of an entire stimulus. The fact that a feature is a template in miniature, so to speak, does mean that some of the questions raised earlier about template-matching processes apply to feature-based systems of pattern recognition as well. For example, such a system must recognize stimuli in novel orientations and novel sizes. How it does this remains poorly understood.

Conceptually Driven Analysis

In Figure 3-7, the sequence of activity is exclusively from left to right; the stimulus is subjected to successively more sophisticated forms of analysis until recognition is achieved. Pattern recognition rarely occurs in exactly this manner. To see why this is so, consider three examples. First look at this pattern:

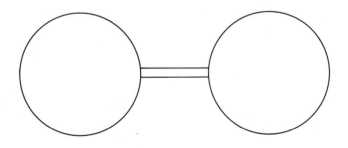

It could be dumbbells or eyeglasses; how people describe it depends upon what they have been led to expect to see (Carmichael, Hogan, & Walter, 1932). Second, read the following brief paragraph (from Bransford & Johnson, 1972, p. 719):

> If the balloons popped, the sound would not be able to carry since everything would be too far away from the correct floor. A closed window would also prevent the sound from carrying since most buildings tend to be well insulated. Since the whole operation depends on a steady flow of electricity, a break in the middle of the wire would also cause problems. Of course the fellow could shout, but the human voice is not loud enough to carry that far. An additional problem is that a string could break on the instrument. Then there could be no accompaniment to the message. It is clear that the best situation would involve less distance. Then there would be fewer potential problems. With face to face contact, the least number of things could go wrong.

The paragraph makes little sense unless you see Figure 3-8 beforehand, for the picture allows you to interpret the words in a particular way. Finally, read the words in Figure 3-9. You probably read the words in that figure as "THE CAT," but notice what must have happened for you to do so. The middle letter in each word actually is ambiguous—it could be either H or A. In fact, it was read as H in the first word because TAE makes no sense in English while THE does. In the second word, the ambiguous letter was interpreted as A for the same reason: CAT is interpretable as a word in English but CHT is not.

These examples demonstrate that pattern recognition is not determined exclusively by the data that the system encounters. Instead, recognition is also determined by a person's intuitions and biases about what pattern to expect, what pattern would make sense in a particular situation. A person's conceptions about what to perceive help to drive the pattern recognition process in a particular direction, hence the name *conceptually driven processing.*

The mechanisms of conceptually driven processing are best understood in the context of letter and word recognition. Most studies have used a procedure devised by Reicher (1969), depicted in Figure 3-10. Subjects are briefly shown either a word or the letters scrambled to form a nonword. This is followed by a ### stimulus to erase or *mask* the icon. Finally, subjects are shown a pair of letters and are asked to decide which of the two

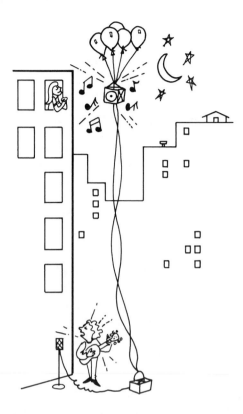

Figure 3-8 *Picture to accompany ambiguous passage in the Brans-ford and Johnson (1972) experiment. (Reprinted with permission from J. D. Bransford & M. K. Johnson, Contextual prerequisites for under-standing: Some investigations of comprehension and recall.* Journal of Verbal Learning and Verbal Behavior, *1972, 11, 717–726. Copyright by Academic Press.)*

Figure 3-9 *An ambiguous figure: The middle letters in the two words are identical. (Reprinted with permission from J. R. Anderson,* Cog-nitive psychology and its implications *[San Francisco: W. H. Freeman and Company, 1980].)*

Figure 3-10   An illustration of the procedures used in Reicher's (1969) experiment. In panel A the subject sees a word for a fraction of a second, followed immediately by a mask over the first three letters and the letters D and K. In panel B the subject sees a nonword followed by the same alternatives. The subject's task is to guess which letter actually appeared.

letters appeared in the designated position in the word (or nonword) just presented. Reicher's basic finding was that subjects were more accurate in selecting the correct letter when it was preceded by a word than by a nonword. In other words, in trying to decide if K or D had been presented, subjects were more accurate if they had seen WORK beforehand rather than OWRK. Somehow the presence of WOR makes it easier to recognize the K.

To incorporate this type of conceptually driven processing, Pandemonium could be modified as shown in Figure 3-11, a modification derived from the work of Adams (1979), McClelland and Rumelhart (1981), and Rumelhart and Siple (1974). Notice that cognitive demons are now called letter demons and that we have added two levels beyond that of letter demons: *Word demons* listen to letter demons and respond when a particular configuration of letter demons—those corresponding to a word—is active; *higher-order demons* is a catchall term used here to point to the fact that identification of words often guides the identification of phrases, which in turn guides the recognition of sentences, and so on. The most important difference, however, between Figures 3-7 and 3-11 is that processing is no longer exclusively from left to right; processing is right to left as well, indicated by the presence of arrows in both directions.

To illustrate the nature of the proposed processing, consider what happens when subjects in Reicher's (1969) paradigm are deciding if D or K was presented, as in Figure 3-10. According to our revised model, when letters are first presented, feature demons scrutinize each character and letter demons monitor the

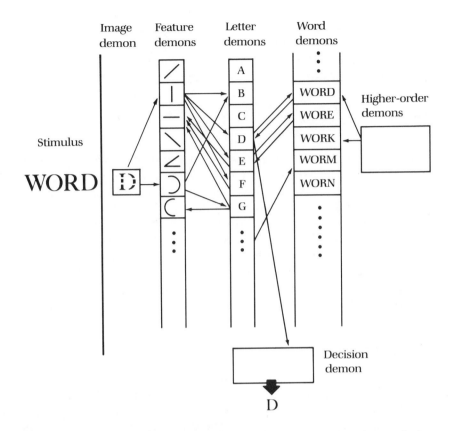

Figure 3-11 A modification of Selfridge's Pandemonium that includes *conceptually driven pattern recognition.*

appropriate configuration of patterns. The novel twist is that word demons also monitor the letter demons. When WORD is presented, word demons for WORD, WORK, WART, and TOAD all become activated—in varying amounts—by the activities of the letter demons W, O, R, and D. In the original Pandemonium model, WORD would have been recognized once each of the four individual letter demons (cognitive demons as we called them then) had persuaded the decision demon to act in its favor. In the revised version, when these word demons become active, they encourage their constituent letter demons to check for their constituent feature demons. In other words, once enough featural information has accumulated to activate word nodes, those words serve as hypotheses about potential letters that might be present, hypotheses that drive the letter recognition process in particular directions. In Reicher's paradigm, words lead to more accurate decisions about letters because nonwords result in negligible activation of word nodes, thus depriving the system of these clues to guide the pattern recognition process.

Summary

Stimulation of the receptors results in a neural representation of the stimulus that is detailed but short-lived. Interpreting this representation, what cognitive psychologists typically call pattern recognition, is based on an analysis of the basic features of the stimulus. Pattern recognition, however, is not determined exclusively by the features of a stimulus. Instead, pattern recognition is more akin to a guessing game: When enough information has accrued to formulate tentative hypotheses about the identity of a stimulus, the aim of subsequent processing is to evaluate those hypotheses.

Activated Memory

One of the paradoxes of human cognition is that although the amount of declarative and procedural knowledge that a person can acquire is virtually limitless, the quantity of information that a person can think about at any one time is severely constrained. Suppose, for example, that you are watching the news and learn, in rapid succession, that the following stocks were the most actively traded that day on the New York Stock Exchange: Grumman, IBM, Sunbeam, Exxon, Mattel, Citicorp, Seagram, Pennzoil, USAir, Pillsbury, Sears, and Massey-Ferguson. These are all relatively familiar national corporations, yet you would probably remember no more than five or six of these companies by the end of the newscast.

Cognitive psychologists have explained these limits by a theory that starts with a neurological metaphor: Just as a neuron (i.e., nerve cell) can be in only one of two states, firing or resting, we assume that any "piece" of a person's knowledge can either be active, meaning that it is currently being processed, or inactive, in which case it is stored in the knowledge base but not being used. For example, upon reading "Thomas Jefferson was the third president of the United States," your knowledge concerning Jefferson and the presidency, which previously had been inactive, became active. According to this theory, processing limitations reflect a ceiling on the number of ideas that can be active at any one time.

As soon as one accepts the notion of a limit on the portion of one's knowledge that can be activated at one time, an obvious next step is to determine that limit precisely. Perhaps the simplest method for measuring the limit of activated memory is the *memory span* task. Stimuli are presented at a rate of one stimulus every one or two seconds, then individuals are asked to recall all of the stimuli in the order in which they were presented. Initially only two or three stimuli are presented; adults will typically recall them perfectly. However, the number of stimuli is increased gradually on successive trials, and, predictably, accurate recall becomes more difficult. A person's span is defined as the number of stimuli in the longest list that is recalled accurately 50% of the time. Adults' span for digits is about 7.7; for colors, 7.1; for letters, 6.35; for words, 5.5; and for geometric shapes, 5.3 (Cavanagh, 1972). These data are nicely consistent in indicating that only five to seven "ideas"—defined in this case as distinct numbers, colors, and the like—can be activated simultaneously.

Unfortunately, all is not this straightforward, as a simple example can demonstrate. Probably no reader could read the following string of sixteen letters and report them from memory with perfect accuracy:

A W T L F N S B C O T A N M B I

But now suppose that we present the letters in the reverse order and group them as follows:

I B M. . .N A T O. . .C B S. . .N F L. . .T W A

The task is transformed so that now most readers would recall all sixteen letters, far exceeding the normative data reported by Cavanagh (1972). The difference, of course, is that when the letters are rearranged, the task is no longer one of remembering sixteen letters but one of remembering five acronyms, and this fact places the accurate recall squarely within the estimates provided by Cavanagh.

More generally, this example demonstrates that to determine the capacity of activated memory, we need to know the functional processing unit in activated memory. Information processing psychologists refer to this unit as the *chunk*, which is defined as the "maximal familiar substructure of the stimulus" (Simon, 1981, p. 80). Thus, the following would all be examples of stimuli consisting of three chunks:

Q, F, X   3 letters

car, seven, pencil   3 words

Old King Cole was a merry old soul;
Humpty Dumpty sat on a wall;
Mary had a little lamb.   3 phrases

By taking a chunk as the unit of analysis, estimates of the capacity of activated memory become more consistent, typically between five and seven chunks.

    Especially convincing in this regard are experiments in which the same stimulus is structured into different chunks by different persons. One good example is the position of pieces on a chessboard. To someone who is ignorant of chess, Figure 3-12 simply depicts twenty-eight pieces scattered about the board; for someone familiar with the game, the pattern of pieces is recognized as the *Fegatello attack*.[2]

Figure 3-12   *The position of chess pieces in the Fegatello attack.*

---

[2]Some readers may recognize this as the "fried liver attack," so called because *fegato* is Italian for "liver."

Expanding on this example, it would seem reasonable that for beginning players, chunks would correspond to individual pieces, while chunks are configurations of pieces for more experienced players. If this analysis is correct, what would happen if we let novice and expert players study a chess board, and we then removed the pieces and asked the players to reconstruct the board (i.e., return the pieces to the positions from which they had just been removed)? First, both players should replace about five to seven chunks but because the experienced player's chunks are larger, the experienced player should replace more pieces accurately. Second, when pieces are placed on the board in distinctly nongamelike positions, so that there are no recognizable configurations, recall by beginning and experienced players should be comparable, at about five to seven pieces.

Chase and Simon (1973) documented each of these predictions in an elegant series of experiments. Similar results have emerged from analyses of other kinds of stimuli that can be structured in different ways depending upon the extent of an individual's experience. Examples include music (Sloboda, 1976), hands in the game of bridge (Engel & Bukstel, 1978), and electronics (Egan & Schwartz, 1979). Chunking has even been used to explain some of the skills of Wayne Gretzky, the most valuable player in the National Hockey League for several seasons:

> What Gretzky perceives on a hockey rink is, in a curious way, more simple than what a less accomplished player perceives. He sees not so much a set of moving players as a number of situations—chunks. Moving in on the Montreal blueline, as he was able to recall while he watched a videotape of himself, he was aware of the position of all the other players on the ice. The pattern they formed was, to him, one fact, and he reacted to that fact. When he sends a pass to what to the rest of us appears an empty space on the ice, and when a team-mate magically appears in that space to collect the puck, he has in reality simply summoned up from his bank account of knowledge the fact that in a particular situation, someone is likely to be in a particular spot, and if he is not there now he will be there presently [Gzowski, 1981, p. 188].

In each of these cases, it appears that a relatively small amount of information can be activated at once, but that experienced individuals pack more information into each chunk.

In our discussion to this point, the contents of activated memory have always been stimuli of some sort. More formally, we have been discussing limits on the amount of declarative knowledge that can be activated at one time. These same limits apply to activation of procedural knowledge. Reading, sewing, running, bicycling, and typing—to name just a few skills—are also affected by the limitations we have been discussing. For example, beginning drivers usually are encouraged to refrain from conversing with their passengers. This advice is based on the realization that driving a car can tax the capacity of activated memory to such an extent that other unnecessary processing should be minimized. Consistent with this advice, adults perform much more poorly on a memory span task when driving a car than when not (e.g., Zeitlin & Finkleman, 1975). Similarly, when adults simultaneously deal cards and remember words, their recall is poorer than when they are performing the memory task alone (Murdock, 1965).

To summarize, whether we are describing the processing of declarative or procedural knowledge, the capacity of activated memory imposes strict limits on the amount of cognitive processing that can occur. Limited capacity might seriously constrain cognitive activity, except that there are ways of bypassing these limits. One way to increase the functional capacity of the processing system to deal with declarative knowledge is to include more information in each chunk, a process known as *recoding*. Thus, the expert chess player in Chase and Simon's (1973) research recalled more positions of chess pieces because his chunks included more information than did the novice's chunks.

There are several other excellent demonstrations of how recoding to form larger chunks can increase the functional capacity of activated memory. Ericsson, Chase, and Faloon (1980), for example, tested one undergraduate, SF, on a digit span task a few days each week for over $1\frac{1}{2}$ years. At the beginning of the project, SF's digit span was essentially seven, perfectly average for his age; and at the end, it was almost eighty digits! SF achieved this remarkable level of memory skill in part by recoding the digits into groups to form meaningful chunks. SF was a competitive long-distance runner, hence one of his methods of recoding was to identify groups of digits that corresponded to times needed to run various distances. For instance, "3492 was recoded as 3 minutes and 49 point 2 seconds, near world-record mile time'" (Ericsson et al., 1980, p. 1181). Consistent with an emphasis on recoding as the basis for SF's memory skill, his span returned to normal levels when he was asked to recall strings of digits that could not be associated with running times or when he was asked to recall strings of consonants.

A similar phenomenon occurs when people improve procedural skills. Earlier we spoke of the advice frequently given to beginning drivers to concentrate on driving and not converse, listen to the radio, and so forth. Few experienced drivers heed these same warnings; indeed, most experienced drivers routinely chat or listen to the radio while driving. The difference between the novice and the experienced driver is that as one gains greater experience, proficient driving (or sewing, swimming, or hitting a baseball) requires less capacity to be performed, thus allowing concurrent processing. That is, people can do two or more things at once, and do so proficiently, as long as the individual processes are simple enough or well mastered, so that the combined demands of the different processes do not exceed the limits of activated memory.

With sufficient practice, a skill may even be performed *automatically;* that is, it makes no demonstrable demands on activated memory. Spelke, Hirst, and Neisser (1976) traced the automatization of one such cognitive skill. The two individuals in their study were asked to read a story and at the same time take dictation. During the first few hours of dictation, they read much more slowly than usual, at about 70% of their normal rates. After ten hours of practice, they read at approximately 80% of their usual rates. Between twenty and thirty hours of practice were needed until these subjects could take dictation and simultaneously read at their normal speeds. In other words, thirty hours of practice seemed to be sufficient to reduce the capacity demands of dictation to the point where the combined demands of reading and dictation no longer exceeded the limits of activated memory.

In summary, the constraints on processing imposed by the limited capacity of activated memory can be reduced by recoding information to form larger chunks or by practicing skills so that they require less capacity for performance. Several similarities about recoding and automatization as memory aids should be noted. First, developing proficient recoding schemes or automatizing skills are quite time-consuming. For example, SF needed $1\frac{1}{2}$ years to develop the recoding schemes that allowed him to increase his digit span so dramatically (Ericsson et al., 1980). Similarly, the over 50,000 different chess patterns familiar to expert chess players take nearly a decade to master (Simon, 1981).

Second, both recoding and automatization are always linked to specific domains of declarative or procedural knowledge. The expert chess player's recall equaled the beginner's when chess

pieces were placed randomly on the board, because these corresponded to none of the patterns known to the expert. Similarly,
when Spelke et al. (1976) changed the nature of their dictating task
slightly—instead of copying the dictated word, subjects named
the category to which it belonged—reading speed again slowed
considerably and required several additional sessions to return
to normal levels.

Third, given the domain-specific nature of recoding and automatization, it should be clear that these processes increase
functional processing capacity but do not alter the actual capacity of activated memory in any way. Recoding and automatization
are ways of improving the efficiency of processing rather than
changing capacity limits per se.

Limited capacity is a salient characteristic of activated
memory, but it is not the only one. We need to mention two other
important properties of activated memory that also critically
influence human information processing.

Accessing Activated Knowledge

Activated knowledge seems to be available immediately to an
individual. Suppose, for example, you read the following pair of
sentences:

> Jeff dove into the pool.
> He swam a mile.

Most readers undoubtedly understood both sentences immediately and effortlessly. But if we consider these two sentences in
some detail, it is apparent that comprehension cannot literally be
instantaneous. For example, the second sentence includes the
pronoun he. To understand this sentence, one presumably must
first identify he as a pronoun used to refer to a male, and then
scan activated memory for an appropriate antecedent. Such scanning of activated memory ordinarily is so fast that a person is
unaware of it. In fact, most readers typically become aware of
such scanning processes only when they fail, as when an antecedent is mentioned only much earlier in a passage or when a
passage contains no appropriate antecedent.

Scanning activated memory for antecedents is a specific instance of a very general cognitive activity. Understanding requires

that an individual relate new information to information that is already active. One basis for comprehension is the pattern recognition process described earlier, for this is how we identify a stimulus. But identifying a stimulus is often only a prerequisite to comprehension; an individual typically must search activated memory for information that allows a meaningful interpretation of the identified stimulus. Consequently, the speed and efficiency of memory scanning may well be an important determinant of the ease with which persons comprehend.

These scanning processes have been studied extensively by information processing psychologists with a paradigm first introduced by Saul Sternberg (1966), shown in Figure 3-13. The task is

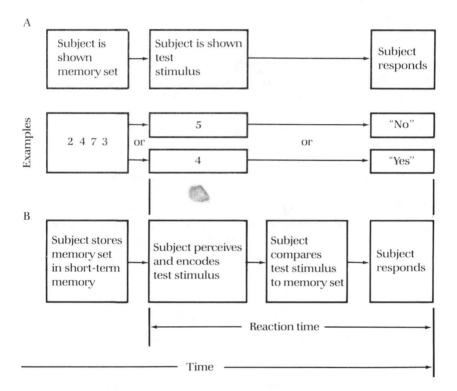

Figure 3-13   Sternberg's memory scanning task. Panel A depicts the steps in the procedure. Panel B depicts the mental events thought to occur in each phase of the experiment. (Reprinted with permission from R. Klatzky, Human memory, *2nd ed. [San Francisco: W. H. Freeman and Company, 1980].)*

simplicity itself: We present a small set of digits to an individual (e.g., 2 9 3) and then immediately present a test digit (e.g., 4). A person merely determines if the test digit was a member of the immediately preceding set. People rarely err on such judgments; instead, it is the speed of their response that is of special interest. Sternberg found a consistent relationship between the number of digits in the set and the amount of time for people to judge if the test digit was a member of the set. Response time increased about 40 milliseconds for each additional digit in the set. In other words, if one set was 2 and 3, and another was 2, 3, and 7, a typical adult would take about 40 milliseconds (about $\frac{1}{25}$ of a second) longer in the second set to determine that a 4 had not been presented. The difference in response times on the two sets apparently reflects the extra time needed to scan activated memory for the additional digit in the second set.

From these findings, we can conclude that a complete scan of the contents of activated memory would take between 200 and 280 milliseconds (40 milliseconds per chunk times five to seven chunks), or roughly a quarter of a second. That is certainly fast enough to be barely perceptible to a person, yet it is a far cry from being instantaneous. To the contrary, it is sufficiently time-consuming that if a person were to scan inefficiently, the extra time would accumulate rapidly. Suppose, for example, that a person needed 50 milliseconds to locate a chunk in activated memory rather than the typical 40 milliseconds. This additional 10 milliseconds seems infinitesimal—it is, after all, only 1/100 of a second—yet it represents a 25% increase in the amount of time needed to access information in activated memory.

Deactivation of Knowledge

Knowledge does not remain active indefinitely, but instead returns to an inert state. Those nodes dealing with Thomas Jefferson and the presidency that were activated a few minutes ago presumably became inactive again (until, of course, you read about them once more in this sentence). A principal cause of deactivation is the fact that earlier you continued reading beyond the sentence about Jefferson and the presidency. The chunks of information read in subsequent sentences became activated and displaced the Jefferson-related chunks from activated memory. According to this account, then, when a maximal number of chunks are already active, activation of additional chunks comes at the expense of deactivating a chunk.

Waugh and Norman (1965) clearly demonstrated such displacement in a variation on the basic digit span task discussed earlier. As before, digits are presented, but now each string consists of sixteen digits. After the final digit is presented, subjects are asked what digit followed the final digit on its first presentation in the list. Given

8 0 5 7 3 4 2 9 1 3 6 1 1 8 0 7 4

a correct answer would be 2 because 2 followed the initial presentation of 4, the final digit in the series.

According to the theoretical framework we have outlined, presentation of the first five to seven digits should activate memory to its limit. At this point, each subsequent digit should result in deactivation of a previously presented digit. A common assumption is that the displaced chunk is the one that has been activated longest (e.g., Gilmartin, Newell, & Simon, 1976). In this case, the first digit would be displaced, meaning that the second through seventh digits would remain active. Carrying out this analysis for all digits, only the eleventh through sixteenth digits should be active when subjects are asked to identify the digit that had followed the probe digit initially.

In fact, Waugh and Norman (1965) found that people were quite accurate (80% or greater) when queried about the twelfth or later digits, moderately accurate on the eleventh digit (about 50%), and much less accurate (40% or less) on the tenth and preceding digits. These results accord nicely, then, with the view that approximately five to seven digits can be activated simultaneously and that successive digits displace preceding ones.

Summary

Activated memory refers to that portion of the knowledge base that is involved in processing at any given moment. There are strict limits on the amount of knowledge that can be activated. For example, five to seven chunks seems to be the maximum quantity of declarative knowledge that can be active. This limit can be bypassed by creating larger chunks of information or by practicing skills until they are done automatically. Either of these schemes, however, is quite time-consuming to learn and is linked to specific components of knowledge.

Accessing an active part of the knowledge base does not occur instantaneously but takes time. In addition, the knowledge base gradually returns to its original inactive status as other parts of the knowledge base become active.

Information Processing and Intelligence

Our overview of human information processing is now complete. According to the view we have presented, human knowledge can be divided into two broad categories: declarative and procedural knowledge. Any element of knowledge—be it procedural or declarative—is thought to exist in one of two states, either inert or active. The amount of knowledge that can be active simultaneously is limited and referred to as activated memory.

What is the relationship between human information processing and human intelligence? Many readers may be tempted to conclude that human information processing and human intelligence overlap but are definitely not one and the same. The reason? Many of the processes that are essential to human information processing we would be reluctant to equate with intelligence. Recognizing a stimulus, for example, somehow seems more of a lower-order process than problem-solving, comprehension, and other similar higher-order processes that we more commonly associate with intelligence.

Let us concretize our intuitions a bit before proceeding. Terms like *higher-order* and *lower-order* imply a continuum of some sort, with sensation and perception at one end and creativity, problem-solving, and comprehension at the other. The exact nature of the continuum is not entirely clear, but complexity of the process is probably as acceptable as any label. The issue, then, is where to place a line dividing the continuum into those processes that are higher order and intelligent from those that are lower order and not intelligent.[3]

---

[3]Recall from Chapter 2 that Galton and Cattell assumed that the *lower*-order processes were the sources of intelligence (Boring, 1950) and that Binet's emphasis on higher processes was quite a controversial proposal at the time.

We believe it is wrong to think of the relationship between human information processing and human intelligence in this fashion, because there is little evidence to support the notion of a continuum of processing complexity. More than once in this chapter we have seen instances indicating that the intuitive distinction between higher and lower mental processes is fuzzy at best and probably unwarranted altogether. In pattern recognition, for example, conceptually driven analysis represents a clear case in which higher processes influence lower ones. The converse is true as well: Such simple processes as verifying the truth of a sentence like "A dog can move" seem to involve inference, which we would typically think of as a higher-order process.

In short, these examples and other evidence indicate that our intuitions of a continuum of processing complexity are probably false. Mental events simply do not lend themselves well to an intuitive ordering from least to most complex. Given this state of affairs, where to place the line dividing intelligent cognitive acts from nonintelligent ones is no longer an issue. Instead, we conclude that most intellectual acts involve a number of processes operating in concert. Included here, of course, are the particular acts that we call intelligence in the sense of performance on particular tests. We may choose to give a label to performance on a particular test (e.g., analogical reasoning), but we must always keep in mind that this is a convenient fiction, for the label actually refers to a set of organized processes.

Once rid of the bias that only higher mental processes are associated with intelligence, it is clear that the information processing approach complements the psychometric approach to intelligence described in Chapter 2. Recall McNemar's (1964) criticism that psychometric theories "never come to grips with the process or operation by which a given organism achieves an intellectual response" (p. 881). Describing these processes is, of course, the forte of information processing psychology. The limitation of the information processing approach for a psychology of intelligence is that, historically, individual differences have been ignored. "The modal paradigm in cognitive research . . . is to hold the subject population constant and to vary the task in a variety of ways to test the implications of a . . . model" (Medin & Cole, 1975, p. 144). One could envision a merger of the psychometric and cognitive approaches that would combine the strengths of both. Such mergers, which have taken place only recently, are the focus of the next section.

Process Analysis of
Intelligence

Early in the history of psychology, the psychometric and cognitive–experimental approaches to intelligence were not as distinct as they are today. Binet, for example, was known for his experimental studies of memory before he began his work on intelligence tests. For most of the twentieth century, however, the psychometric and cognitive–experimental approaches to intelligence have evolved in complete isolation from one another. Cronbach deplored this state of affairs in his presidential address to the American Psychological Association in 1957. He argued: "A true federation of the disciplines is required. Kept independent, they can give only wrong answers or no answers at all regarding certain important problems. It is shortsighted to argue for one science to discover the general laws of mind or behavior and for a separate enterprise concerned with individual minds" (Cronbach, 1957, p. 673). Cronbach's pleas for unity were largely ignored through much of the 1960s, but by the early 1970s there were several fruitful mergers of these previously isolated endeavors. In addressing the 1974 meeting of the American Psychological Association, Cronbach could report that the "hybrid discipline is now flourishing" (Cronbach, 1975, p. 116).

One important part of this hybrid discipline can be traced to the early 1970s when several cognitive psychologists—notably Estes (1974), Glaser (1972), Hunt (Hunt, Frost, & Lunneborg, 1973), and Sternberg (1977)—asked how our general conception of human information processing could help to answer questions about individual differences in cognitive abilities. These psychologists believed that information processing had two important assets for research on human intelligence. First, information processing provided a general theoretical framework that could be used to characterize the mental structures and processes involved in any cognitive performance. Second, information processing psychologists had devised a set of powerful tools for generating and testing explicit models of the cognitive processes involved in any specific task, including those on intelligence tests.

In the remainder of this chapter, we shall examine three cases in which an information processing perspective has been used to study individual differences in intellectual abilities, namely, verbal ability, reasoning ability, and spatial ability. The research described in these sections represents two general approaches that have been used to study the processes underlying individual differences in aptitude. In one approach the aim is to specify the cognitive processes that differentiate persons with high and low levels of aptitude. Tests of aptitude are used to identify subgroups of individuals, such as persons with high and low verbal or quantitative skill. These groups are then compared in their performance on laboratory tasks that involve certain processing skills, as defined by previous experimentation. Thus, in this approach one asks questions of the sort, "What does it mean to have high quantitative skill?" with the answer coming in the form of a link between performance on traditional experimental tasks and scores on psychometric measures.

In a second approach, the focus is performance on existing psychometric measures of aptitude. The objective is to develop models of performance on these tasks and to use the models to reveal processes that differentiate the performance of individuals who are high or low in ability on the task. In other words, here the relevant questions are "What cognitive processes do people use in solving test X?" and "Are these processes the same for individuals who differ in their ability as measured by X?"

Verbal Ability

Earlier in this chapter we discussed some of the basic concepts concerning pattern recognition, accessing activated knowledge, and the structure of knowledge. This research provides a general view of some of the stages involved in processing verbal information. Several investigators have asked whether these and other aspects of information processing are associated with psychometric measures of verbal ability. For example, Earl Hunt and his colleagues (Hunt, Frost, & Lunneborg, 1973; Hunt, Lunneborg, & Lewis, 1975; Hunt & Lansman, 1975, 1982; Hunt, 1976, 1978) have conducted several studies showing that verbal intelligence, as measured by conventional psychometric measures, is related to key components in information processing theories of cognition. In this work, undergraduates with high scores on a measure of verbal ability (part of a college entrance exam) are compared with individuals with lower scores. Typically, the high-ability individuals are from the upper 25% of the distribution of individuals taking the test (which, of course, is far from a random sample of the population at large). Individuals with low scores come from approximately the 30th to the 50th percentiles.

Hunt and colleagues have found that high-verbal under-graduates tend to excel in tasks that require accessing information from the knowledge base and in manipulating information in activated memory. Specifically, verbal ability has been linked to differences in (1) the ability to make a rapid conversion from a physical representation of stimuli to higher-level codes, and (2) the speed with which people can manipulate information in activated memory. We shall briefly illustrate each of these findings.

Coding Speed. Differences between individuals with high and low verbal ability in the speed of accessing different types of information or codes can be shown by examining performance in a simple judgment task. Consider the four pairs of words shown in Table 3-6. The first pair contains physically identical items. The second pair contains items that are not identical physically but are homonyms (i.e., have the same pronunciation). In the third pair, items are not identical either physically or in pronunciation but are from the same semantic category. The fourth pair contains items that differ along all obvious dimensions.

We can present these four types of pairs in tasks that vary the rule for judging that the words are the same. Under one set of instructions, the individual is told to respond "same" only if the words match physically. In this case, subjects should respond "same" to the first pair in Table 3-6 and "different" to the other three. Under a second set of instructions, the individual is told to respond "same" only if the words sound alike, as in the first and second pairs in Table 3-6. A third set of instructions requires that a "same" response be given if words are from the same semantic category, as in the first and third pairs in Table 3-6.

Typically, matches based on physical identity are faster than matches based on identical pronunciations, which in turn are faster than semantic category matches. This pattern is explained in terms of the abstractness of the code or mental representation that must be created before a decision can be made: It takes

Table 3-6   Pairs of words like those used by Goldberg et al. (1977)

Relationship	Words
Physically identical	*bear, bear*
Homophonic	*bear, bare*
In same category	*bear, lion*
Different	*bear, green*

longer to create or access semantic information than acoustic or visual information.

Goldberg, Schwartz, and Stewart (1977) used this type of comparison task to examine differences between high- and low-verbal adults. Their results are shown in Figure 3-14. Of interest is the finding that the difference between high- and low-verbal individuals increases as one moves from matching physical codes to more abstract codes such as acoustic and semantic codes. This basic finding—that high-verbal individuals are faster than low verbals in making semantic category decisions about individual

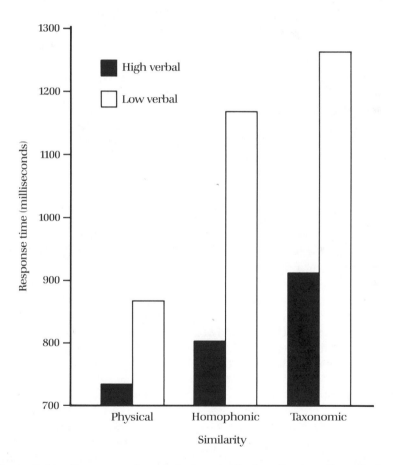

Figure 3-14   Response time to judge similarity of pairs of words for high- and low-verbal subjects and three types of similarity. (From Goldberg, Schwartz, and Stewart [1977].)

words or word pairs—has emerged in other studies involving similar decision tasks (e.g., Hunt, Davidson, & Lansman, 1981).

Accessing Activated Knowledge. Recall that activated knowledge is not available instantly; instead, a brief period of time is typically required to access it. Hunt and his colleagues have shown that individuals with high verbal aptitude access verbal information more rapidly than individuals with low verbal aptitude. In one study, MacLeod, Hunt, and Mathews (1978) demonstrated this difference using a paradigm developed by Clark and Chase (1972). Subjects first read a simple sentence, then see a picture related to the sentence. For example, "Star is above plus" might be the sentence, and $\overset{*}{+}$ might be the picture. However, the sentence and picture do not always correspond. On half the trials the sentence is an accurate description of the picture that follows; on half the trials it describes the opposite relationship (e.g., "Star is above plus" and $\overset{+}{*}$). The subject's task is to decide, as rapidly as possible, if the picture corresponds to the relationship described in the sentence.

MacLeod et al. (1978) found that verbal ability was significantly correlated with the amount of time needed to determine if the sentence was an accurate description of the picture. On the surface, then, these results seem to be consistent with the idea that high-verbal individuals are faster at (1) generating a verbal code for the picture and (2) comparing that verbal code with the code derived from reading the sentence. One other finding of MacLeod et al. represents a serious problem for this explanation, however: A measure of spatial ability correlated just as highly with answering time as did the measure of verbal ability! This is potentially disconcerting because finding that people who have high scores on *any* aptitude test do better on *any* experimental task is not particularly illuminating.

What MacLeod et al. (1978) demonstrated subsequently was that people apparently used one of two different algorithms for determining the correspondence between sentence and picture. One was the *verbal* algorithm described earlier, in which a verbal code generated for the picture is compared with a similar verbal code generated upon reading the sentence. A second, *visual–spatial* algorithm was just the opposite: When the sentence was read, subjects generated an appropriate mental image of a * and + that could be compared directly with the picture when it was presented.

Individuals who used the spatial algorithm spent nearly a full second longer reading the sentence than did individuals using the verbal algorithm, reflecting the time needed to understand the sentence and then generate an image. However, once the picture was presented, individuals using the spatial algorithm responded in about half of the time needed by people using the verbal algorithm: People using the spatial approach simply compared the picture with the mental image, but those using the verbal approach were engaged in the more time-consuming process of generating a verbal code for the picture.

Equally important are the changes in the correlations between the psychometric measures and the time needed to respond to the picture. For individuals using the verbal algorithm, the correlation between verbal ability and response time was significant, $-.52$ (i.e., individuals with high test scores needed less time to judge the correspondence between sentence and picture), but the correlation between spatial aptitude and response time, $-.32$, was not significant. Just the opposite pattern held for individuals using the spatial strategy: The correlation between verbal ability and response time was not significant, $-.33$, but the correlation between spatial aptitude and response time, $-.64$, was.

Thus, for those subjects who used a verbal algorithm, a psychometric measure of verbal ability predicted the speed with which they executed that algorithm, just as a measure of spatial aptitude predicted processing speed for persons using a spatial algorithm. Furthermore, the psychometric measures predicted which individuals were likely to use a particular algorithm: Individuals using the verbal algorithm had higher verbal scores than spatial scores, and the reverse was true for individuals using the spatial algorithm.

More generally, the findings of MacLeod et al. (1978) underscore a point that we have made previously. It is always risky to give a pychological label to a test or task based exclusively on an investigator's intuitions about important psychological processes. Too often individuals use strategies that are altogether different (but effective) from those we presume to represent the logical approach to the task.

Elsewhere Hunt (1978) has speculated that other factors beyond mere processing speed may be required to account for individual differences in verbal ability. He suggests three different sources of individual differences: knowledge, mechanistic processes, and general strategies. The effect of knowledge has been minimized or held constant in most of the studies on the processes underlying verbal ability, chiefly through the use of simple and well-known verbal materials. The mechanics of information processing are divided into two types: automatic and attention-demanding processes. Hunt suggests that automatic processes appear to be stable traits of individuals, as in the case of differences in coding speed. Controlled processes are more flexible and, consequently, may not be effective predictors of cognitive performance. Finally, general strategies include many activities such as the planning, monitoring, and checking that are involved in problem solving. These, too, may be important sources of individual differences in verbal ability, but as yet they are poorly understood.

Summary. On the basis of these and other data, Hunt and his coworkers conclude that measures of verbal ability tap a person's knowledge of language, such as the meanings of words, syntax, and semantic relations between concepts denoted by words, and that they also assess basic information processing capacities that are fundamental elements in experimental studies of cognition.

Reasoning Ability

A pervasive aspect of human thought is the capacity to generalize from specific experiences and form new, more abstract concepts and rules. Although our experiences differ, all people develop a shared set of concepts ranging from concrete ideas (e.g., chair) to complex abstractions (e.g., truth and justice). By analyzing similarities and differences between specific experiences, we extract general characteristics of classes, objects, events, and situations. These become concepts and schemata in our knowledge structure, which can then be applied to new experiences.

The development of general rules, ideas, or concepts from specific instances is known as *induction*. Given the importance of induction in human cognition, it is not surprising that inductive reasoning has been of key importance in both cognitive research (e.g., Greeno, 1978) and theories of human intelligence. As we indicated in Chapter 2, inductive reasoning tasks can be found on virtually any test of general intelligence, and they have come to be viewed as measures of a more general ability known as g_f, or fluid analytic ability (Brody & Brody, 1976). For example, the Cognitive Abilities Test (discussed in Chapter 2) includes five subtests representing induction with verbal, numeric, and geometric stimuli, and these five subtests represent 50% of the entire test!

All inductive reasoning tasks have the same basic property. A set of stimuli is shown, and the individual's task is to infer the pattern or rule present in the set. This general characteristic is manifest in different tasks ranging from simple classification problems to series completion problems to analogy problems. Performance on such tests indicates that people differ widely in their ability to solve classification, series, and analogy problems. The information processing perspective attempts to provide answers to questions about induction that cannot be answered by simply looking at overall differences in test scores. One question concerns the basic cognitive processes involved in solving inductive reasoning problems; a second question concerns the nature of individual differences in performance. In the section that follows, we describe the efforts of cognitive psychologists to answer these questions.

Analogical Reasoning. Of the many tasks that assess inductive reasoning on psychometric tests, the analogy problem (i.e., A is to B as C is to ?) is the most common. As we saw in Chapter 2, analogies have constituted a significant portion of intelligence test items over the course of the entire testing movement. Burt introduced the task in 1911. Thurstone, Otis, and Thorndike all included analogies on tests published in 1919. Examples of the centrality of this type of reasoning with respect to the concept and measurement of intelligence can be found in the writings of individuals such as Spearman (1927) and Raven (1938).

A general description of the cognitive processes required for analogy solution can be derived from the work of several individuals (e.g., Pellegrino & Glaser, 1979; Sternberg, 1977; Whitely, 1977). Here we describe the approach proposed by Sternberg (1977). The processes fall into three general classes. The first class represents *attribute discovery* or *encoding processes:* The important attributes of each individual term in the analogy problem must be represented in memory. For verbal items, this involves activating a set of semantic features associated with a concept. Given the term *dog*, for example, encoding would involve activation of the various links in the knowledge base representing superordinate, subordinate, and other relationships. For figural or geometric items, encoding constitutes a description of individual shapes or elements, their specific properties, and relationships. An example might be a rectangle containing two adjacent circles, one shaded and the other unshaded. Attribute discovery or encoding is essential for executing subsequent processes.

The second set of processes involves comparing attributes

for specific pairs of terms. The first such process is called *inference* and involves the relationship between the first two terms of the analogy (denoted as A and B). For verbal materials, the inference process determines the semantic features that directly or indirectly link the two concepts. For an A:B pair like *dog:wolf,* this might include common features such as *animal* and *canine* as well as differentiating features such as *size, ferocity,* and *domesticity.* When figural or geometric materials are involved, the inference process involves defining a set of feature changes or transformations applied to the A term to produce the B term.

Mapping is a similar process of comparing attributes. It refers to finding the correspondences between the first and third terms (A and C) of an analogy. The third attribute comparison process is referred to as *application.* This involves applying the rule inferred for the A:B pair to the features of the C term to produce a candidate answer. Thus, inference, mapping, and application are attribute comparison processes associated with the stem of an analogy, that is, the A, B, and C terms.

The other major processes necessary for solving analogies are evaluation components. These determine the appropriateness of any completion term that is presented. In simple analogies, where the ideal answer can be generated easily, evaluation is a simple confirmation that the features of the presented completion match the ideal answer. This process leads to rejection of inappropriate answers and selection of the best choice in a multiple-choice test. However, many analogies involve ambiguous rules or have several acceptable answers. In such cases, rule comparison and discrimination processes are required to select the best answer. This general aspect of performance has been called *justification.* The final component process in the theory involves executing an overt response.

To test this type of theory, we begin by assuming that the total time to solve an analogy will be equal to the sum of the times required to execute each process, as shown in Figure 3-15. The theory also specifies that the time to execute each process will depend on the complexity of the item. Consider the different types of items shown in Figure 3-16. They vary in two ways. First, the individual terms have differing numbers of shapes or elements. According to the theory, it should take longer to encode each of the terms in the more complex items. Second, items vary in the number of elements that are changed or transformed in each pair of terms (A:B and C:D). As more features are changed,

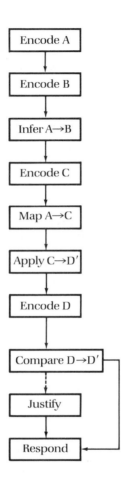

Figure 3-15 *Flow diagram depicting processes involved in solving analogy problems. (Reprinted with permission from S. R. Goldman & J. W. Pellegrino, Deductions about induction: Analyses of developmental and individual differences. In R. J. Sternberg (Ed.),* Advances in the psychology of human intelligence, *vol. 2 [Hillsdale, N.J.: Lawrence Erlbaum Associates, Inc., 1984].*

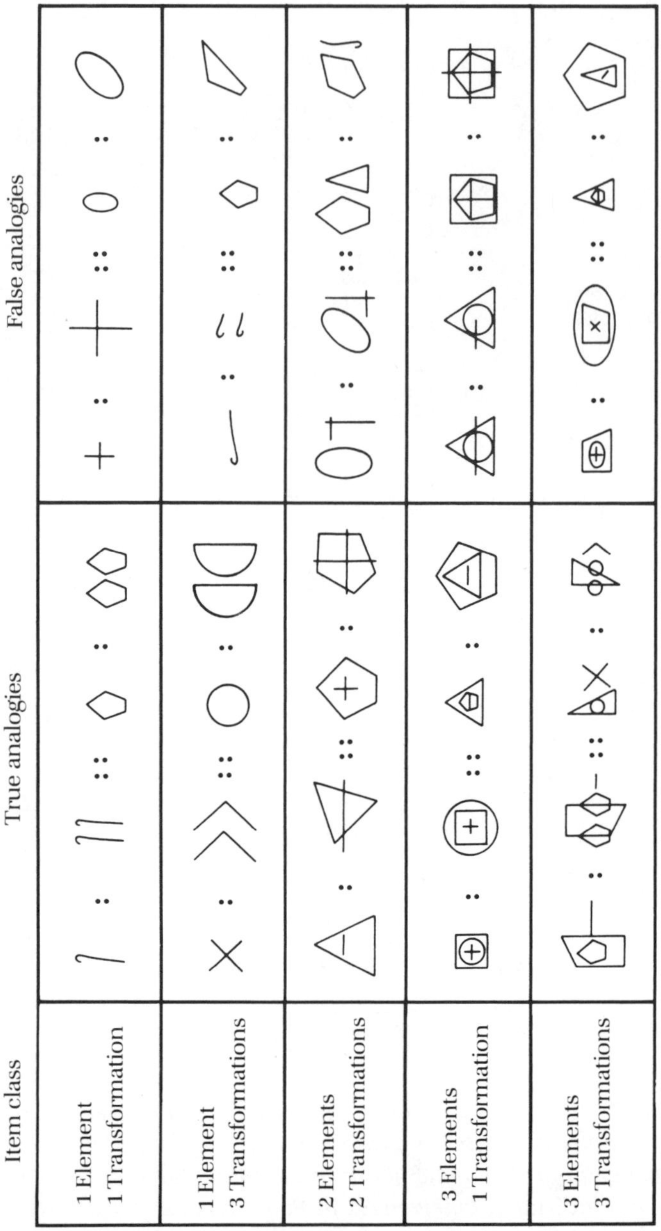

Figure 3-16 *Geometric analogy problems. (Reprinted with permission from T. Mulholland, J. W. Pellegrino, & R. Glaser, Components of geometric analogy solution.* Cognitive Psychology, *1980, 12, 252–284. Copyright by Academic Press, Inc.)*

attribute comparison processes such as inference, mapping, and application should take longer. These two factors, number of elements and transformations, should add together in a systematic way to produce greater total times to solve items.

Exactly this happens. Each element adds approximately 300 milliseconds to solution time; each transformation (i.e., change of a feature) adds approximately 400 milliseconds (Mulholland, Pellegrino, & Glaser, 1980; Sternberg, 1977).

Analyses of individual differences in reasoning ability have focused on the speed and accuracy of executing all the different processes necessary for solving verbal and nonverbal analogies. Correlations are computed between estimates for the time to execute separate processes and performance on a psychometric measure of analogical reasoning ability. The purpose is to determine the components of processing that are most related to differences in reasoning skill.

One source of ability differences is encoding speed. The surprising outcome is that skilled reasoners are actually *slower* at encoding than less skilled reasoners! Sternberg (1977) suggested that such counterintuitive results might reflect a strategy difference between ability groups. High-ability individuals spend more time on encoding because more precise encoding of information in the problem facilitates or speeds up subsequent processes. That is, accurate encodings seem to enhance speed of subsequent processing considerably, as indexed by attribute comparison and response components.

Attribute comparison processes such as inference, mapping, application, and justification have all shown significant latency differences favoring skilled over less skilled reasoners. In solving verbal analogies, for example, Sternberg (1977) determined that skilled reasoners were 243 milliseconds faster than less skilled reasoners in executing the total of attribute comparison processes. Similar results have been obtained with verbal analogies (Pellegrino & Ingram, 1977) and geometric analogies (Sternberg, 1977).

Finally, one of the most consistently observed sources of individual differences involves the response component. Skilled reasoners have shorter latencies for this component of processing when solving verbal and geometric analogies (Mulholland et al., 1980; Sternberg, 1977, 1981). Although the response component may not appear to be a significant cognitive component of inductive reasoning, it has been argued that this measure also reflects executing and monitoring the entire strategy for solving analogies.

To this point, we have been considering relationships between performance on a particular psychometric measure and its laboratory counterpart. Investigators have also considered *classes* of psychometric tasks as well as tasks in isolation. Sternberg and Gardner (1983) reported the results of such a study, in which the performance of eighteen adults was considered over a series of nine different inductive reasoning tasks. The eighteen subjects solved 2880 individual problems representing three tasks—analogy, classification, and series completion—and three types of content—verbal, geometric, and schematic. When performance on all nine tasks was considered together, reasoning scores from a set of psychometric measures were correlated with three aspects of processing. A score representing the combined times for inference, mapping, and application yielded a correlation of −.79 with the psychometric measures. A score representing confirmation speed yielded a correlation of −.75 with the ability measure, and a score for justification produced a correlation of −.48.

All of these scores indicate that individuals with high scores on ability measures need less time to implement the attribute comparison and evaluation processes than do individuals with low scores on the ability measures. That is, differences between adults in reasoning ability are attributable to more efficient execution of component processes involving the attribute relationships between and among individual pairs of analogy terms. Furthermore, skilled reasoners are not only faster in process execution but also more accurate (Alderton, Goldman, & Pellegrino, 1982; Whitely, 1980).

Summary. Information processing psychologists have developed theories and models for induction that are significant both to psychometrics and to experimental psychology. From these efforts, a general theory of inductive reasoning has emerged as well as important information about individual differences in reasoning skill. Nevertheless, as was the case for verbal ability, much remains to be done to understand individual differences in reasoning ability, including the relationship between performance on psychometric test items and routine (i.e., extralaboratory) inductive reasoning.

Spatial Ability

Humans create mental representations of objects (mental images) that preserve many of the properties of the physical stimulus. In addition, people can perform mental operations on these representations, such as changing their size or rotating them in space. These mental operations appear to be analogs of physical operations carried out on actual objects. For example, if a person rotates an object in space, the amount of time to do so will depend upon the distance of rotation (e.g., rotation through 30° is less time-consuming than rotation through 150°). In like manner, mental rotation of an object takes longer for greater mental distances.

Information processing research has revealed a number of important characteristics about the mental representation and mental transformation of stimuli. This research has also provided a basis for studying individual differences in spatial aptitude. The goals are similar to those in research on inductive reasoning: (1) to specify the cognitive processes involved in a range of spatial tasks, (2) to determine the sources of individual differences in spatial aptitude, and (3) from the first two goals, to develop a general, process-based theory of spatial ability and spatial processing. In pursuing these goals, information processing psychologists have studied both spatial-relations tasks and spatial-visualization tasks.

Spatial Relations. Performance on simple spatial-relations problems, such as those found on the SRA Primary Mental Abilities Tests (PMA), has been studied using a general model, proposed by Cooper and Shepard (1973), of the processes required for mental rotation problems. The model was based upon data obtained in a paradigm in which individuals judged, as rapidly as possible, if two stimuli presented at different orientations were the same. This comparison of a pair of stimuli closely resembles the multiple comparisons that must be made to solve problems on the PMA (see Figure 2-5).

An example of the application of this paradigm is a study by Cooper (1975), in which she presented two nonsense shapes that differed in orientation from 0° to 300°; subjects judged whether the shapes were identical or mirror images. Response times in this task increased steadily with increases in the difference in orientation between the two shapes. That is, responses were quite fast when the shapes appeared in a similar orientation and much slower when their orientations differed considerably. This was interpreted as indicating that individuals mentally rotate the stimuli in a manner analogous to the actual physical rotation of the object. Thus, the greater the mental distance to be traveled, the longer it takes to solve the problem.

Cooper and Shepard (1973) presented evidence that response latencies on these problems reflect four distinct stages of processing, illustrated in Figure 3-17. The first stage of processing requires encoding of the stimuli, which involves representing the identity and orientation of the stimuli in activated memory. The second phase involves rotating the mental representation of the

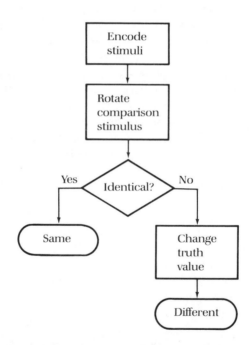

Figure 3-17   *Cooper and Shepard's (1973) algorithm for mental rotation. (Reprinted with permission from P. Carter, B. Pazak, & R. Kail, Algorithms for processing spatial information.* Journal of Experimental Child Psychology, *1983, 36, 284–304. Copyright by Academic Press, Inc.)*

nonvertical stimulus to bring it to the orientation of the vertical stimulus. This phase is followed by a comparison of the two stimulus representations to determine if they are identical. The outcome of the comparison leads to a positive or negative response.

Cooper and Shepard's (1973) analysis of mental rotation provides an obvious scheme for the analysis of individual differences in simple spatial-relations performance. If the processes involved in solving these problems can be determined reliably for individuals, then what remains to be determined is the contribution of each process to individual differences in spatial aptitude. Individual differences in performance on a speeded test such as the PMA Space Test may well be due entirely to speed differences in the cognitive process of mental rotation.

To estimate this possibility, one can calculate correlations between psychometric measures of spatial aptitude and measures of the speed with which people implement the component processes illustrated in Figure 3-17. In this way we can determine the role of encoding speed, rotation, comparison, and response processes in individual differences in spatial aptitude.

An additional, potentially important aspect of performance on a test such as the PMA Space Test may involve the capacity to encode, compare, and rotate unfamiliar stimuli that lack representations and labels in the knowledge base. Mental rotation of unfamiliar stimuli such as PMA characters is slower than rotation of familiar alphanumerics, and more time is needed for encoding and comparison processes on these unfamiliar stimuli (Kail, Carter, & Pellegrino, 1979). Thus, it is necessary to consider the additional times associated with encoding, comparing, and rotating unfamiliar stimuli as potentially important aspects of individual differences on a test like the PMA.

All of these aspects of processing were considered in a study conducted by Mumaw, Pellegrino, Kail, and Carter (in press). We tested a large sample of adults representing the entire range of performance on the PMA Space Test. Each subject was tested individually on a variant of the Cooper and Shepard (1973) paradigm, in which pairs of stimuli were presented on each trial. Half of the trials involved pairs of letters or numbers, and half involved the unfamiliar PMA characters.

We computed correlations between performance on the standard psychometric version of the PMA Space Test and several measures of processing speed. Spatial ability—as defined by the psychometric measure—was associated with two of these measures: (1) the speed with which familiar stimuli are rotated mentally, and (2) the speed with which unfamiliar stimuli are encoded and compared. That is, individuals with high spatial scores rotated stimuli more rapidly than their peers with low scores. In addition, high-ability individuals encoded and compared unfamiliar stimuli more rapidly. However, this difference did not reflect a general advantage in encoding and comparison, for when the stimuli were familiar letters and numbers, ability was unrelated to the speed of encoding and comparison.

Spatial Visualization. The tasks associated with more complex spatial ability, referred to as spatial visualization (see Chapter 2), have also been analyzed from a cognitive-components perspective. Mumaw and Pellegrino (1984) created a laboratory task that emulated the problems on the Minnesota Paper Form Board Test. As shown in Figure 3-18, on the Minnesota Paper Form Board Test, individuals select the pattern that can be assembled from the pieces in the upper left corner. Mumaw and Pellegrino's simplified problems (see Figure 3-19) consisted of a completed figure and an array of puzzle elements. The individual was to determine, as rapidly as possible, if the elements on the right could be arranged to form the completed puzzle on the left. Negative items (i.e., where the correct answer is no) were created by including one or more mismatching elements in the array.

A process model, shown in Figure 3-19, was specified for performance in this task. The core of the model, a cycle that must be executed for each element of the puzzle, is executed repeatedly until the individual has tested all elements or finds a mismatch. According to the model, *encoding, comparison,* and *response* are processes that are required to solve any item; *rotation* and *search* are processes required on only particular kinds of problems.

This model leads to several predictions concerning the time to solve problems. First, for all problems, response time should increase with the number of elements in an item, because the core set of processes in Figure 3-19 must be executed once for each element. Second, the increase in response latency should be more dramatic for more complex problems, because these are likelier to involve the optional processes of rotation and search. Third, when none of these elements matches a piece of the completed puzzle, individuals should be relatively fast in making a different judgment. The basis for this prediction is that an indi-

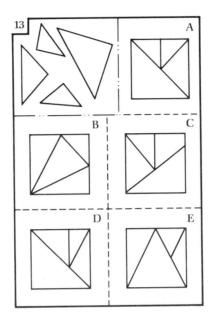

Figure 3-18   *A problem like those appearing on the Minnesota Paper Form Board. (Reprinted with permisson from R. Mumaw & J. Pellegrino, Individual differences in complex spatial processing.* Journal of Educational Psychology, *1984, 76,   920–939. Copyright by the American Psychological Association.)*

vidual will go through the cycle only once, making a response as soon as no matching piece is found.

Mumaw and Pellegrino (1984) tested this model by presenting 300 individual problems to 34 adults who varied in spatial ability. Of particular interest are comparisons between individuals with high spatial ability (defined here as performance on the Minnesota Paper Form Board) and those with low ability. For both groups of individuals, response times on the laboratory task were in accord with the three predictions of the model. Both high- and low-ability individuals apparently solved the problems using the algorithm depicted in Figure 3-19. Of the various processes included in this algorithm, it was the second step—finding corresponding elements—that was the biggest source of ability differences: Individuals with high scores on the Minnesota Paper Form Board were much more rapid in this phase of processing.

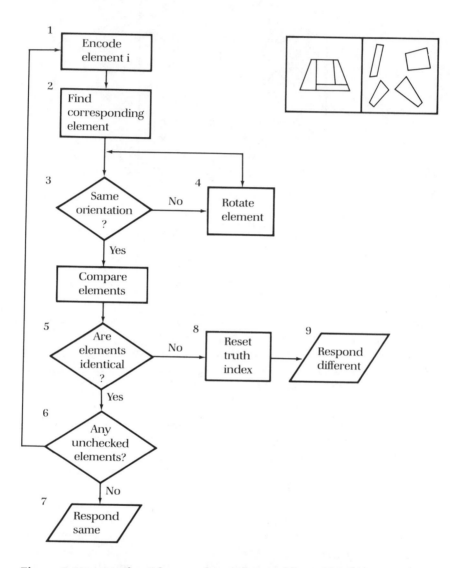

Figure 3-19 An algorithm used to solve problems like those appearing on the Minnesota Paper Form Board. (Reprinted with permission from R. Mumaw & J. Pellegrino, *Individual differences in complex spatial processing.* Journal of Educational Psychology, 1984, 76, 920–939. Copyright by the American Psychological Association.)

Furthermore, their skill in the search phase stemmed, at least in part, from the fact that they had generated a more precise encoding of the problem in the first stage of processing.

Summary. Individual differences in spatial relations and spatial visualization have been studied using models devised by Cooper and Shepard (1973) and Mumaw and Pellegrino (1984). These two spatial domains are consistent regarding the sources of ability differences: High-ability individuals perform mental transformations more rapidly than low-ability individuals, a difference partially attributable to the fact that high-ability individuals are more proficient during the encoding phase. This last finding is particularly significant, because this was also a basis for ability differences in inductive reasoning.

Concluding Remarks

The merger of psychometrics and cognitive psychology represents an effort to explain performance on the psychometric measures in terms of key theoretical constructs drawn from cognitive psychology. That is, the constructs described in the first half of this chapter are used to analyze abilities as they are defined in the psychometric approach described in Chapter 2. Thus far, the approach represented by this merger has been applied to the study of verbal ability, inductive reasoning, and spatial ability.

We must make note of the fact that the psychometric and cognitive approaches, as well as their merger, tend to share a common weakness; they typically describe intellectual functioning at but a single point in the life span, young adulthood. Furthermore, this point is the focus solely on the pragmatic grounds that undergraduates form a readily accessible population for research and not because any special mystique or significance is associated with ages 18 to 22 years. This exclusive focus is obviously a liability; the changes in sheer intellectual power that take place between birth and adulthood are so awesome in scope and consistency that they *must* be addressed in a complete theory of intelligence. Theories of intellectual development represent our third and final approach to human intelligence.

4

The Development of Intelligence

Explaining his hockey prowess, Wayne Gretzky says, "It's all practice. . . . Nine out of ten people think it's instinct, and it isn't. Nobody would ever say a doctor had learned his profession by instinct; yet in my own way I've put in almost as much time as a medical student puts in studying medicine" (Gzowski, 1981, pp. 188–189).

Skills, be they athletic or intellectual, rarely emerge overnight but instead develop gradually. Gretzky first skated when he was not yet 3 years old. It would be nearly a decade and a half before his extraordinary skill would be evident. Even Mozart, the best-known example of a musical prodigy, composed for most of a decade before he wrote what is now recognized as master-calibre music. To address this aspect of intelligence—its acquisition as the individual develops—we turn to cognitive-developmental psychology. In this chapter we begin with the first comprehensive theory of intellectual development, that of Jean Piaget. We then turn to theories that have been proposed to address some of the shortcomings of Piaget's theory.

Jean Piaget's Theory

Piaget's scientific career began at age 10, when he published an article in which he described a partially albino sparrow that he had seen in a local park. In the ensuing three-quarters of a century, Piaget wrote literally hundreds of books and articles in which he touched upon innumerable topics dealing directly or indirectly with the development of intelligence. To summarize this work in a single, brief chapter is obviously out of the question; our goal in the pages that follow is to give the reader a feel for the character and scope of Piaget's theory, so that its unique assets and liabilities can be compared with the psychometric and cognitive approaches to intelligence. For readers interested in learning more about Piaget's theory, a number of excellent books are available, including those by Brainerd (1978), Flavell (1963, 1977), Ginsburg and Opper (1979), and Phillips (1975).[1]

Key Concepts

Piaget's theory is best known for its emphasis on developmental changes in intelligence. Yet Piaget always emphasized that certain concepts are central to intelligence at any age. We begin our account with these key concepts.

Schemes. If you place an attractive toy in front of a 7-month-old, the infant typically will attempt to reach for and play with it. After a minute or so, the infant will seemingly tire of the toy and release it. Now place a different, equally attractive toy in front of the infant and the episode occurs anew. Piaget calls

---

[1]We should point out that to refer to the theory as Piaget's exclusively is misleading, for he had a number of important collaborators through the years, with Barbel Inhelder perhaps the best-known. The reader should recognize that throughout this book, the term *Piaget's theory* is an implicit shorthand for the longer and certainly less elegant phrase "Piaget and his collaborators' theory."

Also, in explicating Piaget's theory, we frequently use examples and analogies. The reader should not be misled to think that Piaget substantiated his theory in this way. To the contrary, much of the theory is worked out in considerable detail using logic and mathematics. These can pose formidable obstacles for a reader first encountering Piaget's theory; hence our use of examples that are less precise but grasped more readily.

this simple action by the child a *scheme*, a concept that is central to his theory. Let us use this example to illustrate several core properties of the scheme construct.

First, scheme is used to denote a *complex, organized sequence of activities*. Note that even simple grasping, as in our example, involves coordinating a number of simpler actions. An infant perhaps detects the presence of an object in its visual field, somehow decides that the object is interesting, calibrates arm movements to bring the hands in proximity to the object, calibrates the movements of the fingers to clutch the object successfully, and finally decides to release the object when it is no longer interesting. The number of actions is large and organized in a particular temporal sequence.

In addition, a scheme is an abstract structure, not simply a set of behaviors. Here Piaget is claiming that a scheme is more than just a term to describe the behaviors that we observe. Instead, the behaviors that we see together are, in fact, a unified entity in the child's mind. That is, Piaget *infers* the presence of a structure that directs the sequence of behaviors we observe, just as the sequence of actions involved in building a house (which we *can* observe) is under the direction of a master plan (i.e., set of blueprints) that we typically do not observe.

Another characteristic of a scheme is that a child activates a scheme again and again. If a child grasped an object only once, we would not attribute "the grasping scheme" to a child. But when we see the child grasp objects repeatedly, this signals that the behaviors are linked together as an entity. In this sense, repetition helps to define what is and what is not a scheme.

Finally, grasping, like all schemes, really refers to a class of similar actions rather than a single set of activities that occurs in exactly the same way on every occasion. The infant's grasping scheme will differ depending upon whether the object is far or near; as the infant grows older, the grasp will be modified according to the size of the object.

The examples we have used thus far to illustrate the scheme concept may suggest that it applies only to infancy. This emphatically is not the case; in Piaget's theory, schemes are fundamental cognitive constructs throughout development. Most adolescents, for example, acquire a *proportionality scheme*, which refers to the individual's understanding of the relationships that can exist between the ratio of quantities a and b and quantities c and d. If $a = 2, b = 4, c = 6$, and $d = 12$, then a and b are proportional to

c and d (i.e., $\frac{2}{4} = \frac{6}{12} = \frac{1}{2}$). Note that this scheme embodies all of the features attributed to the grasping scheme. It refers to an organized set of actions; we infer that these actions exist as a totality in the child's mind; the scheme is applied repeatedly; and the scheme can be applied to diverse objects.

Because schemes are repeatedly applied to different objects, they tend to change in two important ways. First, they become extended to a broader range of objects. Sucking is one of the first schemes to become extended in this way: "According to chance contacts, the child, from the first two weeks of life, sucks his fingers, the fingers extended to him, his pillow, quilt, bedclothes. . . . The newborn child at once incorporates into the global schema of sucking a number of increasingly varied objects" (Piaget, 1952, p. 34). Second, by virtue of being applied to different objects, a scheme will become differentiated into several schemes. The grasping scheme, for example, may result in separate schemes for holding heavy objects, where the object is grasped tightly with both hands and for holding light objects, where a loose grasp of one hand is sufficient. The signal that such differentiation of a scheme has occurred is the fact that objects are grasped consistently in one way or the other, when previously either mode of grasping was likely.

Contents, Functions, and Structures. The central role of schemes in Piaget's theory makes them an excellent means to introduce one of the most important contributions of the theory, at least as far as the aims of this book are concerned. Piaget (1952) distinguished three aspects of intelligence—its contents, its functions, and its structures—which are illustrated in Table 4-1.

Table 4-1   *Components of intelligence in Piaget's theory*

Component	Changes with development?
Contents	Yes
Functions	No
Organization	
Adaptation	
Accommodation	
Assimilation	
Structures	Yes

The contents of intelligence refer to behavioral acts. Included here are such things as grasping an attractive object and determining that $\frac{2}{3}$ and $\frac{4}{6}$ are proportional. Also included under this heading is solving problems like those appearing on the psychometric tests we discussed in Chapter 2. In other words, the contents of intelligence denote the behavioral results of applying a scheme.

Two characteristics of intellectual contents are worth noting. First, the contents of intelligence change considerably with age. As we have seen, schemes for adolescents and infants differ, leading to age differences in behavioral outcomes. Such differences in the contents of intelligence are to be expected between birth and adulthood. Second, Piaget had little interest in intellectual contents per se. Instead, they were of interest chiefly as a means of inferring the nature of the internal mental structures.

Functions refer to characteristics of intelligence that are *unchanging* as the individual develops. That is, functions are principles of intelligence that hold throughout the life span. Because they are constant throughout development, Piaget termed them *functional invariants.*

One functional invariant is *organization.* To illustrate the special meaning this term has for Piaget, imagine that extensive observation of a 10-month-old infant has led us to document several schemes including grasping, sucking, waving, and the like. Earlier we emphasized that each of these schemes is a highly organized set of actions, but what about relations among these schemes? One possibility is that schemes exist essentially as independent entities in the child's mind, with no links to one another or no overarching framework. Piaget emphatically rejected this possiblity. Instead, a child's schemes are always organized to form an *integrated mental structure.*

A second functional invariant is *adaptation.* In biology, adaptation refers to changes in structures or forms that result in a better fit (i.e., greater likelihood of survival) of an animal or plant to its environment. Piaget used the term in much the same way to describe intellectual activity. For example, a 10-month-old attempting to grasp a book may fail if the book is heavy and he uses only one hand. Adaptation in this case would consist of using two hands instead of one.

In fact, intellectual adaptation always involves two complementary processes, *assimilation and accommodation.* To illustrate them, imagine a toddler outdoors with her mother. Successively seeing a robin, blue jay, and sparrow, the youngster names each a "bird." Seeing a butterfly, she says "bird" once again, only to be corrected by her mother. Seeing another butterfly later, she names it appropriately.

The first instance—referring to several visibly different birds by the same generic label—is an instance of assimilation. In assimilation, a child's schemes are used to interpret and organize incoming information. An extreme form of assimilation would be make-believe play, for here the child constructs a fantasy world that is completely derived from his or her schemes, unconstrained by information from the external world (Piaget, 1951).

The complement to assimilation is accommodation, which refers to changes in schemes so that they can incorporate new information. Recall in our example above where the child inaccurately called a butterfly a bird. Apparently the child's initial scheme for bird was very general, referring simply to things that fly. However, after the mother corrected her, she no longer referred to butterflies as birds; what was once one scheme became two. The precise boundaries of these new schemes cannot be identified from our example (e.g., does *butterfly* refer to things that fly and have antennae and *bird* to flying objects with beaks?). The essential point, however, is that a scheme has been differentiated in order to incorporate a wider class of experiences.

In conjunction, the two functional invariants, organization and adaptation, lead to an important implication regarding developmental change. When a scheme is modified, the impact is not specific to that scheme but influences other schemes as well, for all schemes are linked to form one unified mental structure. The implication is that important developmental changes will be *qualitative*, concerning reorganization of these overarching mental structures.

A distinctly nonpsychological example—growth of a butterfly—will help to illustrate the point. The monarch butterfly, like all lepidopterans, goes through four qualitatively different periods en route to adulthood. It starts life as an egg, about the size of a pinhead, on a leaf. From this egg emerges a caterpillar, signaling the onset of the larva stage. About two weeks later the caterpillar spins a cocoon that marks the pupa stage. Finally, the butterfly emerges, marking the onset of adulthood. There *is* marked change within each of these stages. The caterpillar, for example, grows steadily from weighing slightly more than $\frac{1}{2}$ milligram to approximately 1500 milligrams, nearly a 3000-fold increase! Yet it is the qualitative differences between stages—differences in anatomical structure and in behavior—that capture our attention.

Piaget believed that much the same sort of thing occurs in human intellectual development. That is, there are periods of gradual intellectual development that cause an organism to outgrow the existing mental structure, which is replaced by a qualitatively different, more sophisticated structure. Specifically, Piaget proposed that intellectual development can be divided into four periods, which he called the sensorimotor, preoperational, concrete operational, and formal operational periods.

These periods are *explanatory* rather than simply descriptive. To illustrate this distinction, parents commonly say that their children are simply "going through a phase." What they mean is that they have observed some new behavior, one that they expect is temporary. Familiar examples would include a child's constantly saying "no" or "why" in response to requests, recurrence of bed-wetting after toilet training has been established, or teenage rebelliousness. Parents' use of the term *phase* is, in each case, simply a description of a behavior, *not* an attempt to explain the behavior.

Piaget's periods, in contrast, are both descriptions and explanations. The descriptions refer to behaviors associated with a particular period of mental development. There is, for example, a common set of behaviors associated with the preoperational period of intellectual development: Children at this age fail to conserve and are unable to take the perspective of other individuals. The periods are also thought to be explanatory, for associated with each period is a unique mental structure that *causes* the behaviors associated with that period. Hence, saying "Ben is in the preoperational period" is simultaneously a description of certain expected behaviors as well as an explanation for those behaviors.

Another characteristic of Piaget's periods is that they constitute a *universally invariant sequence.* The meaning of sequence is obvious: Piaget's four periods occur in succession. However, adding "universally invariant" imposes two constraints on this sequence. First, just as the egg–larva–pupa–adult sequence is never ordered any other way in the butterfly's development, so too is sensorimotor, preoperational, concrete operational, and formal operational the only ordering of the four periods of intellectual development for all children, regardless of their environment or ability. The second constraint is that all four periods are obligatory; one cannot skip a period in intellectual development, such as moving directly from the preoperational to the concrete operational period, any more than a caterpillar can become a butterfly directly without first going through the pupa period.

Note, however, that insisting on a strict sequence of periods does not mean that a particular period must appear at a specific age. The onset of the concrete operational period typically occurs at approximately 7 years of age, but it may be earlier in precocious children and several years later in retarded children. These variations are inconsequential to Piaget's theory. When we mention ages that are associated with particular Piagetian periods, these should always be considered as rough guides that refer to a "textbook child" rather than as essential parts of the theory.

The fact that the periods emerge in a particular sequence leads us to a third point, concerning the relationships between successive periods. The structures of each period become incorporated into those of its successor. The schemes available during preoperational thought are not eliminated with the onset of concrete operations but instead are transformed as they become part of the concrete operational structure. An apt analogy would be to a corporate reorganization in which the resources of the earlier structure (people, equipment, material, and the like) remain in the new organization but function more effectively after reorganization because of their new relationships to other resources.

Now that the general characteristics of Piaget's periods have been discussed, we shall examine each of the four periods of intellectual development in detail.

The Sensorimotor Period (0–2 years)

Infancy often strikes adults as a special phase of development. For Piaget, too, infancy represents a distinct period of development, called the *sensorimotor* period, which corresponds roughly from birth to approximately two years of age. The research was conducted primarily with Piaget's own three children —Jacquelin, Laurent, and Lucienne. Ordinarily, a sample of only three children would be much too small for one to make *general* conclusions about development with any confidence. However, the outline of the sensorimotor period derived from Jacquelin, Laurent, and Lucienne has been confirmed in subsequent research by investigators using more traditional methods.

The methods used by Piaget have two significant advantages as well. First, Piaget's style was to blend naturalistic observations with informal experimentation. Seeing some intriguing behavior, he would formulate a hypothesis, then try to test that hypothesis in a subsequent experiment. When the hypothesis was validated, Piaget used this new fact to interpret subsequent behaviors. If the hypothesis was not supported, Piaget would propose a new hypothesis to test. Thus, Piaget's constant access to his children, as well as his intimate knowledge of their behavior, allowed him to combine observational study with experimentation in a manner that was—and remains today—quite unusual in psychology.

Second, Piaget was able to study his children over a period of several years. Such *longitudinal* research is rare in developmental psychology because it is time-consuming and expensive. Yet only with longitudinal research can an investigator determine relationships between early behaviors (e.g., those occuring immediately after birth) and later ones (e.g., those coinciding with the onset of language). For this reason, too, Piaget's work provides a perspective on cognitive development that is not typical of most contemporary research.

Stage 1: Use of Reflexes (0–1 month). A newborn's range of behaviors is, obviously, quite limited. Behaviors at this age are chiefly reflexive, including such familiar examples as crying, sucking, blinking, and swallowing, as well as more exotic ones like the Babinski reflex, in which stroking the sole of the foot causes the toes to spread. Yet to dwell on the limitations of reflexive behavior would be a serious error, for Piaget considers them to be the starting point of intellectual development. Piaget saw signs of accommodation in the newborn's reflexive acts. The newborn, for example, modifies the sucking reflex in order to grasp the nipple: At 3 days of age, if Laurent's cheek was stroked, he would open his mouth and turn his head to search for the nipple, but he was just as likely to turn away from the nipple as to turn toward it. By 12 days of age, Laurent consistently turned to the side that was stroked (Piaget, 1952).

This modification of a reflex is perhaps the first evidence of accommodation; there is complementary evidence of assimilation as well. Initially infants suck only a nipple, but soon they extend this activity to other objects as well, such as toys and blankets. By sucking a range of objects, an infant begins the initial assimilations with the environment, learning that some objects, like breasts and bottles, yield nourishment, but others do not.

Stage 2: Primary Circular Reactions (1–4 months). The first stage of sensorimotor thought can be summarized as a month during which reflexes become more finely tuned; the next few months are characterized as a time during which reflexes are changed through experience. The primary vehicle for this learning is the *primary circular reaction.* The essential ingredients of a primary circular reaction are the following: Start with some reflex or reflexlike activity, such as sucking. Next, some novel environmental event triggers the reflex by chance. A child, for example, may accidentally touch her lips with her thumb, initiating sucking and the pleasant sensations that accompany sucking. Finally, the child tries to repeat the triggering event in order to reproduce those pleasant sensations.

Now consider how Piaget describes the emergence of one such circular reaction. (In this and subsequent examples, read "0;2 (7)" as 0 years, 2 months, and 7 days of age.)

> *Observation 53.*—From 0;2 (3) Laurent evidences a circular reaction which will become more definite and will constitute the beginning of systematic grasping; he scratches and tries to grasp, lets go, scratches and grasps again, etc. On 0;2 (3) and 0;2 (6) this can only be observed during feeding. Laurent gently scratches his mother's bare shoulder. But beginning 0;2 (7) the behavior becomes marked in the cradle itself. Laurent scratches the sheet which is folded over the blankets, then grasps it and holds it a minute, then lets it go, scratches it again and recommences without interruption. At 0;2 (11) this play lasts a quarter of an hour at a time, several times during the day. At 0;2 (12) he scratches and grasps my fist which I placed against the back of his right hand [Piaget, 1952, pp. 91–92].

Notice how the primary circular reaction begins with reflexlike activity: Laurent moves his hand in a scratching motion while feeding, a common event among babies as they nurse. This activity is somehow stimulating, and hence Laurent tries to repeat it.

It is easy to see how circular reactions become a critical component of subsequent sensorimotor development. They will form the basis for the first instances of deliberate, intentional behavior by the infant. They provide the first insights into causality, for the infant comes to realize that actions predictably yield certain outcomes. This cause–effect sequence also provides the first clues concerning the concept of time, for the infant learns that the cause precedes rather than follows the effect. All of these achievements do not occur in Stage 2, of course, but it is the emergence of the primary circular reaction in the first few months that provides the basis for these later achievements.

Stage 3: Secondary Circular Reactions (4–8 months). Between 4 to 10 months, most infants learn to sit, to crawl, and perhaps to stand and walk as well. Able to move, the infant can learn much more about its environment. One of the primary bases of such learning, according to Piaget, is the secondary circular reaction. As the name implies, this behavior is a variant of the primary circular reaction seen in Stage 2. The critical difference is that the primary circular reaction results in sensory stimulation directly, and so it often involves the infant's body directly; the secondary circular reaction produces sensory input indirectly and so is usually oriented towards objects and activities beyond the infant's body. Contrast, for example, thumb sucking versus shaking a rattle. The former is a primary circular reaction: in thumb sucking the stimulation is direct. In shaking a rattle, a secondary circular reaction, the focus is on the sounds that come from the rattle when it is shaken.

Piaget described the emergence of such a secondary circular reaction in the following passage:

> At 0;3 (29) Laurent grasps a paper knife which he sees for the first time; he looks at it a moment and then swings it while holding it in his right hand. During these movements the object happens to rub against the wicker of the bassinet: Laurent then waves his arm vigorously and obviously tries to reproduce the sound he has heard, but without understanding the necessity of contact between the paper knife and the wicker and, consequently, without achieving this contact other than by chance. . . . Finally, at 0;4 (6) movement becomes intentional: as soon as the child has the object in his hand he rubs it with regularity against the wicker of the bassinet [Piaget, 1952, pp. 168–169].

Note that with the exception of the focus on objects rather than on the self, the secondary circular reaction has all of the other defining characteristics of the primary circular reaction: It first occurs by chance, the outcome is pleasing, and the infant strives to repeat the event.

The infant performing a secondary circular reaction often seems to be deliberately repeating the interesting activity. To decide whether such behavior is truly intentional, Piaget used three principal criteria. First, the behavior must be object-centered, not self-centered. Second, an action is likelier to be considered intentional as the number of intermediate steps needed to achieve the outcome increases. Thus, kicking an object in a crib to produce movement and sound is less intentional than the sequence of (1) taking a ball from a toy chest, (2) carrying it to another room, and (3) rolling it to a parent. Third, intentionality is inferred when behaviors are not simple repetitions of previous behaviors but instead are adaptations of behaviors to novel situations.

According to these criteria, 1- to 4-month-olds show no intentional behavior, for the primary circular reaction (1) is self-centered, (2) typically involves few intermediate steps, and (3) customarily is a literal repetition of previous behaviors. The secondary circular reaction differs only in the first of these characteristics—it is object- rather than self-centered—and thus constitutes the first inkling of intentional behavior.

Stage 4: Coordination of New Schemes (8–12 months). At first, different secondary circular reactions exist separately; they are not coordinated in any fashion. In Stage 4, however, secondary circular reactions become coordinated so that one activity is used as a means to achieve a second. Piaget (1952), for example, described how Laurent moved obstacles in order to play with a desired toy. Hence, the infant's behavior is now more intentional than was the case in Stage 3, for the infant meets two of Piaget's criteria: The behavior is object-centered and clearly involves an intermediate step to achieve the desired outcome. We do not credit the infant with complete intentionality, though, because of Piaget's third criterion: The infant's behavior still represents a combination of old, familiar circular reactions, not adaptations of them.

Stage 5: Tertiary Circular Reactions (12–18 months). Variation is first systematically introduced into circular reactions with the *tertiary circular reaction.* As in the case of primary and secondary circular reactions, the onset of a tertiary reaction is by accident. And, as before, the consequence is that the infant repeats the event. The critical difference is that now the infant systematically varies the reaction as it is repeated. Furthermore, the infant almost seems to be trying to understand why different objects yield different outcomes. Piaget (1952), for example, described how Laurent, as a 10-month-old, first accidentally dropped an object from his crib. He subsequently dropped a number of different objects and studied the outcome of each fall!

The shift from the self-centered orientation of the primary circular reaction is now complete. The tertiary circular reaction is a method par excellence for learning about the properties of objects. Note also that the infant has now met Piaget's third and final criterion for intentional behavior: Tertiary circular reactions represent active efforts to adapt to a new situation rather than simple repetitions of old behaviors.

Stage 6: Invention of New Means through Mental Combinations (18–24 months).   In the first 18 months of life, infants become capable of ever more complex behaviors, starting with reflexes and ending with tertiary circular reactions. The climax of the sensorimotor period, however, is Stage 6, when infants are capable of *internal* mental representations. The child is now able to use symbols, such as words, to refer to objects not present. For Piaget, several events signal children's use of mental symbols, which begins at approximately 18 months of age. One is that children are capable of *deferred imitation.* Younger children will imitate the actions of other children and adults, but only in their immediate presence. However, deferred imitation refers to imitation that occurs long after the child sees the imitated acts.

Perhaps the most impressive feat of Stage 6—and the origin of its name—is that the active experimentation of tertiary circular reactions from Stage 5 is now carried out *mentally* rather than *behaviorally.* That is, the child no longer literally tries out all possible events to determine their consequences; she is able to *anticipate* some of these consequences mentally:

> At 1;8 (9) [Jacqueline] arrives at a closed door—with a blade of grass in each hand. She stretches out her right hand toward the knob but sees that she cannot turn it without letting go of the grass. She puts the grass on the floor, opens the door, picks up the grass again and enters. But when she wants to leave the room things become complicated. She puts the grass on the floor and grasps the doorknob. But then she perceives that in pulling the door toward her she will simultaneously chase away the grass which she placed between the door and the threshold. She therefore picks it up in order to put it outside the door's zone of movement [Piaget, 1952, pp. 338–339].

This capacity to use mental symbols signals the end of the sensorimotor period. The child has progressed in two years from reflexive acts to the use of mental symbols. Of course, the 2-year-old's use of symbols is far from adultlike; preschool children's mental representations differ systematically from those of older children and adolescents. In fact, the period from 2 to 7 years represents the second of Piaget's four general phases of development, which he called the *preoperational period.*

The Preoperational Period (2–7 years)

The preoperational child's thought often seems to be the mental analog to the infant's sensorimotor actions. Instead of actively experimenting with objects as a 15-month-old might do, a 3-year-old performs exactly the same sequence of actions, only mentally. One can think of these mental representations as mental movies of the behaviors they represent. It is the close connection between mental activities and actual behavior that leads to the prefix *pre* operational thought, for it lacks the flexibility of true symbolic thought.

Conceiving of preoperational thought as a movie in the mind points to a second characteristic of this period. Movies make sense only if they go through a projector in the proper direction; viewed backwards they are meaningless. The preoperational child's thought shares this property: It is essentially *unidirectional;* young children cannot reverse their thinking.

To illustrate this point, let us consider one of Piaget's best-known experiments: conservation of liquid quantity. Children are shown two identical beakers, filled with identical quantities of liquid (see Figure 4-1). Water from one of the beakers is poured into a third beaker differing in shape from the first two. Pre-operational children typically judge the quantities no longer to be equal. Older children judge that the two beakers still contain the same amount of liquid, explaining their answer on the grounds that one can *reverse the operation* to achieve the initial state of equality. These problems, then, are like arithmetic problems in which having started with 4, then having added 2 to obtain 6, one can then perform the inverse of addition—subtracting a 2—to return to the initial value of 4.

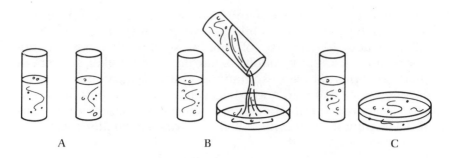

Figure 4-1   Piaget's conservation-of-liquid-quantity problem. Two identical beakers contain the same quantity of liquid (panel A), then the water from one beaker is poured into a different beaker (panel B). Children in the preoperational stage typically believe that the beakers in panel C no longer contain the same quantities of liquid.

The conservation problem reveals another characteristic of preoperational thinking. When asked why they believe there is more water in the taller of the two beakers, preoperational children characteristically refer to the level of the water. In doing so, of course, they ignore the change in the diameter of the beaker that compensates perfectly for the change in height. This tendency to *center* on a particular aspect of a problem to the exclusion of others is a common characteristic of preschool thought.

One sense of this *centration* deserves special attention, for it is one of the hallmarks of preoperational thought. Just as the preschooler has difficulty considering many facets of a problem, so does the young child have difficulty grasping the fact that his or her view of the world—both literally and figuratively—may be but one of many. *Egocentrism* refers to this inability to see the world from another's perspective. Piaget believed that when preschool children ignore the opinions or views of others, this does not reflect stubbornness that they want their own way; instead, preoperational children literally cannot understand that there is another way, that other people have views, opinions, and feelings differing from their own.

One of the first domains in which Piaget demonstrated childhood egocentrism was in children's conversations. Consider this conversation between Pie, a 6-year-old, and Eun, a 4-year-old, described by Piaget (1926, p. 58). Pie begins, "Where could we make another tunnel? Ah, here Eun?" Eun responds, "Look at my pretty frock."

Such egocentric speech develops into mature or *socialized* speech in three phases. The first, corresponding to the first half of the preoperational period, is dominated by egocentric speech of the type illustrated above. The second phase is a transitional phase and corresponds to the second half of the preoperational stage. Much egocentric speech is evident, but there are instances of more sophisticated forms of conversation. Here children will all talk about the same topic, but disregard the previous speaker's comments on the topic. The third and final stage, where egocentric speech is no longer present, coincides with the onset of concrete operational thought.

Similar types of egocentric behavior emerged when Piaget studied children's ability to take the perspective of other persons (Piaget & Inhelder, 1956). In this research, Piaget used what has come to be known as the three-mountain problem (see Figure 4-2). Specifically, a child is shown a model consisting of three mountains that vary in height as well as in color. The model is placed on a table, and the child is asked to view the mountains from one side of the table. Then a doll is placed at various posi-

Figure 4-2   *Piaget's three-mountain problem. A child facing three papier-mâché mountains is asked to decide how the mountains would appear to the doll seated at her right.*

tions around the table, as if it, too, were viewing the mountains. Each time the doll is placed in a new position, the child is asked to select which of several photographs corresponds to the doll's view of the mountains.

As was the case in egocentric speech, Piaget identified three stages in the development of the ability to take the perspective of other persons. The first is the egocentric phase, which typically lasts the entire preoperational period. Here children typically select the photograph that corresponds to their *own view* of the mountains, rather than the doll's view. Preoperational children apparently assume that theirs is the only view of the mountains; anyone viewing the configuration of mountains must see it as they do. A brief transitional period follows, lasting from approximately seven to eight years. In this phase, children rarely make egocentric errors; that is, they are unlikely to judge that the doll sees the array as they do. Yet they often select incorrect photographs. Apparently these children understand that the doll's view must be different from their own, but they do not yet know how to determine precisely what that view is. Finally, beginning at about 9 years of age, children select the photograph corresponding to the doll's view of the mountains.

Concrete Operational Thought (7–11 years)

We have already learned much about concrete operational thinking in examining the preoperational stage of development, for Piaget essentially defines the earlier stage in terms of its shortcomings compared with the later. Thus, the preoperational child's use of symbols often parrots behavioral acts; in contrast, the concrete operational child uses symbols more freely. The preoperational child's thinking is *irreversible, centered,* and *egocentric;* the concrete operational child's is *reversible, decentered,* and *nonegocentric.* A clue to the underlying difference between preoperational and concrete operational thought is provided in the terms themselves: Preschoolers' thinking is somehow *pre*operational; older children have operations of some sort that are available to them.

We illustrated these differences earlier in the conservation-of-liquid problem illustrated in Figure 4-1. Concrete operational children solve these problems correctly and justify their answer in one of two ways. First, they may point out that the liquid could be poured back to the initial container, thereby restoring the original equality. Second, they may argue that the change in the level of the liquid is exactly compensated by the difference in the diameters of the beakers.

Conservation may be Piaget's best-known line of research, but much of his research on concrete operations dealt with children's understanding of classes and the relationships between them. Human thinking and reasoning achieve much of their power from the ability to think of objects as members of classes rather than as isolated entities. Thus, knowing that an object is a member of a class, we can attribute to that object the various properties and features that characterize the class generally. Knowing that a salmon is a fish, we can immediately infer that salmon live in water, swim, do not fly, and the like.

A fundamental aspect of classes that Piaget studied extensively was the *class-inclusion* relationship, or what we might call the *set–subset* relationship. The prototypic task was as follows: Children are shown a set of objects that belong to one of two related but mutually exclusive categories. Furthermore, one of the two categories always contains more elements than the other. Examples would be pictures of four boys and five girls, three dogs and two cats, seven trees and four flowers, and so on. Thus, we can represent the problems as consisting of two subsets, A and A', in which $A > A'$ and which can be summed to form a set B.

After childen are shown the elements, they are questioned about the sizes of the various sets. They might be asked, for example, "Are there more individuals in A (e.g., boys) or in A' (e.g., girls)?", a question that most children answer easily. Of greater interest are children's answers to the following question: "Are there more individuals in A (e.g., boys) or in B (e.g., children)?" Note that a correct answer to this question requires a child to understand that an element can simultaneously be a member of both a subset and a set. In fact, preoperational children typically respond that A is larger. They apparently cannot think of boys as being both a distinct set (i.e., A) and simultaneously a subset of the larger set of children (i.e., B). Hence, the set of children is, for the preoperational child, only the girls (i.e., A'). Not until approximately 8 or 9 years of age do children answer these problems correctly. (For reviews of this work, see Brainerd, 1978, chap. 5; Klahr & Wallace, 1976, chap. 4; Trabasso, Isen, Dolecki, McLanahan, Riley, & Tucker, 1978.)

What are the mental mechanisms responsible for these differences in behavior? For Piaget the answer lies in the *mental operation*. In mathematics, operations refer to such things as addition, subtraction, multiplication, and division; each of these activities can be performed on entities (numbers, typically) that yield some outcome. Piaget proposed that psychological operations are much the same; they are actions that can be performed on entities (objects or ideas) that yield a result. Mental operations, of course, must be inferred because they are in the head. More important is the fact that operations never exist alone or independently; by definition, operations refer to sets of interrelated actions: "A single operation could not be an operation, because the peculiarity of operations *is that they form systems*" (Piaget, 1950, p. 35, emphasis added).

Piaget's description of mental operations relies heavily upon structures drawn from logic and mathematics. Specifically, Piaget proposed that the mental structures of the concrete operational period are described by nine different *groupings*, each grouping referring to an organized set of mental operations. The groupings are much too detailed to be presented in their entirety; instead, we shall describe Grouping I, the simplest of the nine, to illustrate Piaget's use of groupings to characterize the structure of mental operations.

Grouping I concerns ways of combining classes and as such is the grouping that underlies performance on class-inclusion problems. In describing this grouping, symbols will be used to denote various classes and subclasses. Consider the hierarchy of classes shown in Figure 4-3. *A* refers to the category of baseball pitchers; *A'* refers to individuals who play the other positions in baseball. *B* denotes baseball players; *B'* denotes athletes who play other sports. *C* refers to the general category of athletes. At each level in this hierarchy, then, the *unprimed* category refers to a specific class; the *primed* category refers to all other instances *except* those in the unprimed category. Thus, *C'* would refer to all nonathletes.

Grouping I specifies ways in which classes can be combined. In defining legitimate combinations of classes, Piaget uses notation that looks like arithmetic, for the operation of combining two classes is represented by a +. It is not identical to arithmetic operations, however, as the letters represent classes rather than arithmetic values. Also, we shall see that some of the operations yield distinctly nonarithmetic outcomes. The five operations are these:

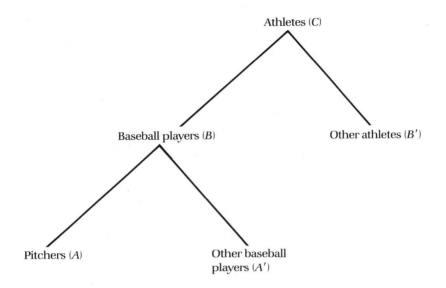

Figure 4-3   A hierarchy of athletes.

1. *Composition.* Combining any two classes results in another legitimate class. Hence, $A + A' = B$; that is, combining pitchers with individuals who play the remaining positions results in the class of baseball players.

2. *Associativity.* The order in which classes are added is irrelevant. For example, the following combinations both yield the same result, C:

$$(A + A') + B' = A + (A' + B')$$

If, as on the left side of this expression, we first combine the pitchers (A) with people who play other positions (A'), the result is the class of baseball players (B); combining this class with all other athletes (B') yields the total class of athletes (C). On the right side, combining all baseball players except pitchers (A') with all athletes except baseball players (B') yields the class of all athletes except pitchers; combining this class with pitchers (A) yields the class of all athletes.

3. *General identity.* When a class is combined with the *null* or *empty* class, the class is unchanged. Thus, if 0 denotes the null class, $A + 0 = A$; combining pitchers with an empty class yields the original class of pitchers.

4. *Reversibility.* For every class, there exists a class that when added to the original class produces the null class. That is, $A + (-A) = 0$. Thus we are defining *subtraction* of classes. If you start with the class of baseball players and subtract from it the class of baseball players, the result is the empty set.

5. *Special identities.* These refer to two properties that are distinctly nonarithmetic in nature. The first is known as *tautology:* $A + A = A$ (not $2A$ as one would expect in algebra). If we add the class of baseball players to the class of baseball players, the result is the class of baseball players. The second property, *resorption,* refers to the related phenomenon that $A + B = B$. Combining the class of pitchers with the class of baseball players, the result is the class of baseball players. Tautology and resorption are called *identities* because they refer to combinations in which classes are unchanged; they are *special identities* because of their nonmathematical nature.

In saying that concrete operational children "have" Grouping I, Piaget certainly does not mean that they can state these principles as we have listed them here, any more than an adult can list all of the grammatical rules that govern his or her fluent speech. Instead, this grouping, along with the other eight, is simply a way of characterizing the mental structures that give rise to concrete operational behavior.

We can easily see how the principles in Grouping I are essential in solving problems dealing with class relationships generally, and class-inclusion problems specifically. When asked if there are more individuals in B or A, the concrete operational child can use the principle of reversibility to realize that $A = B - A'$, that is, that the A class is included in the B class and that the B class is therefore larger than the A class.

It is groupings like this one, then, that give concrete operational thought its power, for thought no longer must mirror actions as in the preoperational period. The groupings give thought flexibility and coherence that are not present prior to the onset of concrete operations.

Formal Operational Thought
(11 years–adulthood)

The concrete operational thought achieved at 7 or 8 years of age certainly represents a quantum leap forward from the intuitive thought of the preoperational period. Yet concrete operational thought does not repesent the pinnacle of human thought in Piaget's account. Two shortcomings are especially noteworthy. First, as the name implies, concrete operations are limited to concrete entities. Children in this stage of development typically are incapable of applying these same operations to *abstract* entities. Concrete operational thought is limited to the tangible and real, to the here and now. Formal operational thought is not so constrained. In fact, "*possibility* no longer appears merely as an extension of an empirical situation or of actions actually performed. Instead, it is *reality* that is now secondary to *possibility*" (Inhelder & Piaget, 1958, p. 251). Such abstract or *formal* thinking is not possible during the concrete operational period, but occurs in the formal operational stage.

A second shortcoming concerns the organization of operations during the concrete operational period. The nine groupings of concrete operations represent an important advance over the isolated, unorganized intuitions that characterize preoperational thought. Yet the concrete operational period still consists of nine separate groupings; not until formal operations is there a single, cohesive cognitive system.

Inhelder and Piaget (1958) used a variety of tasks to highlight the unique assets of formal operational thought. Here we shall focus on experiments on "colored and colorless chemical bodies" (Inhelder & Piaget, 1958, chap. 7). In this research, there were four flasks, each containing what appeared to be the same colorless liquid. In addition, there was a bottle with a dropper. The subject was asked to combine the various clear liquids to create one that was yellow. The four flasks contained (1) diluted sulfuric acid, (2) water, (3) oxygenated water, and (4) thiosulfate; the bottle (labeled g, to be consistent with Inhelder and Piaget's nomenclature) contained potassium iodide. Combining sulfuric acid, oxygenated water, and potassium iodide produces a yellow liquid. Thus, the correct combination was (1) $\times$ (3) $\times$ g. Water is neutral here, so including water as well still yields a yellow liquid. The thiosulfate causes the mixture to revert to its original colorless state.

Let us begin with a description of how a concrete operational child attempts to find the correct combination. (In these protocols, the subject's remarks are italicized; the experimenter's remarks are in roman type.) Consider the efforts of Gay (7;6) who

> limits himself to $4 \times g$, $1 \times g$, $3 \times g$, and $2 \times g$, and discovers nothing else. "Could you try with two bottles together?"— [Silence.]—"Try."—[$4 \times 1 \times g$] "*It doesn't work.*"—"Try something else."—[$3 \times 1 \times g$] "*There it is!*" (Inhelder & Piaget, 1958, p. 111).

Gay is typical of 7-year-olds in that he does not seem to have a well-established plan for identifying the right combination of liquids to produce yellow. He seems to combine liquids arbitrarily hoping that some combination will work.

Contrast Gay's approach with the systematic efforts of the following adolescent:

> Cha (13;0): *"You have to try with all the bottles. I'll begin with the one at the end* [from 1 to 4 with g]. *It doesn't work any more. Maybe you have to mix them* [he tries 1 × 2 × g, then 1 × 3 × g]. *It turned yellow. But are there other solutions? I'll try* [1 × 4 × g; 2 × 3 × g; 2 × 4 × g; 3 × 4 × g; with the two preceding combinations this gives the six two-by-two combinations systematically]. *It doesn't work. It only works with* [1 × 3 × g]." "Yes, and what about 2 and 4?"—"*2 and 4 don't make any color together. They are negative. Perhaps you could add 4 in 1 × 3 × g to see if it would cancel out the color* [he does this]. *Liquid 4 cancels it all. You'd have to see if 2 has the same influence* [he tries it]. *No, so 2 and 4 are not alike, for 4 acts on 1 × 3 and 2 does not.*"—"What is there in 2 and 4?"—"*In 4 certainly water. No, the opposite, in 2 certainly water since it doesn't act on the liquids; that makes things clearer.*"—"And if I were to tell you that 4 is water?"—"*If this liquid 4 is water, when you put it with 1 × 3 it wouldn't completely prevent the yellow from forming. It isn't water; it's something harmful*" (Inhelder & Piaget, 1958, p. 117).

In this protocol, as well as others presented by Inhelder and Piaget (1958), we see the systematic way in which adolescents—that is, formal operational thinkers—proceed in solving this task. Children in the concrete operational stage proceed in the concrete way that we have come to expect. Given some beakers and told to mix them to produce a yellow liquid, they do just that; they show little evidence of trying to formulate a plan for considering all combinations of liquids so that the proper combination is isolated. For adolescents, the reality of the beakers and the act of mixing are subservient to just such a plan. They seem to realize that there is a finite number of possible combinations; proceeding through these combinations systematically is a foolproof way of identifying the critical combination.

Hypothetical-deductive reasoning. The adolescent's more sophisticated thinking represents significant advances on two fronts. The first concerns *hypothetical-deductive reasoning.* Defined informally, deduction is any type of reasoning that starts with a fact, premise, or hypothesis and then draws conclusions.

That is, deductive reasoning is the sort characterized by statements like "if P, then Q." According to Piaget, concrete operational children may sometimes seem to be reasoning in this manner, but on close scrutiny such behaviors are not true deductions but generalizations drawn from their experiences. For example, consider the following:

Premise 1: If a person is a Canadian, that person skis.
Premise 2: Cindy is a Canadian.
Conclusion: Cindy skis.

If a concrete operational child reached this conclusion, it might represent a legitimate instance of deductive reasoning. It might, however, simply represent the fact that the child believes the first premise to be true based on experiences with Canadians. After being told that Cindy is a Canadian, the child infers that Cindy skis.

Why is this not a case of true deductive reasoning? The answer is that conclusions reached by deductive reasoning follow *regardless of the validity of the premises*. Suppose we replace the second premise in our example with the following:

Premise 2A: Abraham Lincoln is a Canadian.

The conclusion "Abraham Lincoln skis" follows from the premises just as necessarily as our earlier conclusion, and formal operational adolescents would draw these conclusions in both cases. For concrete operational children, conclusions are not logically necessary but are derived from the children's experiences. Hence, they would draw the first conclusion but would balk at the second.

In fact, the "if P then Q" type of inference (known formally as *implication*) is but one of sixteen forms of deductive reasoning that provide much of the power of adolescent thought. This power accrues from two sources. First, the sixteen propositional operations "form a single system such that it is possible to move with accuracy from any one of its sixteen elements to each of the others" (Inhelder & Piaget, 1958, p. 303). Such an integrated system of operations affords a flexibility of thought that is not possible with the nine distinct groupings of the preoperational period. Second, the premises and conclusions of propositional logic can denote almost anything. They may refer to concrete entities such as objects or people, but they can just as easily refer to abstractions such as ideas, values, or *even thinking itself.*

Induction: The Formal Operational Schemes. In one of our earlier examples on deductive reasoning, we pointed out that adolescents would conclude that "Abraham Lincoln skis" from two premises, one of which was "Abraham Lincoln is a Canadian." What this example demonstrates, of course, is another important component of reasoning—being able to determine the validity of premises. Making valid generalizations of this sort from experience is known as *inductive reasoning.*

Inhelder and Piaget (1958) proposed that several schemes emerge during formal operations that allow adolescents to induce correct generalizations across different problems that are similar in structure. One of these general-purpose schemes is *proportionality,* which simply refers to the fact that two ratios are equal:

$$\frac{a}{b} = \frac{a'}{b'}$$

It is understanding this basic scheme that allows adolescents to discover a large number of different relationships: (1) when a scale will balance, (2) when two objects will cast shadows of the same size, (3) when two objects are traveling at the same rate of speed, and (4) when two urns, each containing two kinds of objects, are equally likely to contain the desired object. The proportionality concept, then, allows adolescents to evaluate the truth of a wide range of premises. Much the same is true for the other formal operational schemes described by Inhelder and Piaget (1958). These schemes, then, allow the adolescent to systematically explore and discover relationships that exist in the world. Once discovered, the adolescent can draw conclusions about the premises based on the operations available in propositional logic.[2]

---

[2]The specific manner in which the proportionality concept underlies these examples is as follows: The length of a shadow of an object whose length is l is given by $l/(d_1/d_2)$ where d_1 refers to the distance from the object to the source of light and d_2 is the distance from the light source to the screen. Thus, if $a = l$ and $b = d_1/d_2$, two objects will cast similar shadows only when a/b is the same for the two objects. Rate of speed is defined as distance divided by time. So if a

Evaluation of the Theory

Piaget's theory was first introduced to most English-speaking developmental psychologists in the early 1960s. Hunt briefly described the theory in 1961 in an influential book entitled *Intelligence and Experience*. Then, in 1963, Flavell's *The Developmental Psychology of Jean Piaget* appeared. This book included an extensive description of the theory and the relevant evidence, plus a brief evaluation of the theory. The impact of these books was immediate and profound: For the rest of the 1960s and continuing into the 1970s, literally hundreds of studies were published in which the aim was to probe various facets of Piaget's theory.

Such close scrutiny would reveal shortcomings of some sort in any theory, and Piaget's was no exception. Perhaps the most serious problem concerned the logical structures (e.g., Grouping I) that Piaget used to characterize thinking at different ages. Linking the logical structures to performance on particular tasks proved to be extremely difficult, which made it hard to predict exactly what sort of performance was expected on the basis of the theory.

We can illustrate this difficulty with the class-inclusion problem described earlier, in which children might be shown three roses and two daffodils and asked, "Are there more flowers or roses?" This problem can be stated formally: Given the sets A and A' where $A > A'$ and $B = A + A'$, is $A > B$, $B > A$, or $A = B$? Not until age 8 do most children solve these problems. According to Inhelder and Piaget (1964), answering correctly implies that a child "must be aware of B as the sum of $A + A'$, and he must simultaneously be aware of A as the difference $B - A'$. Such simultaneous awareness, which is characteristic of operational thinking, implies the conservation of the whole B" (p. 106).

This analysis implies that all class-inclusion problems that conform to the underlying logical relationships of $A > A'$ and $B = A + A'$ should be equally difficult. They are not; perceptual

---

is distance and b is time, two objects travel at the same speed only when a/b is the same for both objects. Finally, let d refer to objects in the urn that are desired, and u those that are undesired. The probability of selecting a desired object is simply $d/(d + u)$. If $a = d$ and $b = d + u$, then the probability of selecting a desired object from the two urns is equal only when a/b is equal for both urns.

and linguistic variables are known to influence children's performance markedly (e.g., Brainerd, 1978; Klahr & Wallace, 1972; Trabasso et al., 1978). The logical structures and relations of Piaget's theory cannot encompass these effects readily.

Furthermore, the arguments raised here do not apply exclusively to the logic appropriate to the class-inclusion problem; they could be made as well for other aspects of the theory. As a result, during the early 1970s several psychologists (e.g., Bryant & Trabasso, 1971; Case, 1978; Klahr & Wallace, 1970, 1972; Pascual-Leone, 1970) became interested in reformulating some Piagetian notions in information processing terms. These psychologists proposed quite different explanations of children's performance on specific Piagetian tasks, explanations that relied upon information processing constructs like encoding, memory, automaticity, and strategies rather than the logical relations of Piagetian theory.

A second problematic aspect of Piaget's theory concerns the *mechanism* for developmental change. According to Piaget, the complementary sides of adaptation—accommodation and assimilation—are usually in balance, creating a state of cognitive *equilibrium*. There are critical times, however, when *cognitive conflict* produces a state of *disequilibrium*. The result is the creation of the more advanced mental structures of the subsequent Piagetian stage.

An appropriate analogy here would be to revolutions in science. Just as a child's mental structures permit a child to interpret and organize experiences, a theory allows a scientist to interpret and organize scientific observations. Of course, scientific theories are ever changing. Most of the changes are minor adjustments to enable a theory to account for some new observation. Periodically, however, there are conflicting observations that resist simple fine-tuning of a theory. The outcome is a scientific revolution in which a theory is discarded altogether and replaced by a completely new theory that interprets and organizes the data better. Thus, just as Ptolemy's theory that the planets orbit the earth gave way to the Copernican view of the sun as the center of the solar system, so too does conflicting evidence force the preoperational child's view of the world to give way to concrete operational thinking.

Described in this way, conflict seems an intuitively plausible basis for cognitive change, and perhaps for this reason it has long been a part of psychological theories of change (Cantor, 1983).

Nevertheless, Piaget's use of conflict has been faulted on two counts. First, conflict does not always lead to cognitive change, and when it does, the change may not be due to conflict per se (e.g., Zimmerman & Blom, 1983). Second, there are many instances in which cognitive change occurs in the absence of conflict, as in the case where a child spontaneously abandons an inefficient strategy for a task in favor of a more efficient approach (e.g., Groen & Resnick, 1977). These criticisms do not mean that conflict never produces cognitive change; rather it is not the *sole* mechanism for cognitive change (Murray, 1983).

Hence, developmental psychologists of an information processing persuasion have formulated additional mechanisms of growth that are based on constructs described in Chapter 3. Specifically, developmental change has been explained in terms of growth of processing resources as well as increases in processing efficiency.

Information Processing Approaches to Intellectual Development

As we have just described, developmental psychologists have used information processing constructs, first, to explain performance on Piagetian tasks, and, second, to derive alternative mechanisms for growth. In this section, we examine each of these efforts in detail.

Focus on Piagetian Constructs

Information processing psychologists have investigated a number of Piaget's constructs including class inclusion, seriation, and conservation. Here we examine information processing analyses of two other domains: transitive inference and the concept of balance. In the first instance, information processing research leads to an explanation of children's performance that differs considerably from Piaget's account; in the second instance, information processing analyses are generally consistent with Piaget's description, but fill in some important gaps.

Transitive Inference.   On a transitive inference problem, children are given information of the type $A > B$ and $B > C$ and then are asked to determine the greater of A and C. For example, children might be told: "Ellen is older than Ben, and Ben is older than Matt; who is older, Ellen or Matt?" Preschoolers are often perplexed by these problems and typically are just as likely to say "Matt" as "Ellen." According to Piaget's theory (Flavell, 1963), preschool children fail these problems because they lack such concrete operational skills as reversibility. Bryant and Trabasso (1971) provided a much simpler explanation: They showed that preschoolers' difficulty was not in their inability to reason transitively but in their inability to remember the premises of the problem. Young children forget the relationships between Ellen and Ben and between Ben and Matt, and consequently have no way to determine who is older. Bryant and Trabasso showed that if preschoolers are given extensive training on the original pairs of relations, they make inferences almost as accurately as do adults.

Subsequently, Trabasso and his colleagues attempted to describe exactly how children make inferences of this sort. In Piaget's description, the mental processes are analogous to those of formal logic: Given the premises $A > B$ and $B > C$, the child uses the common term, B, to coordinate the two premises; the conclusion that $A > C$ necessarily follows.

Trabasso (1977) suggested a different mechanism. If children are told, "Ellen is older than Ben; Ben is older than Matt," they apparently store this information in memory as a set of ordered relationships along the underlying dimension of age:

Old—Ellen, Ben, Matt—*Young*

When asked a question regarding the relationship between the ages of two persons, the child scans this dimension, beginning at the end mentioned in the question, and answers with the first of the two names (in the question) that is found. In response to "Who is younger, Ben or Ellen?" children begin scanning the dimension from the young end because the comparative in the question is *younger*. Matt was not mentioned in the question, so search continues to the next name, Ben, which was mentioned in the question, so the child answers, "Ben."

Trabasso, Riley, and Wilson (1975) used a reaction-time paradigm to demonstrate that young children represent information in memory in exactly this way. Six-years-olds were taught the relationships between the lengths of five pairs of colored sticks. They learned that $1 < 2$ and $2 > 1$, $2 < 3$ and $3 > 2$, $3 < 4$ and $4 > 3$, $4 < 5$ and $5 > 4$, and $5 < 6$ and $6 > 5$, where 1 refers to the shortest stick and 6 refers to the longest. Following training, children were tested on the relations between all 15 possible combination of sticks.

Of particular interest here are the reaction times to different pairs of sticks. If children represent information about the sticks in memory along an ordered dimension of length, then a specific pattern of reaction times is expected. The pattern is best demonstrated by examining children's solutions to several pairs of sticks. Suppose sticks 2 and 5 are tested. According to the model described earlier, when the question is "Which is longer?", subjects will begin at the long end of the array (i.e., 6) and scan until they find 5. In this case, two items would be scanned, 6 and 5. When the question is "Which is shorter?", search will begin at the short end of the array. Again, two items will be searched in locating 2.

Now suppose we test sticks 2 and 3. When asked "Which is longer?", a child will begin with 6 and continue to 3, scanning four items in the process. "Which is shorter?" will result in two items being scanned, 1 and 2. Averaging the two types of questions, three items will have to be scanned to answer questions concerning sticks 2 and 3.

Because scanning three items presumably takes longer than scanning two, children should have longer response times on judgments of sticks 2 and 3 than on sticks 2 and 5. Furthermore, when this analysis is extended to all pairs of sticks, it leads to the general rule that if children represent information in memory as an ordered array, then response time should increase as the distance between the two sticks decreases.

The resulting reaction times were exactly in accord with these predictions. For example, 6-year-olds' latencies for questions concerning sticks 2 and 3 were approximately a half-second longer than their latencies for sticks 2 and 5. The average latency for sticks 2 and 4 was approximately midway between these two latencies, as would be predicted. Interestingly, when Trabasso et al. (1975) tested 9-year-olds and adults with this procedure, the same relationships among response times were found.

These results, along with those of subsequent investigators (e.g., Brainerd & Kingma, in press), nicely illustrate how performance on a Piagetian task can be explained quite precisely in terms of information processing constructs. In the case of transitive reasoning, processing on the task does not change qualitatively with development: Children seem to reason in fundamentally the same way as adults. Not all information processing analyses lead to this conclusion, as we shall see by considering work on another Piagetian task.

The Concept of Balance. One of Piaget's most interesting tasks is the balance scale. In this task, individuals are shown a balance scale in which identical weights have been placed at various distances to either side of a fulcrum. Individuals simply decide which side of the balance scale will go down, if either, when the supporting blocks are removed. Unlike, for example, the conservation-of-liquid-quantity task, in which children reason correctly by 7 or 8 years of age, even preschoolers have some correct intuitions about the concept of balance, but mature reasoning does not emerge until adulthood.

Inhelder and Piaget (1958) described three distinct stages of reasoning about balance. In Stage I, children do not follow any rule systematically, although by the end of this stage they have intuitions that the number of weights is important. In Stage II, people know that the number of weights is important, as is their distance from the fulcrum; by the end of this stage, they know that weight and distance trade off in some manner. Not until Stage III, however, do individuals discover that the precise form of this trade-off is $w_1 d_1 = w_2 d_2$ where w_j refers to the amount of weight on side j of the fulcrum and d_j its distance.

Siegler (1976) reconceptualized Piaget's stages as a set of developmentally ordered rules that are depicted as flowcharts in Figure 4-4. Typically, 5- and 6-year-olds use Rule I, in which only the number of weights is considered. If the weights are equal on the two sides, the child predicts that the scale will balance; if the weights are unequal, the child predicts that the side with the greater number of weights will go down.

For 9- and 10-year-olds, two rules are common. The simpler of the two, Rule II, is just a variant of Rule I: As before, when the number of weights on the two sides is unequal, children always predict that the side with more weights will go down. When the weights are equal, however, children no longer automatically predict that the scale will balance. Instead, they evaluate the distance of the weights from the fulcrum, then predict. The other rule used frequently by 9- and 10-year-olds (Rule III) involves consideration of both weight and distance. This rule is inadequate only in that it provides no means to resolve conflicts arising when weight and distance lead to different predictions regarding which side of the balance is heavier.

Rules II and III are both used by 13- and 14-year-olds, but Rule III is more frequent. Finally, among 16- and 17-year-olds, some individuals will use Rule II, most will use Rule III, and some will use Rule IV, which is a variant of Rule III that includes procedures for computing and comparing torque.

An advantage of recasting Piaget's account in terms of specific rules is that we can now predict—with no ambiguity—the balance problems that a person will solve. Consider, for example, a problem in which two weights have been placed on each side of a fulcrum but at different distances. A person using Rule I would incorrectly predict the scale to balance, but persons using Rules II through IV would all predict correctly.

These rules also lead to some highly counterintuitive predictions, in which preschool children would answer correctly but adolescents would not. Imagine a problem in which 4 ounces are placed 3 inches to the left of the fulcrum and 2 ounces are placed 4 inches to the right. The left side is heavier, for $4 \times 3 > 2 \times 4$. Notice that a child using Rule I would simply see that the left side has the greater weight and answer correctly, though quite fortuitously. Compare this with the typical 16- or 17-year-old, who would use Rule III: This individual would see that one side has the greater weight but the other side has the greater distance. Lacking a clear-cut rule for such cases, the adolescent guesses. Consistent with these predictions, 5- and 6-year-olds solved 86% of these kinds of problems correctly, but 16- and 17-year-olds solved only 51% correctly (Siegler, 1976).

The chief virtue of the sort of information processing research illustrated by the work of Trabasso and Siegler is that we can describe aspects of cognitive development with great precision. The theories can be used to derive a set of unambiguous predictions; the theories can then be evaluated in terms of the degree of correspondence between the actual data and predictions based on the theory. The result is a precise and detailed characterization of age differences in performance. In some cases, as in Trabasso's work on transitive reasoning, the results are not readily assimilated into Piagetian theory, but in other cases they are much more compatible, as illustrated in Siegler's work on the balance scale.

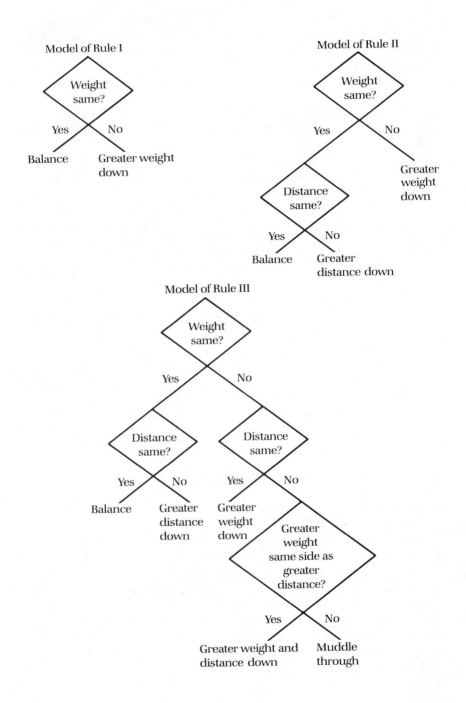

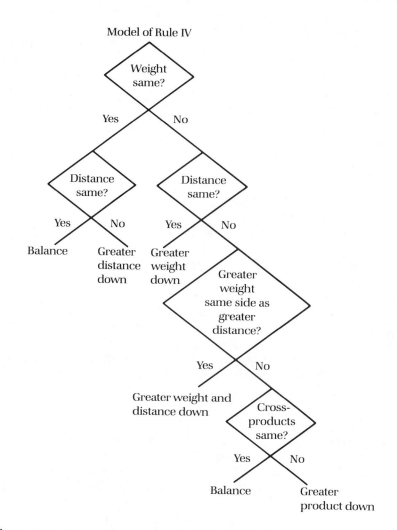

Figure 4-4 *Four rules used to decide which of the two sides of a balance scale is heavier (i.e., will go down when the supporting blocks are removed). (Reprinted with permission from R. S. Siegler, Three aspects of cognitive development.* Cognitive Psychology, *1976, 8, 481–520. Copyright by Academic Press, Inc.)*

Mechanisms of Development

The developmental information-processing work described in the previous section was fundamentally *descriptive* in nature. The theories presented there represent specific statements of *what* people of various ages do as they solve different tasks. What these models do not explain is *how developmental change occurs.* How do children who use a particular approach to solving problems at one age (e.g., 5-year-olds who use Siegler's Rule I) come to use a more sophisticated algorithm when they are older (e.g., Rule IV in young adulthood)? As we noted earlier, information processing psychologists have attempted to explain these changes in terms of increases in processing resources as well as increased processing efficiency.

    Processing Resources. In chapter 3 we used the terms *limited processing resources, limited mental effort,* and *span of awareness* to refer to the simple facts that (1) performance on most tasks is intellectually demanding, and (2) all humans are limited in the intellectual resources they can allocate to those demands. Perhaps the total pool of these intellectual resources increases as children develop, which would explain why children are capable of solving more complex tasks (i.e., tasks with greater processing demands) as they grow older. McLaughlin (1963) was the first to suggest this possibility: He argued that the qualitative developmental changes noted by Piaget might actually reflect changes in memory or attentional capacity. Regrettably, McLaughlin did not test his theory experimentally, and for that reason the theory had relatively little impact.

    However, in 1970 Pascual-Leone proposed a similar theory in which cognitive development was explained in terms of "the size of central computing space M, which increased in a lawful manner during normal development" (p 304). This central computing space is analogous to our assumption that only a limited portion of the knowledge base can be activated at one time. Pascual-Leone proposed that M space could be defined as $e + k$. The first quantity, e, is the amount of space set aside to store general information about how to perform the task. The k refers to the space for storing information from the task and specific procedures for solving the task. The value of e is thought to be invariant developmentally. That is, at different ages, the instructions and general task information occupy the same amount of M space. However, k is thought to increase in discrete steps

Table 4-2   *M values at different developmental levels*

Age	Piagetian substage	M value
3–4	Early preoperational	$e + 1$
5–6	Late preoperational	$e + 2$
7–8	Early concrete operational	$e + 3$
9–10	Late concrete operational	$e + 4$
11–12	Early formal operational	$e + 5$
13–14	Middle formal operational	$e + 6$
15–16	Late formal operational	$e + 7$

Source: Table derived from Case, 1972b.
Note: The value of e is constant across ages and refers to the capacity needed to store information about task instructions.

that are linked directly to a child's chronological age. As can be seen in Table 4-2, Pascual-Leone suggested that k increases by 1 unit every other year between 3 and 16 years of age.

In this theory, then, children who fail on Piagetian tasks do so because the information required to pass the task exceeds the child's available M space. Consider, for example, the conservation-of-liquid-quantity task. Pascual-Leone (cited in Case, 1978) argued that success on this task hinges on storing three units of information: (1) keeping in M space the initial equality of the two beakers; (2) storing the nature of the transformation (i.e., pouring); and (3) storing the rule that pouring liquid from one container to another does not affect its quantity. The three units exceed the 2 available M units for 5- and 6-year-olds, so they fail the task. By 7 or 8 years of age, M has increased to $e + 3$, allowing children to perform the task successfully.

This sort of analysis illustrates how the theory applies to Piagetian tasks but does not test the theory rigorously. For this purpose, we need a task in which the resource demands can be varied systematically. Then the theory can be used to predict those conditions under which children of a particular age (or, more precisely, M power) should succeed as well as those conditions under which they should fail. Pascual-Leone and his colleagues have done this in a number of experiments (Burtis, 1982; Case, 1972a, 1972b; Case & Serlin, 1979; Pascual-Leone, 1970; Scardamalia, 1977).

An experiment by Case (1972b) is illustrative. Childen were shown a series of digits. Their task was to place the last digit in the appropriate place in the series. Shown 3, 8, and 12, they would be asked to place a 10 in the appropriate location (between the 8 and 12). Several practice trials of this sort were given until children had mastered the basics of the task. Then the procedure was modified slightly so that each digit was shown individually for approximately 1 to 2 seconds, then was turned face down. After the last digit was shown, children indicated where it would go in the series.

The 6-, 8-, and 10-year-olds in this experiment were first tested on series where the number of digits presented was equal to the value of k hypothesized for their age. Thus, 6-year-olds saw two digits, while 8- and 10-year-olds saw three and four digits, respectively.[3] Then children were tested on additional series in which the number of digits presented was $k + 1$; thus three, four, and five digits were shown to 6-, 8-, and 10-year-olds, respectively.

The general predictions of Pascual-Leone's (1970) theory are straightforward: When the number of digits is equal to k, all children should solve problems successfully, for available M space equals the quantity of information (i.e., digits) to be remembered. The situation is more complex when the number of digits exceeds k by 1. One digit will be forgotten, and Case (1972b) assumed that all $k + 1$ digits were equally likely to be forgotten. Hence, sometimes the available information will still be sufficient to generate a correct response: Shown 3, 9, and 18 and asked to place the 11, forgetting the 3 should not impair performance. If instead the 11 itself was forgotten, the child would simply have to guess and thus would be correct on one-fourth of the trials.

By examining in this manner the consequences on performance of forgetting each of the individual digits in each problem, Case (1972b) predicted the number of problems that a child should solve correctly when the number of digits is greater than the hypothetically available M space. The number of problems children actually solved correctly was very close to the number predicted by the k values. For example, if 8-year-olds' M space is $e + 3$, Case's analysis led to a prediction that these children will solve approximately 78% of the problems when $n = 5$. In fact, they solved approximately 79% accurately. Thus, Case's (1972b) data, like those of other investigators (e.g., Scardamalia, 1977),

---

[3]The total number of digits always includes the digit to be placed. Thus, two digits were presented to the 6-year-olds, say a 5 then a 7, with the objective to place the 7 to the right of the 5.

seem to provide convincing support for Pascual-Leone's (1970) proposed increase in processing capacity—at least for children between ages 6 to 10 years and for M values $e + 2$ to $e + 4$.

Pascual-Leone's (1970) theory represents, in effect, the combined assets of Piagetian and information processing theories of cognitive processing and cognitive development. In common with Piaget's theory, Pascual-Leone's theory includes the notion of discrete stages in development, stages that are both descriptive and explanatory. However, in Pascual-Leone's theory, the defining characteristic of each stage is its M power, not the logical structures of Piagetian theory.

Also in common with Piagetian theory is the fact that M theory is broad, applicable in principle to performance on completely disparate tasks. In extreme form, Pascual-Leone's theory divides the universe into two classes of tasks: (1) tasks whose informational demands exceed the child's M power, which the child must fail; and (2) tasks whose informational demands are less than or equal to the child's M power, which the child should pass. In fact, of course, tasks cannot be dichotomized in this way, for children will sometimes succeed on tasks in the first category through various ways of circumventing the limitations of his or her M space. In like manner, children may not always pass items in the second category because they lack the necessary processing schemes. The important point, though, is that analysis of a task's demands in terms of M space provides a way of making predictions regarding age differences in performance on tasks that apparently have little in common.

Pascual-Leone's (1970) theory has been scrutinized carefully, at least in part because its claims are so general (Trabasso & Foellinger, 1978; Pascual-Leone, 1978; Trabasso, 1978; Pascual-Leone & Sparkman, 1980). The theory will certainly be modified (see Case, 1978, for one example) and ultimately replaced by other, more sophisticated theories. What is important here is that the M power theory illustrates how the concept of limited processing resources can be used to explain systematic, general cognitive changes that occur as children develop.

Processing Efficiency. An efficiently run company typically produces more goods from the same amount of resources than does an inefficient company. The same could well be true of thinking: An individual who uses resources efficiently may be able to solve more complex tasks than another person with the same resources who uses them less efficiently. This is the crux of another potential mechanism for intellectual development; as children become older, they acquire more efficient information processing skills. Each increment in efficiency means that fewer resources will be required to complete a particular task.

We know of several ways in which processing efficiency increases with age. First, as children grow, they select better algorithms for performing the same task. Young children, for example, are often taught to add $m + n$ by counting first m fingers, then n more; the sum is then obtained by counting the total number of fingers. But within a few months, without instruction, most children abandon this approach in favor of a simpler one in which they simply start with m fingers, then count out n more (Groen & Resnick, 1977).

A related case is that children repeatedly use the same strategy, so that the components of the strategy come to be executed fluidly, ultimately achieving automaticity. A study by Birch (1978) is illustrative. In her experiment, subjects performed two tasks separately as well as concurrently. A tracking task resembled a video game, in that children turned a knob to align a target with a dot that was moving horizontally. In the other task, pairs of words were presented aloud (e.g., *dog* and *cat*, *shirt* and *pants*, *horse* and *cap*), and children judged if the words belonged to the same conceptual category.

Some of the 8-year-olds in Birch's (1978) experiment were tested one time on each task separately, then performed the two tasks concurrently. As we would expect, their performance was much poorer when the tasks were performed concurrently than when they were performed separately. For example, when only judging categories, children erred on 32% of the pairs. When this task was performed in conjunction with the tracking task, the error rate was 49%.

Other 8-year-olds were given extensive practice on the two tasks *separately*, until they had reached the level of performance typical for adolescents. Then, for the first time, they performed the tasks concurrently. Their performance was much better overall than the first group's and, more importantly, was comparable when the tasks were performed alone or concurrently. Error rates on the category-matching task were 16% and 21% for separate and concurrent performance, respectively, a nonsignificant difference. In other words, after training, the task could be performed simultaneously with no loss in the quality of performance, suggesting that the requisite cognitive skills may have been operating automatically (but see Shiffrin & Dumais, 1981, for other criteria of automaticity).

More efficient use of strategies refers to a developmental change in procedural knowledge. A parallel change occurs with declarative knowledge: As individuals develop, their knowledge seems to consist of larger chunks. In other words, in terms of the semantic networks illustrated in Figure 3-3, older individuals typically have more connecting links between nodes and the links are stronger.

This phenomenon is illustrated in work on memory for organized versus disorganized arrays. For example, in a study by Mandler and Robinson (1978), children from grades 1, 3, and 5 were shown eight complex pictures. Half of the individuals in each grade saw the pictures arranged in a meaningful format: A window, chair, ladder, and trunk, for example, might be organized to depict a living room. The remaining individuals saw exactly the same objects but depicted in an unorganized fashion. At all ages, recognition of organized pictures exceeded recognition of unorganized pictures, but the advantage for organized pictures was greater for older children. One interpretation of this finding is that the objects in the organized picture constituted a single chunk for the older individuals but not the younger ones.

Notice that none of these means of achieving increased processing efficiency requires that processing resources remain constant throughout development. To the contrary, processing capacity and processing efficiency may *both* increase with age; the widespread cognitive edge of older children over younger children may be due to the combined effects of having more processing resources available and using those greater resources more efficiently (Kail & Bisanz, 1982).

These two sources of developmental change do differ in a subtle but important way. Increases in processing resources represent fundamental changes in the child's cognitive skill: Increases in resources, as in an increment in M power, should be apparent in performance on *any* resource-demanding task. Developmental increases in processing efficiency are not the same pervasive sort of change. Instead, they occur on a process-by-process basis and are likeliest to occur for those skills that individuals practice extensively. Hence, age differences are not expected on all resource-demanding tasks. In fact, if younger and older individuals use equally efficient strategies, then equal performance is expected.

Developmental Change and Individual Differences

We argued from the outset that a complete theory of intelligence would focus on the cognitive processes underlying individual differences and developmental change. In practice, the sort of research we have in mind would represent a merger of the process analysis of intelligence described in Chapter 3 with the information processing approaches to development described in the second half of this chapter. Only since the late 1970s has there been experimentation of this sort. Hence, we describe it here not so much to present substantive conclusions but to illustrate the nature of this complex merger of different approaches to intelligence.

Consider a study by Keating and Bobbitt (1978). At each of three age levels—9, 13, and 17 years—high- and low-ability individuals were identified based on performance on Raven's (1960, 1965) Standard Progressive Matrices and Advanced Progressive Matrices tests, nonverbal measures of general intelligence, g. The high-ability group consisted of individuals between the 90th and 95th percentiles; low-ability individuals were in the 40th to 45th percentiles. Subjects were shown pairs of letters (e.g., Aa, AA, Ab, and aB). On some trials they judged if the letters were *physically identical* (e.g., AA and bb). On other trials they judged if the letters had the same *name* (e.g., AA and aa as well as Aa and Bb).

The important developmental questions were these: First, will the difference in ability found among adults—where name codes are accessed more rapidly by skilled individuals—also hold for children and adolescents? Second, if a difference is found, will it be the same amount throughout development? One could hypothesize that as some individuals acquire greater verbal skill with age, ability differences will be larger for adolescents and adults than for children.

Keating and Bobbitt's (1978) results, shown in Figure 4-5, provide a clear-cut answer to both of these questions. Note first that individuals in all groups make physical matches more rapidly than name matches, by an amount that varies from 57 to 240 milliseconds. However, the advantage of high-ability individuals is quite constant across the age span studied by Keating and Bobbitt. Compared with physical matches, name matches took high-ability individuals an extra 136, 97, and 57 milliseconds for 9-, 13-, and 17-year-olds, respectively. Corresponding values for

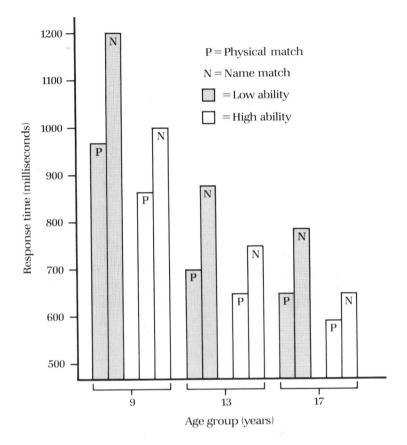

Figure 4-5 *Response time to judge if pairs of letters are identical physically or in name for high- and low-IQ 9-, 13-, and 17-year-olds. (Data from Keating and Bobbitt [1978].)*

low-ability individuals were 240, 180, and 144 milliseconds. At each age, then, the low-ability individuals were slower by approximately 90 milliseconds (e.g., for 9-year-olds, 240 milliseconds for low-ability individuals minus the 136 milliseconds for high-ability individuals yields a 104 millisecond difference). In short, from age 9 years through adulthood, high-ability individuals seem to be able to access a letter's name in approximately $\frac{1}{10}$ of a second less than low-ability individuals.

Such a difference may seem so small that readers may be tempted to conclude it to be trivial, utterly without practical consequences. Nothing could be further from the truth: Small differences in frequently occurring processes will accumulate, resulting in much larger differences in total processing time.

Such developmental consistency in the difference between high- and low-ability persons is not always the case. Keating and Bobbitt (1978), for example, reported an instance where differences between ability groups actually became *smaller* with increasing age. On the Sternberg (1966) task used to measure the speed with which individuals access the contents of activated memory, high- and low-ability groups differed considerably at age 9, moderately at age 13, and not at all at age 17. Put another way, the high-ability groups at all ages accessed activated memory at the same rate; low-ability individuals gradually approached this rate as they grew older.

Findings such as these provide a glimpse of one sort of future research on intelligence that is not provincial, but represents the integration of the psychometric, cognitive, and developmental traditions. For each ability derived from psychometric measures, we seek to specify (1) the age at which high- and low-ability individuals first differ in terms of the speed or accuracy with which they implement component processes, and (2) the extent to which these differences change with development. However, this represents a path towards a future, integrated theory rather than constituting a full-fledged theory of intelligence.

Summary

This chapter concerns the development of intellectual skills. We first considered Piaget's theory, in which intelligence is divided into contents, functions, and structures. Contents refers to behavioral acts, which are by-products of cognitive activities. The functions of intelligence are constant throughout development and include organization and adaptation, with the latter consisting of accommodation and assimilation. The structures of intelligence change developmentally. Piaget identified four: sensorimotor intelligence, preoperational thought, concrete operational thought, and formal operational thought. Each structure is characterized by distinct mental operations.

Piaget's theory has been criticized for its ambiguities in deriving specific predictions and its reliance upon cognitive conflict as a mechanism for growth. Information processing theorists address the first criticism by postulating sets of processes (derived from the general information processing model described in Chapter 3) that are responsible for performance on a particular task. Regarding the second criticism, information processing theorists have suggested that increases in processing resources as well as increased processing efficiency could be responsible for the steady march towards mature intelligence that occurs during childhood and adolescence.

Finally, we examined one instance of a merger between information processing approaches to aptitude like those described in Chapter 3 and an information processing approach to cognitive development. Such mergers are infrequent today, but represent one avenue towards future theories of intelligence.

5

Emerging Perspectives

Each perspective that we have overviewed helps in understanding the important aspects of intelligence and intellectual functioning. We begin this chapter by summarizing these contributions, noting some commonalities among the perspectives and then considering some of their shortcomings.

The psychometric perspective, as the name itself implies, emphasizes the measurement of individual differences. The performances of individuals on a variety of tests are the primary data of interest. Research done within the psychometric perspective typically involves testing large numbers of individuals on many different tasks, each individual obtaining a score on each task. Theories are based upon patterns of relationships among the test scores. These theories attempt to describe the structure of intellect by considering the ways in which individuals differ in intellectual performance. Most theories developed within the psychometric perspective do not focus on how one solves a particular problem or how different cognitive factors or skills interact and interrelate (cf. Guilford, 1982). Instead, the theories represent after-the-fact explanations of individual differences.

The information processing perspective emphasizes theoretical and empirical analyses of performance on simple and complex cognitive tasks. Typically, precise theories of the knowledge and cognitive processes necessary for performing a task are emphasized rather than broad principles and theories of cognitive change, as are emphasized in the cognitive-developmental tradition (cf. Anderson, 1983). No attempt is made to test all the different structures and processes that have been hypothesized from analyses of many different tasks. Instead, research involves a sampling of the knowledge and processes as reflected by a specific task often created to meet the needs of testing a particular theory or model. Finally, there is a strong tendency to ignore differences among individuals and focus instead on data from groups of individuals.

The cognitive-developmental perspective emphasizes general theoretical principles that govern intellectual growth and change. Within this tradition, theory and data focus on characteristics of intellectual development that are common to all individuals rather than emphasizing individual differences as in the psychometric tradition. In the Piagetian tradition, intellectual growth is described as a set of stages that are qualitatively different, reflecting major changes in cognitive structure. The Piagetian tradition also focuses on tasks that can be related to the emergence of reasoning skill. By analyzing the components of different reasoning tasks, hypotheses are derived about the probable success of individuals at different levels or stages of cognitive development. The predictions are based on theoretical assumptions about the cognitive skills and logical abilities available to children at a given stage.

One commonality among the three perspectives, which we mentioned briefly in Chapter 1, is at the general level and concerns the range of knowledge, skills, and activities associated with being or becoming intelligent. This is best illustrated by the shared emphasis on verbal and nonverbal reasoning and on problem-solving skills. Virtually all psychometric theories and tests of intelligence are based upon performance on reasoning and problem-solving tasks, recent work within the information processing perspective has also emphasized problem-solving and reasoning at both a general level and within specific content domains such as mathematics, and Piagetian theory focuses on the development of the cognitive structures necessary for logical reasoning with concrete and abstract concepts.

A second area of overlap among perspectives, also noted in Chapter 1, involves adaptability as an aspect of intelligence. In the psychometric and information processing traditions, this is often implicit, since individuals deal with a succession of novel stimuli and tasks. Measured intellectual skill usually demands the ability to adapt rapidly to a series of new situations. Such adaptation to changing environmental demands is also an explicit component of Piaget's theory, although the period of adaptation and change is of more extended duration.

How has each of these three perspectives helped us to understand human intelligence? That is, to what extent does each perspective lead to theory and research that contribute to a critical understanding of intelligence? Here the clear answer is that each perspective provides a unique but incomplete view of intelligence.

The emphasis on individual differences within the psychometric tradition is certainly relevant to any complete theory of intelligence. A theory of intelligence should take into account similarities and differences among individuals in their cognitive skills and performance capabilities. However, a theory of cognition based solely on patterns of differences among individuals cannot capture all of intellectual functioning unless there is little that is general and similar in intellectual performance.

In contrast, the developmental tradition emphasizes similarities in intellectual growth and the importance of organism–environment interaction. By considering the changes that occur in cognition and the mechanisms and conditions responsible, we can better understand human intellect and its relationship to people's environments. However, this requires that we not only focus on commonalities in a general course of cognitive growth but also consider how individuals differ in their intellectual growth. Such a developmental-differential emphasis seems necessary for a theory of intelligence to have adequate breadth and to move the study of intelligence away from a static, normative view where intelligence changes little over development. That is, a theory of intelligence should capture the dynamic changes in the absolute level of intellectual power that occur with development.

Finally, the information processing perspective contributes to defining the scope of a theory of intelligence by further emphasizing the dynamics of cognition. This stress takes place through the perspective's concentration on precise theories of the knowledge and processes that allow individuals to perform intellectual tasks. Psychometric and developmental theories often lack the focus on specific processes that is necessary for a theory of intelligence to make precise, testable predictions about intellectual performance.

In response to these shortcomings, several psychologists have recently formulated eclectic theories of intelligence, theories that cut across the traditional boundaries of the psychometric, cognitive, and developmental approaches. These new theories draw upon the assets of the distinct approaches to create much broader perspectives on intelligence. Two such efforts that are especially ambitious are the triarchic theory of intelligence, formulated by Robert Sternberg (1984), and the theory of multiple intelligences, proposed by Howard Gardner (1983). We describe each of these theories in detail.

A Triarchic Theory of Human Intelligence

Robert Sternberg was one of the first advocates of the process approach to intelligence, which we described in Chapter 3. In his book *Intelligence, Information Processing and Analogical Reasoning* (1977), Sternberg proposed an information processing theory of individual differences in analogical reasoning. Recently, Sternberg (1984) has proposed a broader theory of intelligence that elaborates the earlier work a great deal. Specifically, his *triarchic theory* includes three subtheories, each addressing issues in defining and measuring human intelligence. The three subtheories also differentiate between aspects of intelligence that are universal and those that are cultural. The three subtheories are termed the *contextual, two-facet, and componential.*

Contextual Subtheory

The main feature of this subtheory is the assumption that the intelligence of an individual's acts must be considered in a cultural context. In its broadest sense, intelligence involves *"purposive adaptation to, shaping of, and selection of real-world environments relevant to one's life"* (Sternberg, 1984, p. 271, emphasis in the original). By *purposive* Sternberg means that intelligence "is directed toward goals, however, vague or subconscious those goals may be" (p. 272). Achieving these goals will typically involve an attempt to *adapt* to one's environment. If that environment stresses intellectual attainment for employment opportunity and personal and financial security, then actions taken to meet those criteria would be considered intelligent.

Given this view, comparisons between different cultural or sociocultural groups cannot be based on a single frame of reference such as traditional test scores or achievement measures; instead, one compares cultures in terms of those behaviors that the cultures deem intelligent (but see Berry, 1974). Furthermore, individuals considered intelligent in one culture may be looked on as unintelligent in another. For example, intelligent individuals living in a North American society might seem quite inept according to the standards of intelligence in African tribal societies or South American Indian societies.

In some cases, there will be a poor fit between an individual's personal goals and the values or societal goals established by the majority in the individual's situation or culture. Examples of this mismatch would include an employee whose goals and interests seem totally at odds with those of an employer or, on a larger scale, minority groups that are systematically persecuted by the majority in a society (e.g., Stohl & Lopez, 1984). In these cases, intelligent behavior can include attempting to change or *shape* that environment. Examples of such behaviors would include urging an employer to do business differently or pressuring governments to insure civil rights and equality of opportunity for all individuals.

Sternberg (1984) claims that many people in diverse occupations are considered intelligent because they both adapt to their environment and modify their environment to capitalize on their particular talents or skills. He writes:

> Consider, for example, the "stars" in any given field of endeavor. What is it that distinguishes such persons from all the rest?. . . Chances are that the stars do not seem to share any one ability, as traditionally defined, but rather share a tendency toward having some set of extraordinary talents that they make the most of in their work. My own list would include a person with extraordinary spatial visualization skills (if anyone can visualize in four dimensions, he can!), a person with a talent for coming up with highly counter-intuitive findings that are of great theoretical importance, and a person who has a remarkable sense of where the field

is going. . . . These three particular persons (and others on my list) share little in terms of what sets them apart, aside from at least one extraordinary talent upon which they capitalize fully in their work [Sternberg, 1984, pp. 272–273].

In some cases, modifying or shaping one's environment is not possible; intelligent action might then consist of selecting another environment that is more suited to one's talents. This alternative environment could be a different job or a different country where one would avoid persecution. The point, however, is that an assessment is made of the options available and then actions are taken to effect a change in one's environment. (Sternberg points out that changing environments is not always an option, as when no jobs are available or when one is prohibited from emigrating.)

The contextual subtheory attempts to broaden the scope of a theory of intelligence by noting the relevance of environment and culture in determining what is and is not intelligent behavior. Assessment of intelligence should not be just a function of test scores or what Neisser (1976) has referred to as "academic intelligence." It needs to be broadened to include everyday intelligence, representing behaviors related to one's environment. Within their environments, individuals develop and refine skills necessary for survival and personal satisfaction.

Two other unique assets of a contextual approach are also noteworthy. First, intelligence has too often been defined—either implicitly or explicitly—in terms of performance on intelligence tests. This view has sometimes led to the absurd situation in which mental tests "come to be viewed as better indicators of intelligence than the criterial, real-world intelligent behaviors they are supposed to predict" (Sternberg, 1984, p. 270). That is, when an individual has exceptional talents yet achieves only modest scores on intelligence tests, we are tempted to believe that the test score is accurate and that the talented behavior is somehow misleading! A contextual view, in contrast, emphasizes that intelligence always refers to real-world behaviors that are valued by individuals in a particular culture.

Second, research on intelligence—especially that by developmental psychologists and cognitive psychologists—typically has concerned the internal, mental processes that comprise intelligence. Neglected here is the fact that these internal processes do not operate in a vacuum but in an environment where certain outcomes are valued but others are not. These cultural values no doubt shape internal processes to some degree, a point that is highlighted in a contextual approach to intelligence.

We should point out (as does Sternberg) that contextual theories are sometimes criticized on the ground that they make all things relative and seem to rule out any components of intelligence that transcend cultures. That is, if intelligence must be considered in its cultural context, then there must be as many theories of human intelligence as there are distinct human cultures. Sterberg's theory avoids this criticism, however, because the other two subtheories that are part of the triarchic theory are not context specific; instead, they are presumed to be universal components of human intelligence.

Two-Facet Subtheory

The basic assumption of the two-facet subtheory is that a task measures intelligence if it requires the ability to deal with novel demands or the ability to automatize information processing. Novelty and automatic processing are two points on a continuum of task or situational experience that can vary over both tasks and individuals.

Let us first consider the novelty end of this dimension. A task or situation can be novel because it requires considerable effort to be understood rather than because the actions required are novel. Many problem-solving tasks and puzzles have this quality, as do many real-world problems. Suppose, for example, that you turn on a television but no picture appears. Often the actual repair is simple—replacing a part. The novelty in such problems for most individuals is in understanding the relationship between the various components of the television and the malfunction.

Conversely, a task or situation can be novel not because of comprehension—in fact, the description may be simple—but because of the actions required for solution. *Insight problems* constitute examples of this type of novelty. Consider the following two problems (Sterberg, 1984, p. 277):

1. If you have black socks and brown socks in your drawer, mixed in the ratio of 4 to 5, how many socks would you have to take out to make sure of having a pair of the same color?

2. Water lilies double in area every 24 hours. At the beginning of the summer there is one water lily on a lake. It takes 60 days for the lake to become covered with water lilies. On what day is the lake half-covered?

Neither of these problems is novel with respect to comprehension. However, they are novel in terms of selecting a solution. Rather than a typical solution involving proportions or progressions, they both have very simple solutions. The trick to solving them is to be selective in encoding, combining, and comparing information.

Sternberg (1984) believes that novel tasks or novel situations are good measures of intellectual ability because they assess an individual's ability to apply existing knowledge to new problems. This ability to adapt to novel tasks or situations is also consistent with people's conceptions of intelligence (Sternberg, Conway, Ketron, and Bernstein, 1981). However, Sternberg points out that a problem should not be so novel that an individual has no relevant knowledge to apply in solving it. Asking children to comprehend and solve a novel problem in thermodynamics, for example, is unreasonable unless they have the prerequisite knowledge.

At the other extreme of the continuum are tasks or situations that are highly automated. For most adults, reading and comprehending the print on this page is a highly automated process; it occurs quickly and with little direct effort. However, reading was not always so easy or automated. Consider the child just learning to read. To such a child, decoding and comprehending print is a novel situation requiring much effort and attention. Ultimately, after much practice, decoding print is such an automatic activity that it can actually serve to interfere with other tasks.

Before going further, it is important to elaborate what is meant by automaticity in information processing, a concept we introduced in Chapter 3. We can distinguish two modes of processing known as *controlled* and *automated*. In controlled processing, effort and attention must be given to selecting the cognitive operations to be performed, their sequence, and monitoring the results of the ongoing process and making adjustments. Each element of the total performance behaves as a single entity, and the transitions between actions are slow and deliberate. Early reading that focuses on letter decoding is a good example. Beginning readers expend so much effort controlling the decoding process—identifying letters or groups of letters—that they are often unable to comprehend what is being read.

Another good example of controlled processing is learning to drive a car with a manual transmission. Someone learning to drive such a car is often so overwhelmed with executing each action and coordinating these actions that it is often difficult to monitor traffic, much less converse with a passenger. The coordination of actions is attention demanding, leaving few resources for doing anything else.

With much practice, however, one moves away from controlled processing to systems that are capable of functioning autonomously without each component being consciously monitored and selected. Transitions between components are now rapid and do not require attention. Recall from Chapter 3, for example, the people in Spelke, Hirst, and Neisser's (1976) experiment who learned to take dictation and read simultaneously. As individuals develop expertise in many different situations, this expertise can be immediately called upon to perform a task automatically, so that a person may perform several tasks simultaneously.

The ability to deal with novelty and the ability to automatize performance bear an interesting relationship to each other. Given two individuals with equivalent experience in a novel situation, the more intelligent individual will be the one who more rapidly copes with the demands of the situation. The faster the adjustment to novelty, the more resources there are that are available for automatized performance. Conversely, the individual who can more rapidly automate performance will also have more resources available to deal with novelty:

> As a result, novelty and automatization trade off, and the more efficient the individual is at one, the more resources are left over for the other. As experience with the kind of task or situation increases, novelty decreases, and the task or situation will become less apt in its measurement of intelligence from the standpoint of processing of novelty. However, after some amount of practice with the task or in the situation, automatization skills may come into play, in which case the task will become a better measure of automatization skills [Sternberg, 1984, p. 279].

Sternberg (1984) suggests that the two-facet subtheory provides a framework for considering what properties make tasks useful measures of intelligence. For example, laboratory tasks have some validity as measures of intelligence because they primarily measure automatization or the ability to automatize. This is partially due to the elementary information processes that are frequently assessed, such as the retrieval of information from semantic memory, and partially due to the repetitive and structured format of the task, which provides the opportunity to automatize processing even if the task format or content was initially novel.

Psychometric tasks, in contrast, are likelier to measure the ability to deal with novelty. This is partially due to the presentation of more difficult items than is customary in the laboratory analogs of paper-and-pencil measures. In addition, the fact that the entire set of items is presented simultaneously (instead of individual items being presented repeatedly, as in laboratory tasks) means that it is less likely that automaticity develops over the course of the testing session.

The two-facet subtheory thus has implications for the selection of tasks to measure intelligence:

> One wishes to select tasks that involve some blend of automatized behaviors and behaviors in response to novelty. . . . The blending may be achieved by presenting subjects with a novel task, and then giving them enough practice so that performance becomes differentially automatized (across subjects) over the length of the practice period. Such a task will thereby measure both response to novelty and degree of automatization, although at different times during the course of testing [Sternberg, 1984, p. 280].

These criteria for task selection also illustrate the difficulty in comparing the task performance of different groups of individuals. The same task may be differentially novel or differentially automated for different individuals. A simple example is presenting the same task to young children and to adolescents or adults. In one case we may be measuring individual differences in the ability to deal with novelty, but in the other we may be measuring individual differences in the level of automatization.

Fortunately, children and adults are not often asked to solve the same problems on intelligence tests, although they may be asked to solve similar types of problems, such as vocabulary items or analogies. The problem *is* likely to arise in comparing individuals with different sociocultural backgrounds, because they lack comparable experiences with the task or situation. Within our own society, individuals of the same age differ substantially in their experience with test-taking situations and the types of problems found on standardized tests, even those tests labeled as "culture fair." These problems in comparing scores on standardized tests for different sociocultural groups within a population have been recognized for some time (e.g., Loehlin, Lindzey, & Spuhler, 1975, chap. 3); the unique contribution of the two-facet subtheory in this regard is that it provides a general theoretical account of the phenomenon.

Summary. The two-facet subtheory goes beyond the contextual subtheory by specifying two broad classes of abilities associated with intelligence and the implications of these abilities for task selection and interpretation. Novelty and automaticity are two sets of skills that must be involved for a behavior to be considered intelligent. An important implication of the subtheory is that these two skills must guide the selection of tasks that measure intelligence: "The subtheory provides an a priori specification of what a task or situation must measure in order to assess intelligence. It [the subtheory] is distinctive in that it is not linked to any arbitrary choice of tasks or situations. These follow from the subtheory, rather than the other way around" (Sternberg, 1984, p. 280).

Componential Subtheory

This subtheory is closely related to the information processing perspective discussed earlier in Chapter 3. A component is a basic or elementary information process that operates on internal representations of objects or symbols. All thought is composed of such units acting in concert to produce a given result— be it comprehending text, answering a question, or solving a problem. Sternberg (1984) distinguishes three broad classes of components. One class of components, referred to as *performance components*, represents the basic operations involved in any cognitive act. In the case of the analogy problems discussed earlier, performance components include encoding and response processes, as well as comparison processes that determine relationships between and among stimuli. These component processes—when organized in a proper sequence— allow an individual to solve analogies correctly.

Tasks vary in the extent to which they share common components. Consider, for example, the difference between inductive reasoning tasks and spatial-relations tasks. Inductive reasoning tasks—be they analogy, classification, or series completion—tend to include the same basic performance components, the most important of these being the encoding and comparison processes. Spatial-relations tasks also involve encoding, comparison, and response processes, but they differ from induction tasks by including a transformation or mental rotation process that is critical for task solution.

Sternberg (1984) believes that such a breakdown of tasks is important for several reasons. First, it provides a way of isolating and organizing the components that are both necessary and sufficient to solve the task. Second, componential analysis can reveal the similarities and differences between various types of tasks. That is, tasks are similar to the extent that they depend upon the same components organized in the same fashion. Third, componential analysis can be used to assess how well—in terms of speed or accuracy—individuals execute different types of mental operations as well as their organization of those operations.

Performance components are only one part of the story, however, in explaining performance in any cognitive task. Components must be selected and organized into a routine to execute a task. In our discussion of information processing in Chapter 3, we made note of the fact that basic operations must be appropriately sequenced into a program or routine analogous to a computer program. Sternberg (1984) refers to these control processes or executive functions as *metacomponents*. They are used in the planning, monitoring, and decision making that frequently occur during task execution. Metacomponents include the following operations: (1) deciding what the problem is that needs to be solved; (2) selecting the appropriate performance components; (3) selecting the type of information representation for a given performance component; (4) selecting a strategy for combining and sequencing performance components; (5) allocating resources for executing the process; (6) monitoring the solution of a problem; and (7) responding to external feedback.

A good example of the need to consider metacomponents in the analysis of cognitive performance can be found in the study by MacLeod, Hunt, and Mathews (1978) described in Chapter 3. Recall that they examined performance on a task in which sentences were matched with simple pictorial representations. Individuals differed in the strategy they used to perform the task. Individuals of high spatial ability tended to select a visualization approach, in which the sentence was transformed into a pictorial representation that could be directly compared with the presented picture. Individuals of high verbal ability tended to adopt the converse strategy: They described the picture in terms of a simple sentence. Thus, the two groups of people produced different patterns of performance. Each group was apparently choosing the set of components and representations that it most preferred.

The MacLeod, Hunt, and Mathews (1978) results emphasize that individuals differ not only in how quickly or accurately they execute specific performance components but also in how they choose to perform a task. Individuals can and do vary in how they approach tasks, how they allocate time and resources, and how well they can monitor their own progress in solving a problem. This is often apparent when one contrasts the performance of young children to older children or of experts to novices (e.g., Chi, Glaser, & Rees, 1982). Thus, in analyzing performance on any cognitive task, one needs to consider both the performance components actually used and the metacomponents or executive operations involved in selecting, organizing, and monitoring the execution of the basic processes.

The last major category of components discussed by Sternberg (1984) are referred to as *knowledge acquisition* components, which are processes used in gaining new declarative or procedural knowledge. These components include *selective encoding, selective combination,* and *selective comparison* of information. Learning often takes place in contexts where much information is presented but only some is new or relevant. For learning to occur, one must be able to sift the relevant from the irrelevant information and combine it into an integrated whole. However, this is often not enough for learning to be effective. One must also be able to compare selectively new information to information already existing in the knowledge base. Doing so provides a basis for integrating new information, thereby assuring that it can be accessed in the future.

Knowledge acquisition components are an essential part of a theory of intelligence because one of the major characteristics of human beings is their capacity to learn and adapt to their environment. Knowledge acquisition is also critical in understanding current measures of intelligence. In Chapter 3, we noted that current intelligence tests assess not only how well individuals can solve reasoning problems but also certain types of declarative and procedural knowledge (e.g., in vocabulary and arithmetic problems). Sternberg (1984) argues that individual differences in knowledge acquisition are more important than individual differences in knowledge per se. What is critical is how individuals differ in their capacity to acquire new information in formal and especially informal contexts.

Summary. The componential subtheory represents an information processing approach to human intelligence and individual differences. In understanding, analyzing, and measuring intellectual ability, we need to consider the basic cognitive operations that individuals perform, how they are selected, organized, and monitored, and how new knowledge is acquired, be it declarative or procedural. The components outlined in this subtheory are considered to be universals applying across all individuals and cultures; that is, they are elements of a general theory of cognition. All individuals are presumed to possess these components to greater or lesser degrees. Intelligence tests are comprised of tasks that are sensitive to these differences. If we want to analyze the nature of the differences exhibited on intelligence tests, then we can use a componential framework to conduct such an analysis. In fact, in Chapter 3 we illustrated how such a framework has been used to analyze verbal ability, reasoning ability, and spatial ability.

Theory of Multiple Intelligences

Sternberg's (1984) triarchic theory, with its contextual, two-facet, and componential subtheories, represents an important effort to merge the distinct perspectives on intelligence that we considered earlier in this book. Another, similarly ambitious theory is described by Howard Gardner in his book, *Frames of Mind* (1983). As implied in the names of both the theory and the book, Gardner's theory is in the tradition of multifactor theories like those of Thurstone (1938) and Cattell (1971), described in Chapter 2. Furthermore, Gardner is not far from the traditional view in arguing that a human intellectual competence must entail a set of skills of problem solving—enabling the individual *to resolve genuine problems or difficulties* that he or she encounters and, when appropriate, to create an effective product—and must also entail the potential for *finding or creating problems*—thereby laying the groundwork for the acquisition of new knowledge [p. 62, emphasis in the original].

These skills or competencies should collectively cover "a reasonably complete gamut of the kinds of abilities valued by human cultures" (p. 62). The emphasis here on finding problems is uncommon (cf. Getzels & Jackson, 1962), but Gardner's general orientation to intelligence does not represent a radical departure from traditional views.

The scope of Gardner's work emerges in the way he establishes distinct intelligences, for here he goes far beyond the garden-variety psychometric evidence to develop his theory. Gardner proposes several "signs" that can be used to identify distinct intelligences. They are signs rather than exact criteria because "this undertaking must be provisional: I do not include something merely because it exhibits one or two of the signs, nor do I exclude a candidate [i.e., possible] intelligence just because it fails to qualify on each and every account" (Gardner, 1983, p. 62). The signs are these:

1. *Isolation by brain damage.* Often injury to the brain results in the loss of a specific intellectual skill. Such *selective impairment* indicates that the affected intellectual skill is at least partially independent of other skills that remain intact following brain damage.

2. *The existence of individuals with exceptional talent.* Some individuals are truly extraordinarily skilled in one intellectual domain but ordinarily skilled—or even retarded—in most other domains. Idiot savants, for example, are retarded persons who have one extraordinarily well developed talent, often in the areas of musical or numeric ability (Hill, 1978). Such selective competence, like selective impairment following brain injury, suggests autonomy of that particular competence.

3. *A distinct developmental history.* If an intelligence is autonomous, it should develop in a distinct manner and in much the same way in all people. That is, we should see a reliable sequence of development in which skills progress through a standard set of initial, intermediate, and advanced stages of development.

4. *An evolutionary history.* Intellectual skills emerge as individuals age; they also have emerged as the human species has evolved. Thus, just as a distinct ontogenic profile suggests the autonomy of an intel-

lectual competence, so too does a well-defined phylogenic sequence help to identify autonomous intelligences.

5. *A set of core operations.* If an intelligence is independent, there should be a distinct mental operation (or set of operations) that is the core of that intelligence. The intelligence may involve other mental operations, but they are secondary to the core processes. For example, many composers are pianists and use the piano as they compose, but skill at the piano is only an adjunct skill for composers; it is not at the core of musical composition.

6. *Experimental evidence.* Independence of intelligence can be demonstrated empirically. In one approach used in laboratory research, individuals perform two tasks simultaneously. In cases where the two tasks are difficult to perform concurrently—such as trying to write and listen to speech—the conclusion is that the two tasks require common skills. Independence of intelligences is implicated when such interference between tasks is minimal. Another tack is based upon the factor analytic approach of examining correlations between performances on different tasks. As we discussed at length in Chapter 2, the abilities tapped by two tasks are presumed to be independent if scores on the first task are uncorrelated with scores on the second task.

7. *Encoding in a symbol system.* Symbols such as words and pictures are fundamental to communication and thought in all human cultures. This universal human proclivity to use symbols leads to Gardner's (1983) final sign of an intelligence. Specifically, he suggests that "while it may be possible for an intelligence to proceed without its own special symbol system . . . a primary characteristic of human intelligence may well be its 'natural' gravitation toward embodiment in a symbolic system" (p. 66).

These signs function collectively as a screening device: Any given intelligence will show many but probably not all of the signs. By the same token, some phenomena may show a few signs, but not enough to qualify as a distinct intelligence. Suppose, for example, that we proposed solving crossword puzzles as a distinct intelligence. We would probably be able to provide some empirical support for its independence, using the interference paradigm described earlier, and one could well imagine a set of distinctive hurdles that a budding crossword puzzle solver would pass en route to completing her first puzzle in the *New York Times.*

Yet on the other signs, solving crossword puzzles fails as an intelligence, and fails miserably. Brain damage does not impair only crossword ability; instead, other language skills are usually lost as well. Crossword puzzle aficionados are usually not completely ordinary in other skills; most often they are articulate persons who have also acquired the odd argot of the crossword puzzle. Finally, there is no reason to believe that a unique set of cognitive processes is in operation when individuals solve these puzzles; to the contrary, the retrieval of words that is the essence of solving a crossword puzzle is not unlike the retrieval of words that occurs in conversation or thought. The retrieval in solving crossword puzzles is simply slowed considerably because the cues in the puzzles that aid retrieval are often unorthodox.

Solving crossword puzzles may seem like a contrived example, because no one would seriously propose such a specific form of intelligence. Hence, consider another example, which illustrates the utility of Gardner's (1983) signs in casting aside some very general conceptions of intelligence. Consider *synthetic ability*, defined as the ability to integrate disparate information to form some new whole. This is surely a more general skill than solving crossword puzzles, as well as being a more plausible intelligence, yet it fares little better against the signs. On the one hand, patients with damage to the left hemisphere of the brain (specifically, in the parietal region of the cortex) sometimes can understand individual words but cannot synthesize those meanings to understand entire sentences. On the other hand, there is no evidence of ordinary people with extraordinary synthetic skills, nor is there a well-defined core of mental operations that defines synthetic intelligence. The ability to synthesize information, then, is not a distinct intelligence but is instead the product of other intelligences.

Using the signs in a manner not unlike our use in these two examples, Gardner (1983) concludes that the cumulative evidence points to six distinct intelligences. Some of these intelligences are not new, including linguistic intelligence, a logical–mathematical intelligence, and a spatial intelligence. (But Gardner does harness some unfamiliar evidence in discussing these familiar intelligences, such as his exploration of the poet's expertise to illustrate components of linguistic intelligence.) Yet his discussions of these intelligences do not greatly differ from accounts of them in previous chapters here, so we shall not discuss them further. Instead, we focus on the three intelligences that are unlike anything we have encountered in previous chapters, namely, Gardner's proposals for musical intelligence, bodily–kinesthetic intelligence, and personal intelligences.

Musical Intelligence

To some readers, a musical intelligence may seem frivolous, at best a secondary or adjunct intelligence in comparison to verbal, logical, and mathematical skills. Gardner (1982) is adamantly opposed to this view; to the contrary, he believes that the appropriate relationship would be for musical intelligence to be central and logical–mathematical skills peripheral:

> For most of humanity, and throughout most of human history, the processes and products involved in artistic creation and perception have been far more pervasive than those enshrined in the sciences. In fact, logical scientific thought can be considered an invention of the West in the wake of the Renaissance—an invention which is still restricted to a small enclave of thinkers; participation in the literary, musical, or graphic arts, on the other hand, has been widespread for thousands of years [p. 299].

Gardner has marshaled an impressive array of evidence to buttress this claim for a musical intelligence.

Core Elements.   The key components of music are *pitch*, the highness or lowness of a sound, *rhythm*, the grouping of successive pitches, and *timbre*, the quality of a tone (i.e., the same notes played on a saxophone and violin produce quite different experiences for a listener, reflecting differences in timbre). Comprehending music, then, involves making sense of pitch, rhythm, and timbre. In fact, the situation is not unlike the processes of pattern recognition discussed in Chapter 3. Recall that pattern recognition occurs in both a bottom–up and a top–down manner. The former refers to the fact that recognition involves the detection of configurations of simple features (e.g., in the case of letters, straight lines and certain types of angles); the latter refers to the fact that recognition is also determined by an individual's hypotheses about what pattern to expect in a particular situation.

Much the same sort of processing occurs in comprehending music in general. For example, in the bottom–up approach to pitch recognition, one emphasizes the fact that nerve cells in the inner ear are triggered by sounds of a particular frequency. Perception of middle C begins when a sound wave with a frequency of 261.63 cycles per second triggers those nerve cells in the cochlea of the ear that are tuned to this particular frequency. The top–down approach emphasizes that a listener's music-relevant knowledge often guides the ability to comprehend pitch. For example, *contour*—the pattern of changes in pitch (i.e., ascending and descending sequences of pitch)—is an important factor in the ability to recognize a piece of music. So important is contour in recognizing musical patterns that if we change the specific pitches in a piece of music but preserve its contour, listeners can often recognize the piece (Deutsch, 1982).

Selective Impairment. Several fascinating case studies of the sequelae to brain damage attest to the independence of musical intelligence. One such case was the Russian composer Shebalin. He was afflicted with Wernicke's aphasia, in which speech remains fluent but comprehension is impaired. Nevertheless, his ability to understand and compose music remained entirely intact. A second case involved a pianist who, like Shebalin, suffered from Wernicke's aphasia. His performance—of both old and new pieces—was unimpaired, as was his ability to recognize pieces and hear errors in a performance. Only when verbal skills were called for—as in identifying a note by name—did his musical skills seem marred by his aphasia (Gardner, 1982).

Exceptional Individuals. Probably no area of accomplishment is so rich with legends of prodigies as musical talent. Undoubtedly the best-known is Mozart, whose talent as both a musical performer and composer was evident early in childhood. Less widely known are *idiot savants*, whose mental retardation is accompanied, inexplicably, by musical talent. Gardner (1983) describes "Harriet [who] was able to play 'Happy Birthday' in the style of various composers, including Mozart, Beethoven, Verdi, and Schubert. . . . At the age of three, her mother called her [i.e., got her attention] by playing incomplete melodies, which the child would then complete with the appropriate tone in the proper octave" (p. 121). Many idiot savants have had the ability to play a tune correctly after hearing it only once or twice, and do so without any formal musical training (Shuter-Dyson, 1982).

Empirical Evidence. Recall the logic of the interference paradigm: Independent intelligences should produce little interference when tasks are performed simultaneously. Deutsch (1975) used this approach to show the independence of musical skill (or, more specifically, that musical intelligence is independent of linguistic intelligence). Individuals in her experiment heard one tone followed 6 seconds later by another. Subjects simply judged if the two tones were the same or different. During the interval between the tones, subjects heard either eight tones or eight digits, which they were told to ignore. This task was easily accomplished when digits intervened, for subjects judged the similarity of the tones with 98% accuracy compared with 60% accuracy when tones intervened. Thus, verbal material produced essentially no interference whatsoever with memory for tones, an outcome consistent with the hypothesis that verbal and musical intelligences are autonomous.

Though not mentioned by Gardner, there is evidence from psychometric studies that supports his view of a musical intelligence. A number of tests of musical aptitude are available that typically assess such skills as the perception of and memory for pitch, sensitivity to rhythm, and "music appreciation" (Shuter-Dyson, 1982). Performance on such measures is only modestly correlated with general measures of intelligence like those discussed in Chapter 2. A correlation of approximately .3 is typical. Most of this relationship is explained by the fact that individuals with low intelligence-test scores typically achieve low scores on measures of musical aptitude. However, musical aptitude is essentially uncorrelated with general intelligence in individuals with IQ scores of roughly 90 or greater.

Development of Musical Competence. One could claim that children learn to sing before they learn to talk: By 2 or 3 months of age, infants coo—that is, they make vowellike sounds (e.g., "oo," "ah," "oh"). In so doing, babies often alternate between high- and low-pitched cooing. In addition, when infant and mother coo together, infants often imitate the pitch and volume of the mother's "song."

The preschool years that follow represent a period of conflict in musical development. On the one hand, the spontaneous musical exploration of the first year of life continues. Children invent their own songs; they also experiment with different intervals between pitches. On the other hand, a certain amount of musical socialization becomes evident, as children learn phrases of familiar songs. Gardner (1983) claims that the conflict is resolved by the end of the preschool years: "The melodies of the dominant culture have won out, and the production of spontaneous songs and exploratory sound play generally wanes" (p. 109).

For most children living in Western cultures, musical ability develops little after the preschool years. Individuals learn more songs and sing them with greater precision and feeling, but we see no further qualitative changes of the Piagetian variety (see also Dowling, 1982). For musically talented youngsters, however, there is a clear progression during childhood and adolescence. In the early elementary-school years,

> the child proceeds on the basis of sheer talent and energy: he learns pieces readily because of his sensitive musical ear and memory, gains applause for his technical skill, but essentially does not expend undue effort. A period of more sustained skill building commences around the age of nine or so, when the child must begin to practice seriously even to the extent that it may interfere with his school and his friendships (Gardner, 1983, pp. 111–112).

A second change occurs in adolescence, when blossoming musicians must "supplement their intuitive understanding with a more systematic knowledge of music lore and law" (Gardner, 1983, p. 111).

The developmental pattern, then, has two tiers. One tier is for all individuals; the second, for the musically talented. Nevertheless, Gardner (1983) speculates that these tiers exist only because most Western cultures tolerate "musical illiteracy." Unlike instruction in reading, science, or math, instruction in music is not emphasized in schools. Perhaps more individuals would progress to the second tier of development if systematic musical instruction were the rule instead of the exception.

Bodily–Kinesthetic Intelligence

A bodily–kinesthetic intelligence—hereafter, simply bodily intelligence—grates on traditional conceptions of intelligence. The notion that the accomplishments of an athlete, dancer, or craftsman are on a par with those of the thinker has never been a popular one in psychology. As Gardner describes it:

> There has been a radical disjunction in our recent cultural tradition between the activities of reasoning, on the one hand, and the activities of . . . our bodies, on the other. This divorce between the "mental" and the "physical" has not infrequently been coupled with a notion that what we do with our bodies is somehow less privileged, less special, than those problem-solving routines carried out chiefly through

the use of language, logic, or some other relatively abstract symbolic system [1983, pp. 207–208].

Gardner argues that this secondary status of bodily intelligence is, like the similar treatment of musical intelligence, a product of the Renaissance invention of rational man. In contrast, the Greeks "sought a harmony between mind and body, with the mind trained to use the body properly, and the body trained to respond to the expressive powers of the mind" (Gardner, 1983, p. 207). Furthermore, among many contemporary non-Western cultures, the mental and the physical are distinguished little, if at all. Hence, Gardner proposes a bodily intelligence that has as its core "control of one's bodily motions and capacity to handle objects skillfully" (p. 206).

The evidence for a bodily intelligence is, in our opinion, somewhat scarce, particularly when compared with some of the other intelligences described by Gardner. This is due, at least in part, to the secondary status of bodily intelligence in Western culture as compared with logical reasoning. The available facts, however, square with Gardner's (1983) claim for a separate bodily intelligence.

Selective Impairment. *Apraxias* are disorders in which, following damage to the brain, movement is limited, even though the necessary muscles are unimpaired (see Roy, 1982). Sometimes apraxias merely take on the appearance of clumsiness: Movements are no longer as fluid as they once were. More stunning are the *ideomotor apraxias,* in which objects are used incorrectly, as in flipping a coin without the coin or using a pencil as a comb (Roy, 1982). Gardner (1983) describes one particularly fascinating case of ideomotor apraxia from the work of Edith Kaplan:

> As part of a test of apraxia, Kaplan asked an apraxic patient to pretend "to saw." . . . This individual proved unable to enact the sawing motion through the representation of the absent implement (holding his clenched hand as if there were a saw in it): instead, in classic apraxic fashion, he treated the hand itself like a saw (moving the edge of the open hand back and forth as if it were itself a saw blade). As Kaplan wanted to ascertain whether the patient could, in fact, carry out the desired motion, she simply asked him to imitate a nonrepresentative act—in this case, that is, to oscillate his hand back and forth as though he were holding an implement, but she did not specify what the implement might be.

The patient performed the apparently arbitrary action in an adequate manner. Pleased with this demonstration, Kaplan declared, "See, you're sawing"—only to find that the instant . . . "saw" left her lips, the patient's fist opened and reverted to the edge-as-a-blade position [p. 222].

Exceptional Individuals. Western cultures abound with individuals whose bodily intelligence is well developed. Athletes come to mind first, but the list would also include dancers, instrumental musicians, craftsmen, and actors.[1] Linking these diverse domains, however, is a common picture of the skilled individual who "has evolved a family of procedures for translating intention into action. Knowledge of what is coming next allows that overall smoothness of performance which is virtually the hallmark of expertise" (Gardner, 1983, p. 209).

Empirical Evidence. Experts often note their inability to capture in words the essence of their performances. Experimental evidence supports this anecdotal finding regarding the independence of verbal and bodily intelligences. Correlations computed between intelligence-test scores and physical prowess are usually low (Cratty, 1979, pp. 193, 203). Evidence from the interference paradigm also points to independence: Asked to remember digits briefly, retention was only 70% if during the retention interval subjects performed a task that involved digits (e.g., addition) versus 91% if they performed the task of moving a lever in a specified direction (Williams, Beaver, Spence, & Rundell, 1969). Exactly the opposite pattern emerges when movements are to be remembered: Intervening digits produce no interference but intervening movements do.

Evolutionary Findings. Bodily intelligence is one domain in which the evolutionary record is clear (Fishbein, 1976, chap. 4). The immediate forerunner of early humans, *Australopithecus habilis*, used simple tools. For example, *Australopithecus* chipped stones to give them a sharper edge. *Homo erectus* shaped stones to make simple hand axes. Tools became more complex with the first *Homo sapiens*, the Neanderthal, who apparently devised

---

[1]Actors may seem to be a surprising entry in this list, but as Gardner (1983) notes, "In all forms of performance, but particularly in acting, one's ability to observe carefully and then to re-create scenes in detail is at a premium" (p. 226). The bodily intelligences are most obvious in the performance of the clown or mime, but are surely just as important in a convincing portrayal of roles as diverse as Hamlet and Superman.

spears and shovels. Advances in tools and their use continued with Cro-Magnon man. "By this time, men had knowledge not only of a wide variety of materials but also of diverse types and classes of tools to be made and used for different purposes, including lances, knives, chisels, needles, and tools for scraping, performing, whittling, serving, and pounding" (Gardner, 1983, p. 219).

A similar pattern of evidence comes from comparative analysis of tools used by different species alive today. Only primates use tools. Animals in lower orders use objects only in specific, stereotyped fashions. The lower primates use tools but infrequently. However, the higher primates, like chimpanzees, show remarkable agility, using tools to increase their reach and to gain mechanical advantage. Impressive as these feats are, Gardner (1983) notes that most are done primarily with one hand; only humans are capable of coordinating two hands to use a tool.

Development of Motor Skill. Though discussed little by Gardner, much evidence indicates that bodily intelligence develops in a very orderly manner. Walking without assistance, for example, is the crowning achievement in a developmental sequence that begins months earlier (Cratty, 1979). Beginning usually in the seventh month, infants will creep: Lying on their stomachs, infants will use their arms (and later their legs as well) to propel their bodies across the floor. Creeping gives way to crawling, in which infants support their bodies with hands and knees. Around the first birthday, infants learn to stand alone and soon thereafter walk when their hands are held. Shortly after the first birthday, infants walk unaided. As with Piaget's stages, the ages of these achievements differ from one infant to another, but the sequence is common to most infants.

During the elementary school years, children gain proficiency at moving in their environments. During these years, children run faster, jump higher and farther, throw (and catch) objects over a greater distance and with more accuracy, and have better balance (Cratty, 1979). The progression is very strongly linked with age, a relationship that reflects the strong dependence of many of these achievements on the child's increased size. However, some of these increases are not size dependent, such as in balance and throwing accuracy.

The developmental endpoint for most individuals is only a modest degree of bodily–kinesthetic intelligence. As is the case with musical intelligence, Western cultures have not ascribed

much significance to the bodily intelligences, providing only minimal instruction in them. But, as with music, with intense instruction and practice, individuals readily progress beyond these
modest levels.

Personal Intelligences

Individuals certainly differ in social and interpersonal skills, and
over the years several theorists have proposed theories of social
intelligence. In Chapter 2, for example, we discussed Guilford's
(1967) cognition of behavioral implications, which referred to an
individual's ability to interpret the significance of another's behavior. Gardner (1983) argues that personal intelligences are just
as central to a theory of human intelligence as the more frequently described logical and mathematical skills. He proposes
two components of personal intelligence. One, which can be described as *intrapersonal intelligence,* refers to a person's ability to
distinguish and identify various feelings and to use them to understand one's own behavior. The second, complementary personal intelligence is *interpersonal* and denotes "*the ability to notice and make distinctions among other individuals* and, in
particular, among their moods, temperaments, motivations, and
intentions" (Gardner, 1983, p. 239, emphasis in the original).

The three sources that provide the most compelling evidence for including personal intelligences in Gardner's (1983)
theory are (1) selective impairment following brain damage, (2) a
distinct developmental pattern; and (3) evolutionary evidence.

Selective Impairment. Zasetsky was a Russian soldier in
World War II whose intellectual skills were devastated as the
result of a serious head wound. He could no longer write letters
or words, add, or carry out simple requests. Yet in the face of this
massive cognitive dysfunction, Zasetsky maintained his personal
intelligence, particularly his sense of self. "He continued to possess will, desire, sensitivity to experience" (Gardner, 1983, p. 262).

Zasetsky's personal intelligence was unimpaired, no doubt,
because his wound left the *frontal lobes* of his brain intact. There
is little doubt that this portion of the brain plays a critical role in
the personal intelligences. Individuals like Zasetsky, in whom
portions of the brain other than the frontal cortex are damaged,
will lose the intelligences described thus far—the number, of
course, depending upon the extent and location of the damage—

but will not lose their sense of self. Indeed, some of these patients, like Zasetsky, are remarkably skilled at reflecting on their own condition and willfully try to improve it.

Just the opposite pattern is seen in individuals whose brain damage is localized in the frontal cortex: These individuals may show little disability in the verbal, logical, musical, or spatial components of intelligence, yet they often undergo marked personality transformations. Gardner (1975) describes one individual whose frontal portion of the cortex had been injured: "In the place of the softspoken, reliable foreman he had been, there now stood a loud-mouthed, obnoxious soul who cursed continuously, exhibited little sense of purpose, and wandered aimlessly until his death . . ." (p. 267).

Development of Personal Intelligence.   During the first year of life, infants gradually become attached to their primary caretakers, typically the mother. This attachment bond is the first manifestation of interpersonal intelligence; many theorists believe that it is the foundation upon which all subsequent interpersonal relationships are based. We also see inklings of intrapersonal intelligence: Infants discriminate other people's emotional responses, they respond to and refer to themselves by name, and they begin to act intentionally.[2]

For Gardner (1983), the preschool years represent a time in which children explore the roles of different individuals:

> Through talk, pretend play, gestures, drawing, and the like, the young child tries out facets of the roles of mother and child, doctor and patient, policeman and robber, teacher and pupil, astronaut and Martian. In experimenting with these role fragments, the child comes to know not only which behavior is associated with these individuals but also something about how it feels to occupy their characteristic niches. At the same time, children come to correlate the behavior and the states of other persons with their own personal experiences. [pp. 246–247].

In other words, role-playing of various sorts allows children to better understand various social relationships (interpersonal intelligence) as well as to understand their own feelings and behaviors (intrapersonal intelligence).

---

[2]Recall, from Chapter 4, Piaget's extensive description of the development of intentional behavior during the sensorimotor stage of development.

Different roles are distinguished in the preschool years, but between the ages of 6 and 12, children become increasingly able to take the social and emotional perspectives of other persons. Toward the end of this phase, children are capable of complex forms of recursive social thinking; for example, "He thinks that I think that he thinks" (Gardner, 1983, p. 250). On the intrapersonal side there is a shift as well: Preschoolers often compare themselves with others primarily by physical attributes such as height or strength, but school-age children are likelier to compare prowess in various domains like reading, arithmetic, or athletics.

During adolescence the complementary nature of intrapersonal and interpersonal intelligences is especially evident. As Gardner (1983) phrases it, "Adolescence turns out to be that period of life in which individuals must bring together these two forms of personal knowledge into a larger and more organized sense, a sense of identity" (p. 251). On the one hand, adolescents are likelier than children to choose their friends on the basis of similar values and knowledge—a case where intrapersonal intelligence seems to be leading interpersonal intelligence. On the other hand, interactions with others are critical in helping adolescents to develop a sense of self. That is, children define themselves in terms of their skills in various domains; adolescents define themselves in terms of more abstract and general underlying constructs like intelligence, generosity, assertiveness, and friendliness (Barenboim, 1977). In this instance, interpersonal intelligence helps to foster intrapersonal intelligence.

The details of this developmental sequence are probably restricted to Western cultures and perhaps even to North American cultures. However, Gardner (1983) claims that all cultures have prescribed routes that eventuate in a balance between interpersonal and intrapersonal intelligence. A culture "ultimately engenders. . . a sense of self, an idiosyncratic but adaptive amalgam of those aspects of experience that are most purely personal and internal and of those that govern and maintain one's relation to the outside community" (p. 270).

Evolutionary Evidence. Personal intelligences are recognizable only in human beings. What factors in the evolutionary history of *Homo sapiens* fostered the development of the personal intelligences? One key may be the relatively long period of childhood in the human species: If the offspring is to survive this prolonged period of dependence on another person, the interpersonal intelligence is essential (particularly when compared with species in which the animal reaches adulthood rapidly). Another critical event was the emergence of human cultures in which large animals were the primary source of food. Hunting such animals (as well as preparing and distributing the resulting meat and skins) was necessarily a group endeavor, which entailed an elaborate structure of roles to be successful.

It is much more difficult to peg key events in the evolution of intrapersonal intelligence. Gardner (1983) believes that the emergence of symbol systems—notably language—is a prerequisite for intrapersonal intelligence. He also speculates that

> one factor that may promote a recognition of oneself as a separate entity is the capacity to transcend the mere satisfaction of instinctual drives. Such an option becomes increasingly available to animals that are not perennially involved in the struggle for survival, have a relatively long life, and engage regularly in exploratory activities (p. 256).

Gardner's hypothesis, then, is that once *Homo sapiens* was no longer totally occupied with survival needs, its symbolic skill was unleashed in various directions, notably the symbolizing of the intrapersonal world.

Commentary

Gardner's (1983) theory of multiple intelligences and Sternberg's (1984) triarchic theory represent the most sophisticated efforts to date to bridge the gaps between the traditional approaches to intelligence. Each is probably best viewed as a general theoretical framework rather than as a fully elaborated, final theory. As Miller (1983) wrote in evaluating Gardner's work, "For his attempt to integrate diverse approaches, Mr. Gardner deserves everyone's gratitude. The fact that he calls his proposal a theory should not frighten off a general reader. It is less a scientific theory than a line on which he hangs out his intellectual laundry" (p. 5). In a similar vein, Sternberg noted that "the subtheories, and especially the contextual one, are in need of more detailed specification" (p. 286). Thus, the contribution of these theories does not lie primarily in our ability to derive from them specific predictions. Instead, their value is in integrating a number of heretofore disparate findings and theories and in providing new frameworks for conceptualizing intelligence, frameworks that will identify the questions that must be answered to understand human intelligence.

Our claim at the outset was that modern theories of intelligence should at the very least encompass the psychometric, developmental, and cognitive traditions. According to this standard, the triarchic theory and the theory of multiple intelligences both fare well. First consider individual differences. In the triarchic theory, individual differences provide one of the links between the three subtheories. That is, the aim of the triarchic theory is to explain individual differences in intelligence; each of the three subtheories provides part but not all of the analytic machinery needed for such an explanation.

Turning to the theory of multiple intelligences, recall that one of Gardner's (1983) signs of an intelligence is that there be psychometric evidence for it. That is, the presence of differences between individuals is one of the criteria that Gardner uses in evaluating a possible intelligence. Furthermore, Gardner believes that individuals will differ in their development of each of his six intelligences: "Some individuals will develop certain intelligences far more than others" (p. 278). Thus, individual differences are prominent both in identifying intelligences and in displaying them.

Both theories also address the development of intelligence. Recall that a distinct developmental profile was one of Gardner's (1983) signs for an intelligence. A developmental perspective on intelligence is less prominent in the triarchic theory; development enters primarily via the two-facet subtheory in the guise of automatization. In Chapter 4 we discussed how developmental increases in automatization might be important in age-related increases in cognitive power. Sternberg (1984) is making a broader version of the same claim: Increased experience and practice on a task can lead to automatization at any point in the life span. These changes are simply more obvious in childhood and adolescence because so many skills become automatized in these years.[3]

Finally, there is the issue of the mental processes that are responsible for intelligent actions. This is clearly the strong suit

---

[3]In fairness to Sternberg, elsewhere (e.g., 1982) he has used many of the constructs from the componential subtheory to formulate an elaborate theory of intellectual development.

of the triarchic theory: The componential subtheory is devoted exclusively to exactly this issue, and it is the componential subtheory that Sternberg (1984) has drawn with great care and precision for nearly a decade. As for the theory of multiple intelligences, Gardner claims that one of the signs of an intelligence is that it be isolable experimentally and that it be identified with a core set of mental operations.

Both theories, then, encompass the three perspectives we have addressed in this book. And they include others as well, such as the contextual perspective in the triarchic theory and the contributions from neuropsychology that are prominent in the theory of multiple intelligences. In short, both frameworks replace the insularity of past theories of human intelligence with the more catholic approach that the phenomenon warrants.

Summary

We began this chapter by reviewing the three traditional perspectives on intelligence, namely, the psychometric, information processing, and developmental approaches. Common to these perspectives is the view that intelligence is associated with reasoning and problem-solving skills. Another common component is the assumption that adaptability is an important component of intelligence. We concluded that each of the these perspectives contributes to our understanding of human intelligence, but that each is incomplete.

We then considered two eclectic theories of intelligence that have transcended the traditional boundaries for theories of intelligence. The first of these was Robert Sternberg's (1984) triarchic theory, an outgrowth of his earlier work on individual differences in reasoning skill. The triarchic theory includes three subtheories: a contextual subtheory, in which intelligent actions are defined relative to particular cultural contexts; a two-facet subtheory, which emphasizes novelty and automaticity as components of human intelligence; and a componential subtheory, which describes the mental operations that give rise to intelligent actions.

The second theory described in this chapter is Howard Gardner's (1983) theory of multiple intelligences. Gardner proposes several signs that can be used to identify a distinct intel-

ligence; in doing so, he argues that the evidence points to six
human intelligences: (1) linguistic intelligence, (2) logical–mathematical intelligence, (3) spatial intelligence, (4) musical intel-
ligence, (5) bodily–kinesthetic intelligence, and (6) personal intel-
ligence.

Neither of these efforts is yet a full-fledged, substantiated
theory. Rather, they are general frameworks or orientations that,
notably, encompass all three traditional perspectives that have
dominated psychological approaches to intelligence in the past.

6

Epilogue: New Perspectives on Old Issues

We began this book by suggesting that psychologists and lay people alike often become embroiled in controversies over intelligence testing, and do so without thoughtful consideration of the construct of intelligence per se. Hence, the bulk of this book has explored that construct in detail; in the process, we have discussed three traditional views and two new, eclectic views. At this point, we return briefly to those social controversies, for the different perspectives on intelligence do have ramifications that extend beyond purely theoretical concerns.

In fact, some of these disputes are seen in a much different light when the underlying conception of intelligence is not derived from the psychometric tradition. One such controversy is the appropriate use of mental tests; a second concerns differences in intelligence between individuals of various cultural groups. In addressing these issues, we make no pretense of discussing them fully; each warrants and has received book-length treatments (e.g., Jensen, 1980; Kamin, 1974; Loehlin, Lindzey, and Spuhler, 1975; Willerman, 1979). Our intent in presenting them is merely to establish that nontraditional conceptions of intelligence can provide novel vistas from which to behold these issues.

Use of Mental Tests

Binet and the other early test constructors did not labor in a social vacuum. By the end of the nineteenth century, education was compulsory in many Western cultures. As a result, educators grappled with diversity in individual talents and goals that far exceeded anything they had experienced previously. Hence, early in the twentieth century, tests began to be seen as one solution to this problem of diversity, for example, by allowing educators to decide which students should be encouraged to pursue higher education and which would probably need special programs to master minimal educational goals. Thus, the primary aim of early mental tests was *selection*, placing students on the appropriate track in the educational system (Glaser, 1981).

This function led to an unmistakable definition of a good test: It accurately predicted scholastic outcomes. By extension, an improved test was more highly correlated with the behavior to be predicted. For example, the average correlation between the Numerical Ability Subtest of the Differential Aptitude Tests (Bennett, Seashore, & Wesman, 1974) and grades in secondary school mathematics courses is approximately .51. This test would be improved, by traditional criteria, if the items of the test were modified in such a way that the correlation increased by a statistically significant amount.

For some time consensus among psychometricians has been that the predictive level of mental tests is probably about as high as possible, given the typical constraints of the testing situation. As Estes (1974, p. 740) phrased it, "Long ago, efforts to increase the predictive power of intelligence tests began to run into sharply diminishing returns, and it now seems quite possible that we are near the maximum attainable, given the usual limitations on time and expense of testing."

Nor is there reason to hope that a measure with a greater predictive power will emanate from developmental psychology or information processing. There have been efforts to create standardized tests of intelligence for school-age children based on items derived from Piagetian tasks. The modal outcome here is that the Piagetian-based scales predict school success less accurately than do traditional mental tests (e.g., Dodwell, 1961; Kaufman & Kaufman, 1972; Tuddenham, 1970). Concerning information processing, we know of no serious efforts to create a standardized measure of intelligence based on information processing tasks (see Rose, 1979, for the closest approximation). However, based on correlations scattered through the literature between various measures of achievement (e.g., reading achievement) and information processing parameters, there is little reason to expect that such a measure would have greater predictive power than psychometric measures.

However, predictive power is not the only criterion by which to evaluate a test. The historical emphasis on predictability stems from the use of tests for selection purposes. Implicit in this use is a view that intelligence is relatively stable and inert. That is, the assumption underlying traditional mental testing is that some mental entity—call it *g*—determines success in school and similar intellectual endeavors. By measuring *g* accurately, one can then predict a person's success in such endeavors.

The basis for the psychometric belief in the stability of *g* comes from longitudinal research projects in which individuals have taken an intelligence test for several years in succession—beginning in infancy or the preschool years and continuing through adolescence and sometimes into adulthood. In these cases, one can compute correlations between intelligence in an adult and intelligence at various points earlier in the adult's development. Put another way, one can use mental-test scores obtained in childhood and adolescence to predict an individual's intelligence-test performance as an adult.

In fact, test scores obtained from infancy typically correlate poorly with adult intelligence (McCall, 1979; Yang, 1979); however, scores obtained in the preschool years correlate significantly with adult intelligence, and by the elementary school years the correlations are quite large. Bayley (1949), for example, reported a correlation of .86 between scores on intelligence tests administered at 6 and 18 years of age. In other words, a person whose test score was one of the lowest in a sample at age 6 would be quite likely to have one of the lowest test scores as an 18-year-old. This and other comparably large correlations provide the traditional basis for the conclusion that intelligence is relatively stable from the preschool years on.

Ignored here is the fact that the terms *stability* and *change* can have two meanings. *Relative level of performance* refers to one's position relative to the positions of others in a sample. This is the stability demonstrated in the correlational analyses of test scores obtained in longitudinal research. *Absolute level of per-*

formance concerns change or stability in one's performance from an initial level. Finding that a person recalls two digits as a 2-year-old, three as a 5-year-old, and six as a 15-year-old indicates little absolute stability in digit span, for span increases consistently between 2 and 15 years of age.

These two senses of stability and change are completely independent mathematically. To see this, imagine that four individuals enter a physical fitness program. At the beginning of the program, individuals A through D run 1500 meters (the so-called metric mile) in 20, 15, 12 and 10 minutes, respectively. Ten weeks into the program, corresponding times are 12, 10, 8 and 7 minutes. In this example there is perfect relative stability: The individuals are rank-ordered (from slowest to fastest) A, then B, then C, and finally D both at the beginning and at the end of training. There is, however, no evidence for absolute stability: All individuals improve substantially, ranging from D's 30% improvement to A's 40% improvement.

This example illustrates that from a practical standpoint, large changes in absolute levels of performance can make the question of relative levels of performance quite beside the point. Suppose we substitute for our physical fitness example a totally hypothetical program of mathematics instruction. Prior to instruction, individuals A through D solve, respectively, 2, 4, 6, and 9 algebra problems correctly out of 100. Following instruction they solve, respectively, 91, 92, 94, and 99 problems correctly. Again, we have perfect relative stability, but it is the massive changes in the absolute level of performance that matter from an educational standpoint.

Of course, changes in absolute level of performance have been central to Piaget's theory. Information processing psychologists as well have studied these phenomena, either in the context of studying learning or of comparing the special skills of experts with those of novices. (Recall from Chapter 3, for example, the expertise of SF with his 80+ digit span.) From these perspectives, it is more reasonable to start with the point of view that intellectual skills are malleable rather than fixed.

If it is assumed that intelligence is malleable, the predictive value of tests is no longer a prime concern. If we believe that intelligence is malleable, then what educators need to know are those experiences that are likeliest to assist a student in achieving particular educational goals. If a child is struggling with addition or subtraction, what specific form of instruction will help the child most? What experiences will allow a mathematically talented youngster to grasp the essentials of calculus? Believing that intelligence is malleable, the value of tests lies in their ability to provide some of the information needed to design instruction appropriate for an individual. According to Glaser (1981, p. 924):

> Teachers and schools need information on individuals that is oriented toward instructional decision rather then prediction. Tests in a helping society are not mere indexes which predict that the individual child will adjust to the school or which relieve the school from assisting the student to achieve as much as possible. The test and the instructional decision should be an integral event.

Thus, the important criterion for evaluating a test becomes its *diagnostic* value.

If tests are to be used to devise instruction for the individual—rather than the more traditional emphasis on placing an individual in the appropriate niche in a fixed instructional system—how should we proceed? One position is that tests should be able

> to describe the initial state of the learner in terms of processes involved in achieving competent performance. This would then allow us to influence learning in two ways: (a) to design instructional alternatives that adapt to these processes, and (b) to attempt to improve an individual's competence in these processes so that he is more likely to profit from the instructional resources available [Glaser, 1976, p. 14].

Mental tests derived from the psychometric tradition are not terribly useful in this regard (Estes, 1974; Glaser, 1972, 1976). Why? The outcome of almost any mental test is a score that simply indicates a person's standing relative to a normative sample. Based on such information about a person's relative performance, it is essentially impossible to design appropriate instruction. In this regard, mental tests are not unlike a thermometer as a measure of physical health. The thermometer provides a rough index as to whether a person is healthy or not; in the latter instance, the thermometer provides precious little in the way of specific diagnostic information.

Analysis of processes involved in performance has been the heart of the information processing and, to a lesser extent, the

Piagetian perspectives. In Piaget's theory, performance on any test—the cognitive contents—is always a by-product of the interaction between the functional invariants and the person's current mental structures. In information processing, performance is determined by the combined effects of pattern recognition processes, the knowledge base, and activated memory. One could anticipate, then, that by combining the focus on process exemplified in the Piagetian and information processing approaches with existing psychometric measures, it would be possible to devise instruments that are no more predictive than their predecessors but that provide more extensive diagnostic information about an individual's cognitive assets and liabilities.

In fact, research of this sort has begun. Given the relative newness of process analyses of intelligence, it is not too surprising that there are as yet few instances of such diagnostically based instruction. Here we consider one example to demonstrate that such instruction is in fact possible.

Series completion items are found at several developmental levels on many standardized tests. Such items may be letters, numbers, pictures, or geometric figures. In all cases, the structure of the task is the same: Elements comprising the series are ordered according to specific interitem relationships; the individual's task is to extract the basic relationships and to generate the next item(s) in the series. Letter series problems, for example, were developed by Thurstone and Thurstone (1941) as a test of the primary mental ability of *induction* (i.e., inductive reasoning). An example of such an item is the series "npaoqapraq . . . . "

Simon and Kotovsky (1963; Kotovsky & Simon, 1973) developed a model of the component processes necessary to solve these tasks. Their model distinguishes the declarative knowledge and the procedural knowledge required. The declarative knowledge for letter series problems is limited to knowledge about the order of letters in the alphabet as well as the concepts of *identity*, *next*, and *backwards-next* (i.e., reverse ordering).

The model is more detailed concerning procedural knowledge and breaks down the completion of any letter series problem into a set of four processes. The first is the detection of the interletter relations in a problem. The common relationships included in the model are the identity, next, and backwards-next relationships just mentioned (also see Table 6-1). The second phase is to extract the *period length* of the pattern within the problem. The period length is the regular interval at which a

Table 6-1　　*Interletter relationships in the Simon–Kotovsky model*

Relationship	Example
Identity	ab*m* cd*m* ef*m* . . .
Next	ur*tus* tu*t* tu . . .
Backwards-next	ab*y* ab*x* abw . . .

Note: In each example, the italicized letters illustrate the relationship.

relation or a break in a relation occurs. For instance, in the series "aaabbbcccdd . . . ," the identity relation repeats every three letters, so this series has a period of 3.

The third process is generating a rule involving both the relations and the periodic structure of the problem. For instance, to complete the series "cdcdcd . . . ," one must recognize the occurrences of the identity relation and recognize that the period length is 2. Then the information must be assembled into a rule that defines the relationships of letters between and within periods. Thus, for "cdcdcd . . . ," a person must formulate the rule that the first letter of every period is related to the first letter in each of the other periods by identity, that the second letter of all periods are also related by identity, and that the two letters within a period are related by next relationship. The final process involved in solving letter series problems is *extrapolation*. A person must use the rule generated in the third phase to continue the generation of the series.

Holzman, Glaser, and Pellegrino (1976) used the Simon and Kotovsky (1963; Kotovsky & Simon, 1973) model as the basis for instruction to improve children's performance on letter series problems. The study involved direct training for discovering relations and periodicity (i.e., the first and second phase of the Simon–Kotovsky model) with children in grades 1 through 6. Both the training group and the control group were given a pretest with fifteen problems. The training group then received approximately two hours of instruction in identifying relations and periodicity. Both the training group and the control group were then asked to solve fifteen new problems that were identical in structure to the original problems but used different letters. The training group showed a significant gain in performance compared with the control group: Errors decreased by 32% in the training group compared with 13% in the control group. In addition, the training group showed significantly greater gains on the problems with more difficult interletter relationships (e.g., next relations).

The study by Holzman, Glaser, and Pellegrino (1976) is in many ways a naive form of diagnostically based instruction. No attempt was made to determine the particular components of performance that were responsible for the intermediate levels of competence shown by individuals of different ages. The training that was administered was the same for all individuals and varied in its success. However, there is no particular reason why future instructional studies could not use the model of task performance as a basis for both the initial diagnostic assessment of individual cognitive strengths and weaknesses as well as the subsequent training designed to improve those skills. Holzman, Glaser, and Pellegrino (1976) have at least shown that a process model of series completion performance can be translated into a set of procedures for explicit training in cognitive processes.

Similar work is under way on a number of other mental tests (see Detterman & Sternberg, 1982). Collectively, this research leads us to be optimistic about the development in the near future of diagnostic mental tests that can lead directly to specific programs of instruction.

Group Differences in Intelligence

1. Females have greater verbal ability than males.
2. Males have greater spatial ability than females.
3. Whites have higher IQ scores than blacks.

Each of these statements has been made at one time or another with various forms of supporting evidence (Loehlin, Lindzey, and Spuhler, 1975; Maccoby & Jacklin, 1974). Common to each claim is a contrast between subgroups within a population that is based on performance on mental tests. Such differences per se need not be controversial. What has made them so is that, throughout much of the history of psychometrics, theorists have claimed that these differences can be traced to differences at birth, differences in inherited ability. That is, psychometricians have often assumed that intelligence is determined or fixed at birth by genetic inheritance.

Galton was the first to make this claim and support it with evidence: In his *Hereditary Genius* (1869), he showed that many of the eminent professionals in Britain were not randomly drawn from the population at large but instead came from the same few families. Another noteworthy figure was Henry Goddard, who first introduced the Binet test in the United States. In *The Kallikak Family: A Study in the Heredity of Feeblemindedness* (1912), Goddard traced the descendants of Martin Kallikak (a pseudonym), a soldier in the American Revolution. One branch of descendants came from his wife, a woman of "good stock." The other branch resulted from an affair with a "feebleminded" tavern maid. According to Goddard, the branches were as dissimilar as one could imagine: "We find on the good side of the family prominent people in all walks of life . . . . On the bad side we find paupers, criminals, prostitutes, drunkards, and examples of all forms of social pest with which modern society is burdened" (Goddard, 1912, p. 116).

Neither Galton nor Goddard paid much attention to the likely effect of environment on producing these differences. As ardent hereditarians, the genetic basis was obvious to them. Subsequent psychometricians—among them Lewis Terman and Cyril Burt—also believed that human intelligence was largely determined by inherited factors.[1] To support their views, they drew upon sources more reliable than the pedigree research of Galton and Goddard. Among them were the studies of correlations between IQ scores at various ages (described earlier in this chapter), studies of intelligence in identical and fraternal twins, and studies of intelligence in adopted children (Hunt, 1961; Loehlin, Lindzey, and Spuhler, 1975).

The proper interpretation of these and other relevant sources of data has been one of the most extensively and heatedly debated topics in the recent history of social science (Kamin, 1974). We have no intention here of adjudicating the issue, instead, we simply want to make the modest point that information processing and developmental psychologists are likely to see the issues in a quite different light. On the one hand, relevant evi-

---

[1]Alfred Binet was an important exception, believing that intelligence was a reflection of environmental factors, notably schooling.

dence aside, the psychometrician's belief in a fixed intelligence is, in many ways, a natural state of affairs:

> The very significance of his research and practice lies in the capacity of the tests to predict performance at a later time and to predict other kinds of performance. *A faith in intelligence as a basic and fixed dimension of a person is probably the faith on which one can most readily rest such a professional function.* With such a faith, when the exigencies of a testing effort fail, one can proceed in the hope that better instruments will improve the state of affairs [Hunt, 1961, p. 14, emphasis added].

Developmental and information processing psychologists do not necessarily share this professional commitment. Neither is prone to view intelligence as fixed or predetermined; to the contrary (as we discussed earlier in this chapter) both are more inclined toward a plastic view of intelligence. In the remainder of this section we illustrate how these views lead developmental and information processing psychologists to analyze group differences, using the second of the group differences with which we began this section, namely, sex differences in spatial skill.

A Psychometric Account

Men routinely achieve higher scores than women on most of the tests of spatial aptitude described in Chapter 2. For many years, the favored explanation of this difference was that superior spatial skill depended upon a sex-linked recessive gene. Three predictions were derived from this hypothesis (Bock & Kolakowoski, 1973; Harris, 1978). One concerned correlations between parents' spatial ability and that of their offspring. If a sex-linked recessive gene is involved, fathers' spatial aptitude should be related to their daughters' spatial aptitude but not to that of their sons; just the opposite pattern should exist for mothers. A second prediction concerned correlations between siblings' spatial aptitudes: Correlations between spatial ability scores should be largest for sisters, smaller for brothers, and smaller still for siblings of the opposite sex. Finally, the genetic model also made predictions regarding the distribution of spatial ability in males and females.

The distribution should be bimodal for both males and females but more distinctively so for males.

Several early studies resulted in findings consistent with one or more of these predictions. Stafford (1961), for example, found the predicted pattern of correlations between parents' spatial ability and that of their children. In more recent studies involving larger samples of subjects and more extensive psychometric testing of spatial aptitude, evidence regarding the recessive gene hypothesis has been inconclusive at best (Boles, 1980). Because of these outcomes, more complex genetic models of spatial aptitude are being suggested (e.g., DeFries, Ashton, Johnson, Kuse, McClearn, Mi, Rashad, Vandenberg, & Wilson, 1976).

An Information Processing Approach

Process analysis of intelligence, as described in Chapter 3, can readily be extended to the study of group differences. That is, given group differences in performance on a psychometric measure, one can ask (1) whether individuals in the groups of interest solve the problem using the same algorithm and (2) if they do, whether they execute the component processes of that algorithm with comparable speed. This approach can be applied to the question of sex differences in spatial aptitude using many of the methods already described in detail in Chapter 3.

In fact, research of this sort comparing the performance of men and women leads to two conclusions with reasonable consistency. First, males and females use similar algorithms for solving these problems. On spatial-relations problems, for example, their response times typically conform equally well to the predictions of the Cooper and Shepard algorithm (Figure 3-17) that includes encoding, rotation, comparison, and response phases (e.g., Kail, Carter, & Pellegrino, 1979; Kail, Stevenson, & Black, 1984). Second, men are faster than women in performing the rotation component of the algorithm, but men and women execute the other processes at much the same rate (Carter, Pazak, & Kail, 1983; Kail, Carter, & Pellegrino, 1979; Tapley & Bryden, 1977). In short, at least for problems concerning spatial relations (see Figure 2-5), men and women use the same general approach to solving the problems; the sex difference in performance appears to be localized in one component of that approach.

A Developmental Approach

As a first step in understanding sex differences in spatial aptitude, a developmental psychologist would want to know the typical period in development when the sex difference first emerges. Here the evidence is clear: Sex differences in spatial aptitude are infrequent prior to adolescence and thereafter are seen routinely (Maccoby & Jacklin, 1974).

Armed with this information, a developmental psychologist would next determine what is critical about adolescence for the emergence of these sex differences. One theory (Harris, 1978; Waber, 1977) is that hormonal changes in adolescence may produce functional differences in the central nervous systems of boys and girls, differences that make girls less able to perform spatial tasks successfully. Specifically, hormonal changes during adolescence may result in a greater division of labor between the left and right hemispheres of the brain in males. The greater specialization of male's right hemisphere for spatial processing is responsible for males' advantage in spatial skill.

Another explanation emphasizes that experiences during childhood and adolescence are not the same for most boys and girls, and that boys' experiences may be more conducive to the development of spatial aptitude (Harris, 1978). For example, exploring and manipulating objects—an experience thought to aid the development of spatial skill—is sometimes found to be more common in boys' play than in girls'. According to this explanation, the sex difference in spatial skill emerges only in adolescence because "several years are required before the *culturally* prescribed different learning experiences for boys and girls become expressed in actual skill differences" (Harris, 1978, p. 426, emphasis in the original).

The available evidence does not allow us to rule out either approach categorically, nor is future evidence likely to allow us to do so. Rather, in the likeliest model genetic and environmental components will both play important and *interactive* roles. That is, the group differences that we measure in adults unfold over the lifetime of those individuals. The nature of that unfolding is dictated by genetic components (e.g., the release of hormones during adolescence) as well as individuals' experiences (e.g., direct training in spatial skills).

In this regard, spatial aptitude is probably typical of most intellectual skills. For any intelligence—be it general, verbal, or bodily–kinesthetic—inheritance is the starting point for the analysis, not the entire explanation. As Scarr-Salapatek (1975) described it, "The degree to which an individual's genotype is expressed in his or her intellectual development depends upon many environmental factors that are critically present in adequate or inadequate amounts during the developmental process" (p. 6).

Hence, from a developmental perspective, group differences in intelligence are unlikely to be seen as etched in stone. Instead, such differences are recognized for what they are: the product of life histories of groups of individuals living in particular environments. Anything that alters the nature of organism–environment interactions—illness, malnutrition, war, or depression—will alter the developmental record of individuals and the cultural groups to which they belong. In the process, group differences may be accentuated, eliminated, or even reversed.

Summary and Concluding Remarks

A working assumption of most psychometricians is that intelligences are fixed. This assumption is a necessity for the psychometric enterprise, for if intelligence were to fluctuate erratically—like stocks, for example—psychometricians would be little more than brokers of the mind, making hunches about intelligence, having best bets, but not predicting with confidence. Psychometrics has flourished because intelligence does possess relative stability; a person's standing compared with his or her peers is not erratic but reasonably consistent (at least in Western cultures after the preschool years).

The information processing psychologist and the developmental psychologist base their analyses of intelligence on different assumptions. Both psychologists agree (1) that performance on mental tests represents the orchestration of numerous distinct mental processes and (2) that it is possible to alter the orchestration and thereby improve an individual's performance. Information processing psychologists have focused on the first of these claims. The fruit of their labor is a large and growing catalog of descriptions of the precise manner in which individuals solve items on mental tests. Developmental psychologists have studied the second claim and have shown that the mental orchestration changes systematically as children develop.

If, as developmental and information processing psychologists generally believe, intelligence can change, there is little point in simply predicting a negative outcome and then sitting idly, allowing it to occur. This is true whether the situation involves either test results for a single child that indicate meager educational accomplishments in the future or mental-test results that indicate differences between groups. In either case one would intervene to promote a more favorable outcome. However, if instructional intervention is to be systematic rather than haphazard, it is essential to know an individual's current intellectual assets and liabilities. It is process analysis of test performance, which is only in its infancy, that will allow test scores to be interpreted in such a diagnostic fashion.

In summary, whether discussing the practical issue of the use and misuse of tests or the more theoretical facets of intelligence, the conclusion is much the same: Psychometric dogma, though it has held center stage for nearly a century, is no longer sufficient to address the pressing theoretical and applied issues associated with intelligence. Information processing and developmental psychology are playing ever larger roles in the analysis of intelligence and will probably continue to do so in the future. Waiting in the wings and likely to dominate the twenty-first century are eclectic theories of intelligence, like those of Gardner (1983) and Sternberg (1984).

References

Adams, M. J. (1979). Models of word recognition. *Cognitive Psychology*, *11*, 133–176.

Anderson, J. R. (1983). *The architecture of cognition*. Cambridge: Harvard University Press.

Anderson, J. R. (1980). *Cognitive psychology and its implications*. San Francisco: W. H. Freeman and Company.

Alderton, D. L., Goldman, S. R., & Pellegrino, J. W. (1982). *Multitask assessment of inductive reasoning skill*. Paper presented at the annual meeting of the American Educational Research Association, New York.

Baltes, P. B., & Schaie, K. W. (Eds.). (1973). *Life-span developmental psychology: personality and socialization*. New York: Academic Press.

Barenboim, C. (1977). Developmental changes in the interpersonal cognitive system from middle childhood to adolescence. *Child Development*, *48*, 1467–1474.

Bayley, N. (1949). Consistency and variability in the growth of intelligence from birth to eighteen years. *Journal of Genetic Psychology*, *75*, 165–196.

Bennett, G. K., Seashore, H. G., & Wesman, A. G. (1974). *Differential Aptitude Tests*. New York: The Psychological Corporation.

Berry, J. W. (1974). Radical cutural relativism and the concept of intelligence. In J. W. Berry & P. R. Dasen (Eds.), *Culture and cognition: Readings in cross-cultural psychology*. London: Methuen.

Binet, A., & Henri, V. (1896). La psychologie individuelle. *Année Psychologie, 2,* 411–465.

Binet, A., & Simon, T. (1908). Le développement de l'intelligence chez les enfants. *Année Psychologie, 14,* 1–94.

Birch, L. L. (1978). Baseline differences, attention, and age differences in time-sharing performance. *Journal of Experimental Child Psychology, 25,* 505–513.

Bock, R. D., & Kolakowski, D. (1973). Further evidence of sex-linked major-gene influence on human spatial visualizing ability. *American Journal of Human Genetics, 25,* 1–14.

Boles, D. B. (1980). X-linkage of spatial ability: A critical review. *Child Development, 51,* 625–635.

Boring, E. G. (1923). Intelligence as the tests test it. *New Republic,* June, pp. 35–37.

Boring, E. G. (1950). *A history of experimental psychology* (2nd ed.). New York: Appleton-Century-Crofts.

Bower, G. H., Black, J. B., & Turner, T. J. (1979). Scripts in memory for text. *Cognitive Psychology, 11,* 177–220.

Brainerd, C. J. (1978). *Piaget's theory of intelligence.* Englewood Cliffs, NJ: Prentice-Hall.

Brainerd, C. J., & Kingma, J. (in press). Do children have to remember to reason? A fuzzy-trace theory of transitivity development. *Developmental Review.*

Bransford, J. D., & Johnson, M. K. (1972). Contextual prerequisites for understanding: Some investigations of comprehension and recall. *Journal of Verbal Learning and Verbal Behavior, 11,* 717–726.

Brody, E. B., & Brody, N. (1976). *Intelligence: Nature, determinants and consequences.* New York: Academic Press.

Bryant, P. E., & Trabasso, T. (1971). Transitive inferences and memory in young children. *Nature, 232,* 456–458.

Buros, O. K. (1974). *Tests in Print II: An index to tests, test reviews, and the literature on specific tests.* Highland Park, NJ: Gryphon Press.

Buros, O. K. (1978). *The eighth mental measurements yearbook.* Highland Park, NJ: Gryphon Press.

Burt, C. (1949). The structure of the mind: A review of the results of factor analysis. *British Journal of Educational Psychology, 19,* 100–111, 176–199.

Burt, C. (1954). The differentiation of intellectual ability. *British Journal of Educational Psychology, 24,* 76–90.

Burtis, P. J. (1982). Capacity increase and chunking in the development of short-term memory. *Journal of Experimental Child Psychology, 34,* 387–413.

Cantor, G. N. (1983). Conflict, learning, and Piaget: Comments on Zimmerman and Blom's "Toward an empirical test of the role of cognitive conflict in learning." *Developmental Review, 3,* 39–53.

Carmichael, L., Hogan, H. P., & Walter, A. (1932). An experimental study of the effect of language on the reproduction of visually perceived form. *Journal of Experimental Psychology, 15,* 73–86.

Carter, P., Pazak, B., & Kail, R. (1983). Algorithms for processing spatial information. *Journal of Experimental Child Psychology, 36,* 284–304.

Case, R. (1972a). Learning and development: A neo-Piagetian interpretation. *Human Development, 15,* 339–358.

Case, R. (1972b). Validation of a neo-Piagetian mental capacity construct. *Journal of Experimental Child Psychology, 14,* 287–302.

Case, R. (1978). Intellectual development from birth to adolescence: A neo-Piagetian interpretation. In R. Siegler (Ed.), *Children's thinking: What develops?* Hillsdale, NJ: Lawrence Erlbaum Associates.

Case, R., & Serlin, R. (1979). A new processing model for predicting performance on Pascual-Leone's test of M-space. *Cognitive Psychology, 11,* 308–326.

Cattell, R. B. (1963). Theory of fluid and crystallized intelligence: A critical experiment. *Journal of Educational Psychology, 54,* 1–22.

Cattell, R. B. (1971). *Abilities: Their structure, growth, and action.* Boston: Houghton-Mifflin.

Cavanagh, J. P. (1972). Relation between the immediate memory span and the memory search rate. *Psychological Review, 79,* 525–530.

Chaille, S. E. (1887). Infants: Their chronological progress. *New Orleans Medical and Surgical Journal, 14,* 893–912.

Chase, W. G., & Simon, H. A. (1973). The mind's eye in chess. In W. G. Chase (Ed.), *Visual information processing.* New York: Academic Press.

Chi, M. T. H., Glaser, R., & Rees, E. (1982). Expertise in problem solving. In R. J. Sternberg (Ed.), *Advances in the psychology of human intelligence* (Vol. 1). Hillsdale, NJ: Lawrence Erlbaum Associates.

Clark, H. H., & Chase, W. G. (1972). On the process of comparing sentences against pictures. *Cognitive Psychology, 3,* 472–517.

Cooper, L. A. (1975). Mental transformation of random two-dimensional shapes. *Cognitive Psychology, 7,* 20–43.

Cooper, L. A. & Shepard, R. N. (1973). Chronometric studies of the rotation of mental images. In W. G. Chase (Ed.), *Visual information processing.* New York: Academic Press.

Cratty, B. J. (1979). *Perceptual and motor development in infants and children* (2nd ed.). Englewood Cliffs, NJ: Prentice-Hall.

Cronbach, L. J. (1957). The two disciplines of scientific psychology. *American Psychologist, 12,* 671–684.

Cronbach, L. J. (1975). Beyond the two disciplines of scientific psychology. *American Psychologist, 30,* 116–127.

DeFries, J. C., Ashton, G. C., Johnson, R. C., Kuse, A.R., McLearn, G. E., Mi, M. P., Rashad, M. N., Vandenberg, S.G., & Wilson, J. R. (1976). Parent-offspring resemblance for specific cognitive abilities in two ethnic groups. *Nature, 261,* 131–133.

Detterman, D. K. & Sternberg, R. J. (1982). *How and how much can intelligence be increased?* Norwood, NJ: Ablex.

Deutsch, D. (1975). The organization of short-term memory for a single acoustic attribute. In D. Deutsch & J. A. Deutsch (Eds.), *Short-term memory.* New York: Academic Press.

Deutsch, D. (1982). The processing of pitch combinations. In D. Deutsch (Ed.), *The psychology of music.* New York: Academic Press.

Dodwell, P. (1961). Children's understanding of number concepts: Characteristics of an individual and of a group test. *Canadian Journal of Psychology, 15,* 29–36.

Dowling, W. J. (1982). Melodic information processing and its development. In D. Deutsch (Ed.), *The psychology of music.* New York: Academic Press.

Dye, N. W., & Very, P. S. (1968). Growth changes in factorial structure by age and sex. *Genetic Psychology Monographs, 78,* 55–88.

Egan, D. E., & Schwartz, B. (1979). Chunking in recall of symbolic drawings. *Memory & Cognition, 7,* 149–158.

Engel, R. W., & Bukstel, L. (1978). Memory processes among bridge players of differing expertise. *American Journal of Psychology, 91,* 673–689.

Ericsson, K. A., Chase, W. G., & Faloon, S. (1980). Acquisition of a memory skill. *Science, 208,* 1181–1182.

Estes, W. K. (1974). Learning theory and intelligence. *American Psychologist, 29,* 740–749.

Fishbein, H. D. (1976). *Evolution, development, and children's learning.* Pacific Palisades, CA: Goodyear.

Flavell, J. H. (1963). *The developmental psychology of Jean Piaget.* Princeton, NJ: Van Nostrand.

Flavell, J. H. (1977). *Cognitive development.* Englewood Cliffs, NJ: Prentice-Hall.

French, J. W., Ekstrom, R., & Price, L. (1963). *Kit of reference tests for cognitive factors.* Princeton, NJ: Educational Testing Service.

Galton, F. (1869). *Hereditary genius: An inquiry into its laws and consequences.* London: MacMillan.

Gardner, H. (1975). *The shattered mind.* New York: Knopf.

Gardner, H. (1982). Artistry following damage to the human brain. In A. W. Ellis (Ed.), *Normality and pathology in cognitive functions.* London: Academic Press.

Gardner, H. (1983). *Frames of mind: The theory of multiple intelligences.* New York: Basic.

Garrett, H. E. (1946). A developmental theory of intelligence. *American Psychologist, 1,* 372–378.

Getzels, J. W., & Jackson, P. W. (1962). *Creativity and intelligence.* New York: Wiley.

Gibson, E. J. (1969). *Principles of perceptual learning and development.* New York: Appleton-Century-Crofts.

Gilmartin, K. J., Newell, A., & Simon, H. A. (1976). A program modeling short-term memory under strategy control. In C. N. Cofer (Ed.), *The structure of human memory.* San Francisco: W. H. Freeman and Company.

Ginsburg, H., & Opper, S. (1979). *Piaget's theory of intellectual development* (2nd ed.). Englewood Cliffs, NJ: Prentice-Hall.

Gladwin, T. (1970). *East is a big bird.* Cambridge: Harvard University Press.

Glaser, R. (1972). Individuals and learning: The new aptitudes. *Educational Researcher, 1,* 5–13.

Glaser, R. (1976). Components of a psychology of instruction: Toward a science of design. *Review of Educational Research, 46*, 1–24.

Glaser, R. (1981). The future of testing. *American Psychologist, 36*, 923–936.

Goddard, H. H. (1912). *The Kallikak family: A study in the heredity of feeblemindedness.* New York: Macmillan.

Goldberg, R. A., Schwartz, S., & Stewart, M. (1977). Individual differences in cognitive processes. *Journal of Educational Psychology, 69*, 9–14.

Goodenough F. L. (1949). *Mental testing.* New York: Rinehart.

Greeno, J. G. (1978). Natures of problem-solving abilities. In W. K. Estes (Ed.), *Handbook of learning and cognitive processes* (Vol. 5). Hillsdale, NJ: Lawrence Erlbaum Associates.

Groen, G. J. & Resnick, L. B. (1977). Can preschool children invent addition algorithms? *Journal of Educational Psychology, 69*, 645–652.

Guilford, J. P. (1964). Zero intercorrelations among tests of intellectual abilities. *Psychological Bulletin, 61*, 401–404.

Guilford, J. P. (1967). *The nature of human intelligence.* New York: McGraw-Hill.

Guilford, J. P. (1977) *Way beyond the IQ: Guide to improving intelligence and creativity.* Buffalo, NY: Creative Education Foundation.

Guilford, J. P. (1982). Cognitive psychology's ambiguities: Some suggested remedies. *Psychological Review, 89*, 48–59.

Guilford, J. P., & Hoepfner, R. (1971). *The analysis of intelligence.* New York: McGraw-Hill.

Gzowski, P. (1981). *The game of our lives.* Toronto: McClelland and Stewart.

Harris, L. J. (1978). Sex differences in spatial ability: Possible environmental, genetic, and neurological factors. In M. Kinsbourne (Ed.), *Asymmetrical function of the brain.* Cambridge: Cambridge University Press.

Hayes-Roth, B., & Hayes-Roth, F. (1977). Concept learning and the recognition and classification of exemplars. *Journal of Verbal Learning and Verbal Behavior, 16*, 321–338.

Hill, A. L. (1978). Savants: Mentally retarded individuals with special skills. In N. R. Ellis (Ed.), *International Review of Research in Mental Retardation* (Vol. 9). New York: Academic Press.

Holzman, T. G., Glaser, R., & Pellegrino, J. W. (1976). Process training derived from a computer simulation theory. *Memory & Cognition,* 4, 349–356.

Horn, J. L. (1968). Organization of abilities and the development of intelligence. *Psychological Review,* 75, 242–259.

Horn, J. L., & Cattell, R. B. (1967). Refinement and test of the theory of fluid and crystallized ability intelligences. *Journal of Educational Psychology,* 57, 253–270.

Horn, J. L., & Knapp, J. R. (1973). On the subjective character of the empirical base of Guilford's structure of intellect model. *Psychological Bulletin,* 80, 33–43.

Horn, J. L., & Donaldson, G. (1976). On the myth of intellectual decline in adulthood. *American Psychologist,* 31, 701–719.

Horn, J. L., & Donaldson, G. (1979). Cognitive development II: Adulthood development of human abilities. In O. G. Brim & J. Kagan (Eds.), *Constancy and change in human development: A volume of review essays.* Cambridge: Harvard University Press.

Hunt, E. (1976). Varieties of cognitive power. In L. B. Resnick (Ed.), *The nature of intelligence.* Hillsdale, NJ: Lawrence Erlbaum Associates.

Hunt, E. (1978). The mechanics of verbal ability. *Psychological Review,* 85, 109–130.

Hunt, E., Davidson, J., & Lansman, M. (1981). Individual differences in long-term memory access. *Memory & Cognition,* 9, 599–608.

Hunt, E., Frost, N., & Lunneborg, C. (1973). Individual differences in cognition: A new approach to intelligence. In G. Bower (Ed.), *Psychology of learning and motivation* (Vol. 7). New York: Academic Press.

Hunt, E., Lansman, M. (1975). Cognitive theory applied to individual differences. In W. K. Estes (Ed.), *Handbook of learning and cognitive processes* (Vol. 1). Hillsdale, NJ: Lawrence Erlbaum Associates.

Hunt, E., & Lansman, M. (1982). Individual differences in attention. In R. J. Sternberg (Ed.), *Advances in the psychology of human intelligence* (Vol. 1). Hillsdale, NJ: Lawrence Erlbaum Associates.

Hunt, E., Lunneborg, C., & Lewis, J. (1975). What does it mean to be high verbal? *Cognitive Psychology,* 7, 194–227.

Hunt, J. McV. (1961). *Intelligence and experience.* New York: Ronald Press.

Inhelder, B., & Piaget, J. (1958). *The growth of logical thinking from childhood to adolescence.* New York: Basic Books.

Inhelder, B., & Piaget, J. (1964). *The early growth of logic in the child: Classification and seriation.* London: Routledge and Kegan Paul.

Jensen, A. R. (1980). *Bias in mental testing.* New York: Free Press.

Johnson, R. C., McClearn, G. E., Schwitters, S. Y., Nagoshi, C. T., Ahern, F. M., & Cole, R. F. (1984). Galton's data a century later. Unpublished manuscript.

Kail, R., & Bisanz, J. (1982). Information processing and cognitive development. In H. W. Reese (Ed.), *Advances in child development and behavior* (Vol. 17). New York: Academic Press.

Kail, R., Carter, P., & Pellegrino, J. (1979). The locus of sex differences in spatial ability. *Perception & Psychophysics, 26,* 102–116.

Kail, R., Stevenson, M. R., & Black, K. N. (1984). Absence of a sex difference in algorithms for spatial problem solving. *Intelligence, 8,* 37–46.

Kamin, L. J. (1974). *The science and politics of IQ.* Potomac, MD: Lawrence Erlbaum Associates.

Kaufman, A. S., & Kaufman, N. L. (1972). Tests built from Piaget's and Gesell's tasks as predictors of first-grade achievement. *Child Development, 43,* 521–535.

Keating, D. P., & Bobbitt, B. (1978). Individual and developmental differences in cognitive processing components of mental ability. *Child Development, 49,* 155–167.

Klahr, D., & Wallace, J. G. (1970). An information processing analysis of some Piagetian experimental tasks. *Cognitive Psychology, 1,* 358–387.

Klahr, D., & Wallace, J. G. (1972). Class inclusion processes. In S. Farnham-Diggory (Ed.), *Information processing in children.* New York: Academic Press.

Klahr, D., & Wallace, J. G. (1976). *Cognitive development: An information processing view.* Hillsdale, NJ: Lawrence Erlbaum Associates.

Kotovsky, K., & Simon, H. A. (1973). Empirical tests of a theory of human acquisition of concepts for sequential patterns. *Cognitive Psychology, 4,* 339–424.

Lambert, N. (1981). Psychological evidence in *Larry P. v. Wilson Riles. American Psychologist, 36,* 937–952.

Loehlin, J. C., Lindzey, G., & Spuhler, J. N. (1975). *Race differences in intelligence.* San Francisco: W. H. Freeman and Company.

Lohman, D. (1979). *Spatial ability: A review and reanalysis of the correlational literature* (Tech. Rep. No. 8). Aptitude Research Project. Stanford, CA: Stanford University, School of Education.

Luchins, A. S. (1942). Mechanization in problem solving. *Psychological Monographs, 54* (6, Whole No. 248).

Luchins, A. S., & Luchins, E. H. (1959). *Rigidity of behavior: A variational approach to the effects of Einstellung.* Eugene: University of Oregon Books.

McCall, R. B. (1979). The development of intellectual functioning during infancy and the prediction of later I.Q. In J. Osofsky (Ed.), *Handbook of infant development.* New York: Wiley.

Maccoby, E. E., & Jacklin, C. N. (1974). *The psychology of sex differences.* Stanford, CA: Stanford University Press.

McClelland, J. L. & Rumelhart, D. E. (1981). An interactive model of context effects on letter perception: Part 1. An account of basic findings. *Psychological Review, 88,* 375–407.

McGee, M. G. (1979). *Human spatial abilities: Sources of sex differences.* New York: Praeger.

McLaughlin, G. H. (1963). Psycho-logic: A possible alternative to Piaget's formulation. *British Journal of Educational Psychology, 33,* 61–67.

MacLeod, C. M., Hunt, E., & Mathews, N. N. (1978). Individual differences in the verification of sentence-picture relationships. *Journal of Verbal Learning and Verbal Behavior, 17,* 493–507.

McNemar, Q. (1964). Lost: Our intelligence? Why? *American Psychologist, 19,* 871–882.

Mandler, J. M., & Robinson, C. A. (1978). Developmental changes in picture recognition. *Journal of Experimental Child Psychology, 26,* 122–136.

Medin, D., & Cole, M. (1975). Comparative psychology and human cognition. In W. K. Estes (Ed.), *Handbook of learning and cognitive processes* (Vol. 1). Hillsdale, NJ: Lawrence Erlbaum Associates.

Miller, G. A. (1983). Varieties of intelligence. [Review of *Frames of mind* by H. Gardner.] *New York Times Book Review,* December 25, p. 5.

Mulholland, T. M., Pellegrino, J. W., & Glaser, R. (1980). Components of geometric analogy solution. *Cognitive Psychology, 12,* 252–284.

Mumaw, R. J., & Pellegrino, J. W. (1984). Individual differences in complex spatial processing. *Journal of Educational Psychology, 76,* 920–939.

Mumaw, R. J. Pellegrino, J. W., Kail, R. V., & Carter, P. (in press). Different slopes for different folks: Process analyses of spatial aptitude. *Memory & Cognition.*

Murdock, B. B. (1965). Effect of a subsidiary task on short-term memory. *British Journal of Psychology, 56,* 413–419.

Murray, F. B. (1983). Equilibration as cognitive conflict. *Developmental Review, 3,* 54–61.

Neisser, U. (1976). General, academic, and artificial intelligence. In L. B. Resnick (Ed.), *The nature of intelligence.* Hillsdale, NJ: Lawrence Erlbaum Associates.

Neisser, U., & Bellar, E. K. (1965). Searching through word lists. *British Journal of Psychology, 56,* 349–358.

Norman, D. A., & Rumelhart, D. E. (Eds.) (1975). *Explorations in cognition.* San Francisco: W. H. Freeman and Company.

Pascual-Leone, J. (1970). A mathematical model for the transition rule in Piaget's developmental stages. *Acta Psychologica, 32,* 301–345.

Pascual-Leone, J. (1978). Compounds, confounds, and models in developmental information processing: A reply to Trabasso and Foellinger. *Journal of Experimental Child Psychology, 26,* 18–40.

Pascual-Leone, J., & Sparkman, E. (1980). The dialectics of empiricism and rationalism: A last methodological reply to Trabasso. *Journal of Experimental Child Psychology, 29,* 88–101.

Pellegrino, J. W., & Glaser, R. (1979). Components of inductive reasoning. In R. E. Snow, P. Federico, and W. E. Montague (Eds.), *Aptitude, learning, and instruction, vol. 1. Cognitive process analyses of aptitude.* Hillsdale, NJ: Lawrence Erlbaum Associates.

Pellegrino, J. W., & Ingram, A. L. (1977). *Components of verbal analogy solution.* Paper presented at the annual meeting of the Midwestern Psychological Association, Chicago.

Pellegrino, J. W., & Kail, R. (1982). Process analyses of spatial aptitude. In R. J. Sternberg (Ed.), *Advances in the psychology of human intelligence* (Vol. 1). Hillsdale, NJ: Lawrence Erlbaum Associates.

Peterson, J. (1925). *Early conceptions and tests of intelligence.* Yonkers, NY: World Book.

Phillips, J. L. (1975). *The origins of intellect: Piaget's theory* (2nd ed.). San Francisco: W. H. Freeman and Company.

Piaget, J. (1926). *The language and thought of the child.* London: Kegan Paul.

Piaget, J. (1950). *The psychology of intelligence.* New York: International Universities Press.

Piaget, J. (1951). *Play, dreams and imitation in childhood.* New York: Norton.

Piaget, J. (1952). *The origins of intelligence in children.* New York: International Universities Press.

Piaget, J., & Inhelder, B. (1956). *The child's conception of space.* London: Routledge and Kegan Paul.

Raven, J. C. (1938). *Progressive matrices: A perceptual test of intelligence* (individual form). London: Lewis.

Raven, J. C. (1960). *Guide to the standard progressive matrices.* London: Lewis.

Raven, J. C. (1965). *Advanced progressive matrices.* London: Lewis.

Reicher, G. M. (1969). Perceptual recognition as a function of meaningfulness of stimulus material. *Journal of Experimental Psychology, 81*, 274–280.

Rose, A. M. (1979). Information-processing abilities. In R. E. Snow, P. Federico, and W. E. Montague (Eds.), *Aptitude, learning, and instruction, vol. 1. Cognitive process analyses of aptitude.* Hillsdale, NJ: Lawrence Erlbaum Associates.

Roy, E. A. (1982). Action and performance. In A. W. Ellis (Ed.), *Normality and pathology in cognitive functions.* London: Academic Press.

Rumelhart, D. E., & Siple, P. (1974). The process of recognizing tachistoscopically presented words. *Psychological Review, 81*, 99–118.

Scardamalia, M. (1977). Information processing capacity and the problem of horizontal *décalage:* A demonstration using combinatorial reasoning tasks. *Child Development, 48*, 28–37.

Scarr-Salapatek, S. (1975). Genetics and the development of intelligence. In F. D. Horowitz (Ed.), *Review of child development research* (Vol. 4). Chicago: University of Chicago Press.

Schaie, K. W. (1983). The Seattle longitudinal study: A twenty-one year investigation of psychometric intelligence. In K. W. Schaie (Ed.),

Longitudinal studies of adult psychological development. New York: Guilford Press.

Schaie, K. W., & Strother, C. R. (1968). A cross-sequential study of age changes in cognitive behavior. *Psychological Bulletin, 70,* 671–680.

Schaie, K. W., Labouvie, G., & Buech, B. U. (1973). Generational and cohort-specific differences in adult cognitive functioning: A fourteen year study of independent samples. *Developmental Psychology, 9,* 151–166.

Schaie, K. W., & Labouvie-Vief, G. (1974). Generational versus ontogenetic components of change in adult cognitive behavior: A fourteen year cross-sequential study. *Developmental Psychology, 10,* 305–320.

Schank, R. C., & Abelson, R. (1977). *Scripts, plans, goals and understanding.* Hillsdale, NJ: Lawrence Erlbaum Associates.

Selfridge, O. G. (1959). Pandemonium: A paradigm for learning. In *The mechanisation of thought processes.* London: H. M. Stationery Office.

Shepard, R. N., & Metzler, J. (1971). Mental rotation of three-dimensional objects. *Science, 171,* 701–703.

Shiffrin, R. M., & Dumais, S. T. (1981). The development of automatism. In J. R. Anderson (Ed.), *Cognitive skills and their acquisition.* Hillsdale, NJ: Lawrence Erlbaum Associates.

Shuter-Dyson, R. (1982). Musical ability. In D. Deutsch (Ed.), *The psychology of music.* New York: Academic Press.

Siegler, R. S. (1976). Three aspects of cognitive development. *Cognitive Psychology, 8,* 481–520.

Simon, H. A. (1981). *The sciences of the artificial* (2nd ed.). Cambridge: MIT Press.

Simon, H. A., & Kotovsky, K. (1963). Human acquisition of concepts for sequential patterns. *Psychological Review, 70,* 534–546.

Sloboda, J. A. (1976). Visual perception of musical notation: Registering pitch symbols in memory. *Quarterly Journal of Experimental Psychology, 28,* 1–16.

Smith, I. M. (1964). *Spatial ability.* San Diego: Robert R. Knapp.

Spearman, C. (1904a) "General intelligence" objectively determined and measured. *American Journal of Psychology, 15,* 201–293.

Spearman, C. (1904b). The proof and measurement of association between two things. *American Journal of Psychology, 15,* 72–101.

Spearman, C. (1927). *The abilities of man.* New York: Macmillan.

Spelke, E., Hirst, W., & Neisser, U. (1976). Skills of divided attention. *Cognition, 4,* 215–230.

Stafford, R. E. (1961). Sex differences in spatial visualizing as evidence of sex-linked inheritance. *Perceptual and Motor Skills, 13,* 428.

Sternberg, R. J. (1977). *Intelligence, information processing and analogical reasoning.* Hillsdale, NJ: Lawrence Erlbaum Associates.

Sternberg, R. J. (1981). Intelligence and nonentrenchment. *Journal of Educational Psychology, 73,* 1–16.

Sternberg, R. J. (1982). A componential approach to intellectual development. In R. J. Sternberg (Ed.), *Advances in the psychology of human intelligence* (Vol. 1). Hillsdale, NJ: Lawrence Erlbaum Associates.

Sternberg, R. J. (1984). Toward a triarchic theory of human intelligence. *Behavioral and Brain Sciences, 7,* 269–287.

Sternberg, R. J., Conway, B. E., Ketron, J. L., & Bernstein, M. (1981). People's conceptions of intelligence. *Journal of Personality and Social Psychology, 41,* 37–55.

Sternberg, R. J., & Gardner, M. K. (1983). Unities in inductive reasoning. *Journal of Experimental Psychology: General, 112,* 80–116.

Sternberg, S. (1966). High speed scanning in human memory. *Science, 153,* 652–654.

Stohl, M., & Lopez, G. (1984). *The state as terrorist.* Westport, CT: Greenwood Press.

Strauss, M. S. (1979). Abstraction of prototypical information by adults and 10-month-old infants. *Journal of Experimental Psychology: Human Learning and Memory, 5,* 618–632.

Tapley, S. M., & Bryden, M. P. (1977). An investigation of sex differences in spatial ability: Mental rotation of three-dimensional objects. *Canadian Journal of Psychology, 31,* 122–130.

Thurstone, L. L. (1938). *Primary mental abilities.* Chicago: University of Chicago Press.

Thurstone, L. L., & Thurstone, T. G. (1941). *Factorial studies of intelligence.* Chicago: University of Chicago Press.

Thurstone, L. L., & Thurstone, T. G. (1949). *Manual for the SRA Primary Mental Abilities.* Chicago: Science Research Associates.

Trabasso, T. (1977). The role of memory as a system in making transitive inferences. In R. V. Kail & J. W. Hagen (Eds.), *Perspectives on the development of memory and cognition.* Hillsdale, NJ: Lawrence Erlbaum Associates.

Trabasso, T. (1978). On the estimation of parameters and the evaluation of a mathematical model: A reply to Pascual-Leone. *Journal of Experimental Child Psychology, 26,* 41–45.

Trabasso, T., & Foellinger, D. B. (1978). Information processing capacity in children: A test of Pascual-Leone's model. *Journal of Experimental Child Psychology, 26,* 1–17.

Trabasso, T., Isen, A. M., Dolecki, P., McLanahan, A. G., Riley, C. A., & Tucker, T. (1978). How do children solve class-inclusion problems? In R. Siegler (Ed.), *Children's thinking: What develops?* Hillsdale, NJ: Lawrence Erlbaum Associates.

Trabasso, T., Riley, C. A., & Wilson, E. G. (1975). The representation of linear order and spatial strategies in reasoning: A developmental study. In R. Falmagne (Ed.), *Reasoning: Representation and process in children and adults.* Hillsdale, NJ: Lawrence Erbaum Associates.

Tuddenham, R. (1970). A "Piagetian" test of cognitive development. In W. B. Dockrell (Ed.), *On intelligence.* Toronto: The Ontario Institute for Studies in Education.

Vandenberg, S. G. (1971). A test of three-dimensional spatial visualization (based on the Shepard-Metzler "mental rotation" study). Boulder: University of Colorado.

Vernon, P. E. (1961). *The structure of human abilities* (2nd ed.). London: Methuen.

Vernon, P. E. (1965). Ability factors and environmental influences. *American Psychologist, 20,* 723–733.

Waber, D. P. (1977). Biological substrates of field dependence: Implications of the sex difference. *Psychological Bulletin, 84,* 1076–1087.

Waugh, N. C., & Norman, D. A. (1965). Primary memory. *Psychological Review, 72,* 89–104.

Wechsler, D. (1974). *Manual for the Wechsler intelligence scale for children.* New York: Psychological Corporation.

Whitely, S. E. (1977). Information processing on intelligence test items: Some response components. *Applied Psychological Measurement, 1,* 465–476.

Whitely, S. E. (1980). Modeling aptitude test validity from cognitive components. *Journal of Educational Psychology, 72,* 750–769.

Willerman, L. (1979). *The psychology of individual and group differences.* San Francisco: W. H. Freeman and Company.

Williams, H. L., Beaver, W. S., Spence, M. T., & Rundell, O. H. (1969). Digital and kinesthetic memory with interpolated information processing. *Journal of Experimental Psychology, 80,* 530–536.

Willis, S. L. (1984). Toward an educational psychology of the older adult learner: Intellectual and cognitive bases. In J. E. Birren & K. W. Schaie (Eds.), *Handbook of the psychology of aging* (2nd ed.). New York: Van Nostrand Reinhold.

Wissler, C. (1901). The correlation of mental and physical traits. *Psychological Monographs, 3,* 1–62.

Woodworth, R. S. (1944). James McKeen Cattell: 1860–1944. *Psychological Review, 51,* 201–209.

Yang, R. (1979). Early infant assessment: An overview. In J. Osofsky (Ed.), *Handbook of infant development.* New York: Wiley.

Zeitlin, L. R., & Finkleman, J. M. (1975). Subsidiary techniques of digit generation and digit recall as indirect measures of operator loading. *Human Factors, 17,* 218–220.

Zimmerman, B., & Blom, D. (1983). Toward an empirical test of the role of cognitive conflict in learning. *Developmental Review, 3,* 18–38.

Name Index

Subject Index